"'Application integration is hard,' says Anne the nature of the beast is to expect and demand easy answers to hard problems, and the management, technology and deployment problems are legion in application interoperability. Nevertheless, we have no choice if we want to create a more streamlined, efficient enterprise, and lower the cost of interacting with our suppliers and customers. Anne Thomas Manes gives the most cogent and clear explanation to date of how the Web Services revolution can help an enterprise reach those goals. Together with an architecture decision process and an IT organization that understands the business and architecting solutions, this book goes a long way toward helping us integrate business processes with IT."

—Richard Soley, Chairman and CEO
Object Management Group

"Ann Manes has done an admirable job of stripping away the hype and confusion surrounding Web services and describing the essential concepts in language that managers can use. If only we who are working on the Web services specifications could write so clearly!"

—Michael Champion, Advisory R&D Specialist
Software AG

"The reasons for using Web services are not always clear, creating a lot of uncertainty around their adoption in IT. Most Web services books focuses on the technology, and don't provide enough overall context to help decision makers. Anne Thomas Manes' book does, clearly identifying the applications of Web services, separating current reality from future promises, and comparing the strengths and weaknesses of the various vendor products."

—Eric Newcomer, CTO, IONA Technologies
Author of *Understanding Web Services*

"This is the one book I would recommend for professionals looking for the inside story on Web services. Indeed, this book cuts through the hype, getting to the meat of the technology, highlighting what value this technology brings to your enterprise."

—Dave Linthicum, CTO
Mercator Software

"The Web services paradigm suffers badly from the two great technology ills: marketing hyperbole and engineering technobabble. Making sound business decisions about application development can be nearly impossible. Luckily, *Web Services: A Manager's Guide* cuts through the hyperbole and rises above the technobabble. Any IT manager even thinking about Web services should read it cover to cover."

—Kevin Dick, Founder of Kevin Dick Associates
Author of *XML: A Manager's Guide*

"Anne's book cuts through the hype surrounding Web Services to explain in a cogent, rational, and well-written manner what these technologies are all about and how they can be used to solve real business problems."

—Daniel Appelquist, Senior Architect, Vodafone
Author of *XML and SQL:Developing Web Applications*

Web Services

Addison-Wesley Information Technology Series
Capers Jones and David S. Linthicum, Consulting Editors

The information technology (IT) industry is in the public eye now more than ever before because of a number of major issues in which software technology and national policies are closely related. As the use of software expands, there is a continuing need for business and software professionals to stay current with the state of the art in software methodologies and technologies. The goal of the **Addison-Wesley Information Technology Series** is to cover any and all topics that affect the IT community. These books illustrate and explore how information technology can be aligned with business practices to achieve business goals and support business imperatives. Addison-Wesley has created this innovative series to empower you with the benefits of the industry experts' experience.

For more information point your browser to http://www.awprofessional.com/itseries

Sid Adelman, Larissa Terpeluk Moss, *Data Warehouse Project Management*. ISBN: 0-201-61635-1

Sid Adelman et al., *Impossible Data Warehouse Situations: Solutions from the Experts*. ISBN: 0-201-76033-9

Wayne Applehans, Alden Globe, and Greg Laugero, *Managing Knowledge: A Practical Web-Based Approach*. ISBN: 0-201-43315-X

David Leon Clark, *Enterprise Security: The Manager's Defense Guide*. ISBN: 0-201-71972-X

Frank P. Coyle, *XML, Web Services, and the Data Revolution*. ISBN: 0-201-77641-3

Kevin Dick, *XML, Second Edition: A Manager's Guide*. ISBN: 0-201-77006-7

Jill Dyché, *e-Data: Turning Data into Information with Data Warehousing*. ISBN: 0-201-65780-5

Jill Dyché, *The CRM Handbook: A Business Guide to Customer Relationship Management*. ISBN: 0-201-73062-6

Patricia L. Ferdinandi, *A Requirements Pattern: Succeeding in the Internet Economy*. ISBN: 0-201-73826-0

David Garmus and David Herron, *Function Point Analysis: Measurement Practices for Successful Software Projects*. ISBN: 0-201-69944-3

John Harney, *Application Service Providers (ASPs): A Manager's Guide*. ISBN: 0-201-72659-9

International Function Point Users Group, *IT Measurement: Practical Advice from the Experts*. ISBN: 0-201-74158-X

Capers Jones, *Software Assessments, Benchmarks, and Best Practices*. ISBN: 0-201-48542-7

Ravi Kalakota and Marcia Robinson, *e-Business 2.0: Roadmap for Success*. ISBN: 0-201-72165-1

Ravi Kalakota and Marcia Robinson, *Services Blueprint: Roadmap for Execution*. ISBN: 0-321-15039-2

Greg Laugero and Alden Globe, *Enterprise Content Services: Connecting Information and Profitability*. ISBN: 0-201-73016-2

David S. Linthicum, *B2B Application Integration: e-Business-Enable Your Enterprise*. ISBN: 0-201-70936-8

David S. Linthicum, *Enterprise Application Integration*. ISBN: 0-201-61583-5

David S. Linthicum, *Next Generation Application Integration: From Simple Information to Web Services*. ISBN: 0-201-84456-7

Sergio Lozinsky, *Enterprise-Wide Software Solutions: Integration Strategies and Practices*. ISBN: 0-201-30971-8

Anne Thomas Manes, *Web Services: A Manager's Guide*. ISBN: 0-321-18577-3

Larissa T. Moss and Shaku Atre, *Business Intelligence Roadmap: The Complete Project Lifecycle for Decision-Support Applications*. ISBN: 0-201-78420-3

Bud Porter-Roth, *Request for Proposal: A Guide to Effective RFP Development*. ISBN: 0-201-77575-1

Ronald G. Ross, *Principles of the Business Rule Approach*. ISBN: 0-201-78893-4

Karl E. Wiegers, *Peer Reviews in Software: A Practical Guide*. ISBN: 0-201-73485-0

Ralph R. Young, *Effective Requirements Practices*. ISBN: 0-201-70912-0

Bill Zoellick, *CyberRegs: A Business Guide to Web Property, Privacy, and Patents*. ISBN: 0-201-72230-5

Web Services
A Manager's Guide

Anne Thomas Manes

✦ Addison-Wesley

Boston • San Francisco • New York • Toronto
Montreal • London • Munich • Paris • Madrid
Capetown • Sydney • Tokyo • Singapore • Mexico City

Many of the designations used by manufacturers and sellers to distinguish their products are claimed as trademarks. Where those designations appear in this book, and Addison-Wesley was aware of a trademark claim, the designations have been printed with initial capital letters or in all capitals.

The author and publisher have taken care in the preparation of this book, but make no expressed or implied warranty of any kind and assume no responsibility for errors or omissions. No liability is assumed for incidental or consequential damages in connection with or arising out of the use of the information or programs contained herein.

The publisher offers discounts on this book when ordered in quantity for bulk purchases and special sales. For more information, please contact:

U.S. Corporate and Government Sales
(800) 382-3419
corpsales@pearsontechgroup.com

For sales outside of the U.S., please contact:

International Sales
(317) 581-3793
international@pearsontechgroup.com

Visit Addison-Wesley on the Web: www.awprofessional.com

Library of Congress Cataloging in Publication Data is available.

Copyright © 2003 by Anne Thomas Manes

All rights reserved. No part of this publication may be reproduced, stored in a retrieval system, or transmitted, in any form, or by any means, electronic, mechanical, photocopying, recording, or otherwise, without the prior consent of the publisher. Printed in the United States of America. Published simultaneously in Canada.

For information on obtaining permission for use of material from this work, please submit a written request to:

Pearson Education, Inc.
Rights and Contracts Department
75 Arlington Street, Suite 300
Boston, MA 02116
Fax: (617) 848-7047

ISBN 0-321-18577-3
Text printed on recycled paper
1 2 3 4 5 6 7 8 9 10—CRW—0706050403
First printing, June 2003

In memory of Tucker and Sheba

Contents

Foreword — xv
Preface — xxiii
Acknowledgments — xxvii

1. The Application Integration Crisis

Hershey's Integration Nightmare	2
Integration Helps Your Business	3
All Applications Require Integration	4
Calculating Return on Investment	5
Application Integration Is Hard	6
Approaches to Application Integration	7
Building Integration Hooks	9
Exposing Interfaces Across the Network	11
Middleware Styles	13
Traditional Middleware Blues	16
Pervasiveness and Heterogeneity	16
Total Cost of Ownership	18
Extending Integration to Work Across the Internet	20
Using the Internet as an Integration Platform	21
Using Web Services for Integration	22
Web Services Have Tactical and Strategic Value	23

2. Web Services Basics

What Is a Web Service?	27
Why Web Services?	28
Defining "Web" and "Service"	29
Building Services	32
Web Evolution	33

Contents

Defining Characteristics of Web Services — 35
Understanding the Scope of Web Services — 35
Web Services Business Models — 37
    Google — 38
    Kinko's — 39
    Amazon — 40
    UPS — 41
    T-Mobile — 41
    Internal Integration — 43
Executive Summary — 44

3.
Web Services Technologies

The Web — 48
    The Web Versus Other Networks — 50
XML — 50
    XML Schema — 53
    XSLT — 54
    XML Versus Other Data Representations — 55
SOA — 57
WSDL, UDDI, and SOAP — 59
    Description (WSDL) — 60
    Advertising and Discovery (UDDI) — 65
    Communication (SOAP) — 70
    Extending SOAP — 73
    SOAP Versus Other Communication Systems — 76
Other Web Service Technologies — 77
    ebXML — 78
Executive Summary — 80

4.
Standardizing Web Services Technologies

The History of SOAP — 84
    Challenges with SOAP 1.1 — 85

WS-I	86
W3C and OASIS	88
The History of WSDL	88
Challenges with WSDL 1.1	89
The History of UDDI	92
UDDI Business Registry	93
Private UDDI Registries	95
Programming Standards for Web Services	97
Java Standards for SOAP	99
Java Standards for WSDL	101
Java Standards for UDDI	101
Executive Summary: Status Check	102

5.
Advanced Web Services Standards

Web Services Security Standardization Efforts	105
Confidentiality and Integrity	107
Authentication and Authorization	110
Using XML Security in Web Services	115
Web Services Management Standardization Efforts	117
Transactions, Orchestration, and Choreography	122
Transactions	123
Orchestration and Choreography	126
Reliability	130
Portlets and Interactive Applications	132
Other Advanced Efforts	133

6.
The Promise of Web Services

Web Services Hype	135
Super-powered PDA	136
Software-as-a-Service	137

Contents

Dynamic Discovery of Business Partners	140
Enabling Dynamic Discovery	142
Dynamic Binding	147
What Makes Web Services Special	150
Web Services Adoption	151
Clear Benefits	153
Truth in Hype	154

7.
When to Use Web Services

Bell Ringers	158
Heterogeneous Integration	158
Unknown Client Environment	159
Multichannel Client Formats	160
Other Web Services Applications	162
Point-to-Point Integration	162
Consolidated View	163
Managing Legacy Assets	165
Reducing Duplicative Applications	165
Managing Portal Initiatives	167
B2B Electronic Procurement	170
Trading Partner Network	171
Software-as-a-Service	172
When Not to Use Web Services	174
Executive Summary	177

8.
Web Services Infrastructure

Core Products	180
Web Services Platforms	181
Web Services Management Extensions	206
Infrastructure-Level Web Services	210
Associated Products	214

9.
Evaluation Guidelines

Characterizing Your Project	219
Making the Initial Cut	221
Language and Operating System	221
Selecting a Java Platform	222
Licensing and Support Issues	224
Evaluating Your Requirements	226
Performance and Scalability	226
Standards Support and Interoperability	227
Extensibility Features	229
Security	231
Tools	234
UDDI Registries	236
Platform Considerations	237
Standards Support	239
User Interfaces	240
Administration and Management	241
Security	242
Executive Summary	244
Base Your Selection on Project Requirements	244
Charting Your Course	246

Appendix A
Web Services Product List

.NET Platform	249
COM Platform	250
Portable C and C++ Platforms	251
Java Platforms	252
J2EE Platforms	252
J2SE Platforms	255
J2ME and KVM Platforms	258

Contents

Other Languages and Platforms — 259
    Scripting Languages — 259
    Programming Languages — 261
UDDI Registry Servers — 262
    Embedded UDDI Registries — 263
    Standalone UDDI Registries — 264

Appendix B
Requirements Questionnaire

Operating Platform Attributes — 267
Client Platform Attributes — 267
Licensing Requirements — 267
Performance and Scalability Requirements — 268
Extensibility Features — 268
Security Requirements — 268
Developer Preferences — 269
UDDI Requirements — 269

Glossary — 271

Index — 307

Foreword: Understanding the Power (and Limitations) of Web Services

This book performs a valuable service for managers seeking to harness the business potential of Web services technology. Web services represent a major step in the direction of service-oriented architectures, and these, in turn, will provide a foundation for extraordinary innovation in business practices and industry structures.

As with any new technology, there is enormous confusion, generated by the hype machines of major technology vendors and assorted enthusiasts. Will Web services enable dynamic composition of applications from hundreds of micro-services? Will Web services truly allow all applications to finally connect seamlessly with all other applications? Will we finally overcome the barriers created by generations of proprietary technology layered on top of and around each other? Will XML really provide a lingua franca that can transcend all the fragmented dialects that make communication among applications so challenging?

This confusion is dangerous for several reasons. At the very least, it will slow down adoption of the technology. Managers have been burned by exaggerated claims from previous generations of technology many times in the past. They are understandably gunshy at this point and develop an allergic reaction to any suggestion of hype surrounding a new technology.

But there is an even bigger danger. Some managers might actually believe the hype and launch implementation efforts that far exceed

Foreword

the capabilities of the technology. If they are lucky, the implementation effort will merely fall short of expectations and fail to deliver the anticipated return on investment. A few will be truly unlucky and find that they have compromised key business activities because of limitations in the technology. If that happens, the broader impact of Web services technology will be seriously compromised as a backlash gathers force and creates a serious obstacle for anyone interested in implementing this technology.

If Web services technology is the first step in the direction of much more ambitious service-oriented architectures, it is essential that the first step be a solid one, free from stumbles and moving the business briskly forward. For that to happen, we need absolute clarity regarding the capabilities of the technology and, even more importantly, the limitations of the technology as it exists today.

This book by Anne Thomas Manes does precisely that. Bringing a real practitioner's experience to the task, Anne carefully walks managers through the fundamentals of the technology, taking particular care to point out the limitations. She clearly sees the potential of the technology, but she also understands that, to realize this potential, expectations must be managed carefully and potential adopters need to be clear about the performance boundaries of the technology.

With this book in the hands of CIOs and business strategy executives, we will be much more likely to see accelerated adoption of Web services. Confident that they understand the technology, these executives will be more likely to deploy Web services in production environments. Alert to the limitations of the technology, they will be assured that Web services will deliver the functionality required to generate real business impact. As the compelling return on investment supporting this technology becomes apparent, executives will broaden the deployment of Web services, and the technology providers will be motivated to continue to invest heavily in enhancing Web services capabilities.

This is a deceptively disruptive technology. Enterprises are adopting Web services to support very mundane technology "plumbing" in order to deliver tangible operating savings. Nothing very disruptive about that. Most Web services enthusiasts find such implementations very uninteresting. On the other hand, most business executives are very excited about the prospect of achieving substantial operating savings with modest investment and relatively short lead times measured in months instead of years. Achieving these near-term savings does not require any major changes in business practices or organizations.

As the technology penetrates the enterprise, it begins to create more degrees of freedom for managers. Exploiting this freedom *will* require disruptive change in terms of business practices and business organization. Those who have the understanding and commitment necessary to confront these disruptions will reap the real economic rewards of Web services.

What is the source of this disruptive power in Web services technology? It begins with the notion of contract-driven integration embedded in key Web services standards. Web services standards define the foundations for a service-oriented architecture. As Anne points out, one of the three basic artifacts of this architecture is the service contract. The Web Services Description Language (WSDL), a key early Web services standard, specifies the format for this service contract. This service contract describes what will be offered (the service type), what procedures must be used to access and use the service (the binding), and where the service can be found (the endpoint).

Foreword

Now, service contracts in themselves are not a major breakthrough, as Anne points out. Previous generations of service-oriented architectures also used standardized ways of describing service contracts. The big difference, though, is that these earlier forms of service contracts only supported one way of communicating with the service and required all users to install the same middleware in order to locate the service to begin with. In other words, these service contracts were still tightly coupled—they required all users to conform to the same communication protocols and the same middleware platforms.

Service contracts implemented with Web service standards support much more loosely coupled connections. Services can be located, accessed, and used over a variety of middleware platforms. The standards assume that providers and users of Web services will operate across a broad range of technology platforms and therefore seek to provide maximum flexibility in creating and supporting connections.

This flexibility is key to the power of Web services technology and related service-oriented architectures. The real opportunity (and challenge) is to extend this philosophy of loose coupling to asynchronous transactions. As Anne points out, one of the key sources of operating inefficiency in business processes involves the difficulty in automating long-running, loosely coupled asynchronous transactions—multistep business processes that span extended periods of days or weeks. The operating inefficiencies are especially significant when these business processes span multiple enterprises.

By addressing this opportunity, Web services and service-oriented architectures will provide the technology foundation required for a very different approach to management of business processes. In contrast to the hard-wired approaches used throughout business today, we will see the spread of loosely coupled business processes.

These business processes will be designed in a modular fashion so that orchestrators of these processes can quickly assemble the right set of activities to tailor the process to the needs of specific customers or products.

Of course, to realize the potential of this technology foundation, additional elements will need to fall into place. In particular, we would highlight the need for service grids and for a very different management approach based on trust rather than control.

Service grids assemble a diverse set of specialized enabling services required to support the connections across applications enabled by Web services technology. For example, specialized enabling services would include security, directory services, data transformation, and performance auditing. These services are essential to deliver mission critical functionality.

Rather than implementing them at each node, creating significant complexity and expense for each party participating in the connection, service grids would make these services available on a shared basis. The various enabling services required to compose a service grid are likely to be assembled in a federation from a variety of sources. Some of the more specialized ones may be provided from within enterprises participating in the connections, while most of them will likely be sourced from specialized third parties that view these services as their core business.

This would create significant efficiency in terms of avoiding replication of functionality at each node. It would also provide a powerful platform for accelerated learning and performance improvement, offering providers of these shared services much broader visibility into the requirements for performance in many different operating environments simultaneously. Service grids are only now beginning to emerge. They will need to evolve significantly in order to

Foreword

handle the challenges of long-running, loosely coupled business processes. For more information about service grids, see our white paper "Service Grids: The Missing Link in Web Services" available at www.johnhagel.com.

Service grids are essential to enhance the performance of the technology itself. But to really harness the economic value of the technology, management will need to shift to a very different management approach. Most executives today are experienced practitioners of a control-based management approach. Shaped within the enterprise, this management approach assumes a single point of control. It specifies activities in great detail and then seeks to monitor those activities at a granular level to ensure quick intervention if actions deviate from their prescribed course. In part, previous generations of technology shaped this management approach. Tightly coupled technology platforms required detailed specification of activities in advance and strict adherence to these activity flows.

Two forces have been increasing stress on this control-based management approach. First, companies have realized that enhancing value for the customer requires coordinating activities within business processes across multiple enterprises. Thus, the assumption of a single point of control, so essential to the effective functioning of control-based management approaches, becomes questionable. Federated models of decision making become essential. Second, intensifying competition and accelerating change make it more difficult to specify detailed activities in advance. It becomes even more difficult to adhere to these specifications as countless unanticipated events and exceptions disrupt operations. Flexibility becomes essential.

These stresses are creating a need to move to a trust-based management approach. This approach starts with the assumption that multiple enterprises will need to come together to deliver value to customers. Rather than a single point of control, this approach focuses on the need for an orchestrator—someone who will identify and recruit participants with the required capabilities, clearly specify and communicate expectations regarding deliverables, and create the appropriate incentive structures to motivate each participant to perform as expected. Rather than specifying activities, the orchestrator specifies outcomes. Rather than seeking complete transparency regarding all activities in the process, the orchestrator seeks selective visibility from each participant regarding events that might put outcomes in jeopardy.

Realizing the full economics of Web service technology will in the end require significant changes in management approaches. As more loosely coupled business processes emerge, shaped by trust-based management approaches, executives will realize they have far more options in terms of organizing their business. Activities that previously were internal to the enterprise will now be dispersed to enterprises that have far more capability. More distinctive activities will remain within the enterprise, but they will be made available to other enterprises on an as-needed basis. As this process unfolds, enterprises will need to be rearchitected, in terms of business models, governance approaches, and organizations. In parallel, industry architectures will rapidly evolve in response to the new economic and competitive dynamics generated from service-oriented technology architectures and loosely coupled business processes.

What started as a relatively benign way to achieve near-term operating savings will reveal its true disruptive potential. Substantial economic value will be created as these disruptions unfold. At the same time, substantial economic value will also be destroyed. Managers who understand the true business potential of this technology will be in the best position to create, rather than destroy, value.

Foreword

But that is another story. For now, we need to focus on the first steps. Anne does a superb job of helping managers to understand this technology so that they can move with sure footing and avoid potentially harmful stumbles along the way.

John Hagel, III
John Seely Brown
February 12, 2003

Preface

This book provides an overview of Web services. Its purpose is to help you make more informed decisions about adopting Web services in your company.

This guide gives an overview of Web services

Unlike most books you'll find on the subject, this guide is written for managers and not for engineers. I've tried to limit the use of computer jargon and acronyms. I don't assume that you know how to write software. I do assume that you are familiar with the way businesses use software.

It's written for managers

I present the technology in business terms. I've tried to cut through the hype by presenting both the advantages and the disadvantages of this technology. My goal is to help you understand how Web services can benefit your business. I've identified tactical and strategic projects in which Web services offer the greatest advantages. You will find the information in this book helpful when trying to cost-justify a project.

It's business-oriented

It seems that nearly every hardware and software vendor is touting a Web services strategy. I've made an effort to present the technology in a completely vendor-neutral fashion. I also provide some guidelines that you can use to help you evaluate and select a Web services technology provider.

It's vendor-neutral

Information about Web services standards and vendor products is current as of this writing. I will publish periodic status updates on my Web site. Please visit http://www.bowlight.net.

The information will be updated online

If you're planning a Web services project, you should read this book thoroughly. If you want only a basic introduction to Web services,

You can read this guide selectively

Preface

read the first two chapters. If you already feel comfortable with the basics and you want more specific information about Web services applications or vendor offerings, you can read selective chapters. You can also skim the book by scanning the "fast track" summary in the outer margin and then selectively drilling down into specific sections.

It provides summaries of key concepts and a Glossary

I've found it impossible to discuss this technology without using some jargon and acronyms. To minimize confusion, I include a number of Executive Summaries of key concepts throughout the book. I also provide a Glossary, which has definitions for all terms that appear in **boldface** throughout the book.

Book Outline

Chapter 1 talks about the challenges associated with application integration

Chapter 1, The Application Integration Crisis, identifies the motivation behind Web services. In nearly every survey taken during the past 10 years, managers consistently list application integration as one of the top three technology issues facing business. Application integration provides both tactical and strategic value to a business. From a tactical perspective, application integration improves operational efficiency, resulting in reduced costs. From a strategic perspective, application integration enables better access to information, allowing decision makers to make better decisions. Unfortunately, most businesses have a hodgepodge of application systems, developed using different technologies and running on a variety of platforms. It is hard to integrate heterogeneous systems. The issue becomes much more challenging when a business tries to integrate its systems with those of its partners, suppliers, and customers. Web services technology addresses this challenging issue.

Chapter 2, Web Services Basics, provides a basic explanation of Web services in business terms. It contains an overview of what

Preface

Web services are and why you might want to use them. I explain how Web services technology is different from previous integration technologies. I also explore Web services business models using case studies.

Chapter 2 provides a business-oriented introduction to Web services

Chapter 3, Web Services Technologies, is the most technical chapter in the book. I provide an overview of the core technologies that support Web services, including the Web, XML, and the Service Oriented Architecture (SOA). I then look at WSDL, UDDI, and SOAP, the three most popular technologies used to implement the SOA. I explain how these technologies can make your application systems much more powerful and flexible.

Chapter 3 gives a technical overview of the Web, XML, SOA, WSDL, UDDI, and SOAP

Chapter 4, Standardizing Web Services Technologies, recounts the history of SOAP, WSDL, and UDDI, and it explores the efforts under way to define formal industry standards. Although many people view SOAP, WSDL, and UDDI as formal standards, they were developed by private companies. Now these technologies are being standardized by W3C and OASIS. Another organization, WS-I, is defining guidelines for Web services interoperability.

Chapter 4 talks about the standardization efforts for SOAP, WSDL, and UDDI

Chapter 5, Advanced Web Services Standards, looks at the current standardization efforts to define advanced features for Web services, such as security, management, transactions, and portal integration. Some efforts, including security and portal integration, are making great headway. Other efforts are less far along.

Chapter 5 talks about advanced standardization efforts, such as security and portal integration

Chapter 6, The Promise of Web Services, dispels the hype around Web services. It examines some of the more popular science fiction stories told to explain the promise of Web services and recasts them into something a bit more realistic. Then it focuses on the progress in the industry that is helping to make these promises come true.

Chapter 6 takes a realistic look at what you can do with Web services

xxv

Preface

Chapter 7 provides a number of case studies

Chapter 7, When to Use Web Services, explores the scenarios and applications that would benefit most from using Web services. Each of these scenarios is illustrated using a case study.

Chapter 8 examines the various products you need to build Web services

Chapter 8, Web Services Infrastructure, examines the software products that you can use to build Web services. It seems as if every software vendor now sells a product that "supports" Web services. But what does that mean? This chapter categorizes the various types of products and explains how they work together and how they fit into your existing IT infrastructure. This chapter also provides a comparison between Java and .NET.

Chapter 9 provides guidelines to help you evaluate and select products

Chapter 9, Evaluation Guidelines, furnishes basic guidelines that a business manager should follow when evaluating Web services products. Chances are high that you will use different products for different applications. You should choose products based on the requirements of each application.

Appendix A provides a list of products

Appendix A, Web Services Product List, provides a listing of the most popular Web services products, categorized by product type and supported environments.

Appendix B provides a list of evaluation questions

Appendix B, Requirements Questionnaire, is a list of questions that can help you identify your application requirements during your evaluation.

The Glossary defines terms

The Glossary defines all the terms that appear in **boldface**.

Acknowledgments

I'd like to thank all the people who helped me write this book. In particular I'd like to thank my technical reviewers, including Daniel Applequist, John Seely Brown, Kevin Dick, Chris Ferris, Chris Kurt, Wendell Lansford, David Linthicum, Joel Munter, Eric Newcomer, and Ed Roman. Your comments were invaluable. Simon Phipps also supplied me with invaluable input as I was framing my ideas. The editorial and production crew at Addison-Wesley were fantastic. I want to thank all the brilliant folks at Systinet, especially Jan Alexander, Ian Bruce, Petr Dvorak, Radovan Janecek, Kamila Kilayko, Jacek Kopecky, Roman Stanek, and Zdenek Svoboda. I'd like to thank Bob Atkinson, Don Box, and Dave Winer for starting this whole mess. And I'd like to thank all the folks who participate in the Web services standards efforts. I can't tell you how fantastic it is to see such a phenomenal level of dedication and cooperation.

Thanks to Google for supplying the industry's best glossary service. I used it extensively when compiling my glossary.

And, of course, I want to thank Matthew, Sasha, Peter, Cally, and Ojibway.

1

The Application Integration Crisis

If you look at any survey of CIOs taken during the past 10 years, you'll notice that application integration is always one of the most critical issues facing information technology (IT) managers. Application integration is any mechanism that allows different software systems to share, route, or aggregate information. **Web services** help you integrate your applications.[1]

Application integration is one of the most critical IT issues

Your application systems implement and automate your company's business processes. The more effectively these systems work, the more smoothly your business operates. You have many different application systems, each performing a different part of the process. Consider a typical array of business systems. One system manages materials requirement planning (MRP). Another system manages inventory control. A third system manages the distribution process. Yet another manages customer orders, and one more keeps track of customer information. Meanwhile, a completely different system generates sales forecasts. To coordinate the process of building products to fulfill customer orders, these systems need to share information. Sharing and routing information among these application systems is fundamental to the business process. Without it, this process breaks down. And when your process breaks down, you lose money.

Application integration is fundamental to the business process

---

[1] See Chapter 2 for a thorough definition of Web services. For now, just consider Web services as a technology that lets applications communicate using XML and the Web.

Chapter 1   The Application Integration Crisis

Hershey's Integration Nightmare

Hershey experienced an ERP integration nightmare

Hershey Foods Corporation is the leading North American manufacturer of quality chocolate and nonchocolate confectionery and chocolate-related grocery products. In 1999, Hershey spent $112 million on an enterprise resource planning (ERP) integration project involving software from SAP, Manugistics, and Siebel. Unfortunately, it blew up in Hershey's face.

Hershey's plan was aggressive

Admittedly Hershey was taking a huge gamble because it was trying to deploy a four-year project in only 30 months. It started the project in 1997 and went live with SAP financial, purchasing, materials management, and warehousing modules in January 1999. In July it added SAP modules for order processing and billing as well as planning and scheduling modules from Manugistics and a pricing promotions package from Siebel.

Order processing didn't work

That's when things started to go wrong. Just as the back-to-school and Halloween season set in, Hershey started experiencing severe order fulfillment problems. Orders weren't being processed properly. Shipments were delayed or delivered incomplete. And Hershey had no idea what was going on. It had to call its customers to find out how much candy they had received.

Hershey experienced a 19% drop in profits

Chocolate started to pile up in the warehouse. By the end of September, product inventories were up more than 25 percent over those of the preceding year. Hershey blamed the subsequent 19 percent drop in third quarter profits on these system problems.

Hershey needed to improve information flow

Hershey didn't say whether the problems were caused by software quality, implementation issues, or a combination of the two. It did indicate, though, that one of its highest priorities for fixing the problem was to improve the way information flowed between the different applications.

Three years later, Hershey is much happier with its systems. Staying with SAP, it started another ERP upgrade in July 2001 and went live in May 2002. This upgrade went smoothly, and it came in 20 percent under budget. Hershey has consolidated more than 95 percent of its revenue and business transaction processing within a single system, and this arrangement gives the organization greater consistency, visibility, and real-time access to critical business information.

Now Hershey has integrated 95% of its business processing

The new integrated system helps Hershey reduce costs, improve quality, increase efficiency, and make better decisions. The upgrade includes a number of process enhancements such as materials management invoice verification, military distributor credit processing, and pick list processing. These enhancements help reduce costs and processing times, and Hershey now has a near zero-defect production environment. Using business analytics, Hershey can perform real-time impact analysis of sales and marketing activities, resulting in reduced packaging stock outs.

The new integrated system produces numerous benefits

Integration Helps Your Business

As Hershey can attest, when application systems don't communicate effectively, your business process suffers. When application systems do communicate effectively, your business works better. From a tactical point of view, application integration can reduce errors and friction in the production process, thereby improving quality, increasing productivity, and reducing costs. From a strategic point of view, application integration helps people get access to the information they need to be more effective at their jobs. Employees can work more efficiently. Analysts can get a better sense of the big picture. Decision makers can make more informed decisions. Better knowledge makes your business more competitive, resulting in higher profits.

Effective application integration provides both tactical and strategic advantages

Chapter 1 The Application Integration Crisis

All Applications Require Integration

Nearly every IT project involves integration

Application integration is at the heart of nearly every IT project. Very few application systems work in a vacuum. In many cases, a "new" application aggregates information from some number of legacy applications or perhaps provides a new, integrated interface to the business process functionality implemented by an assortment of legacy applications. In both cases the integration makes employees more efficient and effective at their jobs.

Business process automation and workflow rely on integration

Application integration forms the foundation for business process automation and workflow applications. The goal of these applications is to streamline operations by automating the process by which applications interact with humans and with other applications. A set of business rules guides the process, determining the next task and specifying which application or human should perform it.

Portals require integration

A portal is another example of an application integration project. A portal provides a consolidated doorway into countless application systems and information resources. Thus, a portal must have integrated connections to every system and resource.

KM/BI systems aggregate corporate information

Knowledge management (KM) and business intelligence (BI) systems aggregate information from multiple business applications and make it available to analysts and decision makers via reports, multi-dimensional databases, and data mining tools. You must give these tools access to all applications if you want to achieve a unified view of your business.

ERP, PLM, CRM, SFA, FFA, SCM, and DCM are integration initiatives

Most major IT initiatives, such as ERP, product lifecycle management (PLM), customer relationship management (CRM), sales force automation (SFA), field force automation (FFA), supply chain management (SCM), and demand chain management (DCM), are, in fact, application integration initiatives. These initiatives have far-reaching goals to improve employee efficiency, reduce errors, streamline operations, and give decision makers more accurate and timely information.

Application integration can also extend beyond your corporate boundaries, enabling your application systems to converse directly with those of your suppliers, distributors, partners, and customers. Business-to-business (B2B) integration is inherently more challenging than internal integration because you have control over only half of the equation.

B2B initiatives cross corporate boundaries

Calculating Return on Investment

In some cases it's quite easy to measure the return on an application integration investment. If you deploy a new customer care application that makes your telephone support staff more efficient, the application can reduce the amount of time workers spend on each call, allowing fewer people to handle more calls. In this case you have a clear metric (time per call) that you can measure before and after an integration project.

Metrics make it easy to calculate ROI

Perhaps, over time, you might also notice a drop in your customer attrition rate. It's hard to say definitively what generates this benefit. Was it the new customer care application? Perhaps the quality of the product improved. Perhaps the competition wasn't working as aggressively to woo your customers away. Perhaps your new customer-retention marketing program should get the credit.

It's hard to identify the source of secondary benefits

It's often difficult to measure the ROI for strategic investments. When managers have the right information, they make better decisions. They can determine which products or services are most or least profitable. They can recognize conditions that might affect demand for a particular product in a particular geographic region

It's hard to measure the effects of better decision making

Chapter 1   The Application Integration Crisis

and adjust inventory accordingly. Without the right information, they might make poor decisions that could increase costs or jeopardize an important contract. They also might not recognize a golden opportunity. How can you measure the cost of an unknown lost opportunity?

Application Integration Is Hard

Integrating applications isn't always easy

As you've no doubt experienced, nearly every application, at some point in its lifecycle, needs to share information with at least one other application. Unfortunately it isn't always easy to make your application systems talk to one another. Web services make it easier to connect your applications.

You probably have many different applications

Most likely your enterprise has a hodgepodge of application systems, deployed over the years as necessary. Some of these applications were developed in-house, others purchased from a variety of software vendors, and still others acquired in mergers and acquisitions.

Web services simplify heterogeneous communication

If yours is like most companies, you probably have to deal with a heterogeneous environment. No doubt you've built your corporate application systems using a variety of hardware platforms and software technologies. Having heterogeneous systems makes integration hard. Your application systems simply don't speak the same language. Web services provide a common, platform-independent language that simplifies heterogeneous application integration.

Most application systems aren't designed to communicate

One of the biggest issues, though, is that most application systems aren't designed to talk to other application systems. When you build in-house systems, expedience tends to drive development. You have a set of well-defined requirements for the application system, and your goal is to deliver that functionality as quickly as possible. It takes a lot more time and effort to design an extensible application that can support future, unknown requirements.

Packaged application systems are notorious for being closed and proprietary. Vendors have strong incentives to limit the integration capabilities of their applications. They want you to buy all your software from them. During the 1980s and 1990s software packages started growing in size and complexity as the vendors strove to provide a theoretically "complete" solution. Unfortunately, no single vendor supplies a complete solution, so you're always faced with the task of external integration. Only recently have these vendors started to respond to customers' demands for more versatile integration capabilities.

Packaged application software rarely supports external integration

Approaches to Application Integration

Application integration strategies fall into two basic categories: data-level integration and application-level integration. Figure 1-1 shows the difference.

There are many ways to integrate applications

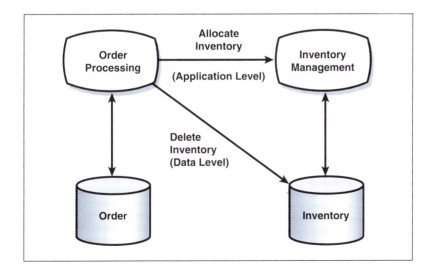

Figure 1-1: Allocating inventory for an order. In data-level integration, the order processing application reaches directly into the inventory database and deletes the inventory, bypassing the business rules in the inventory management application. In application-level integration, the order processing application calls the inventory management application and asks it to allocate inventory.

7

Chapter 1 The Application Integration Crisis

Data-level integration is well suited for read-only aggregation

With data-level integration, applications can share information simply by sharing their databases. This approach is less costly and less invasive than application-level integration. Generally you don't need to modify your existing application systems to implement data-level integration. It's a useful way to implement retrieval-only information aggregation. An application can extract information from multiple databases, aggregate it, and produce useful reports. You frequently use this type of integration to build a data warehouse.

Data-level integration is dangerous for transactional and update applications

But you need to be very careful using this approach for update operations. I view data-level integration as a quick and dirty way to integrate systems. As a rule, you should not attempt to implement transactional or update applications using this technique. Data-level integration doesn't let your applications share business logic—the code that implements your business rules. For example, in your inventory application, your business logic implements the business rules used to allocate inventory. If you build an integration application that accesses the inventory database directly without using the inventory application, that application will bypass the business rules that you have defined to establish priorities and resolve conflicts. You must either duplicate the business logic in the new application or risk violating the business rules. A number of vendors of packaged applications view direct manipulation of the database as a violation of your support agreement.

Application-level integration allows applications to share information and business logic

In many cases it's a much better idea to integrate at the application level. Compared with data-level integration, application-level integration takes more time and effort, but it offers much more versatility and maintains business consistency. In this approach, an application makes its information *and* its business logic available to other applications through an **application programming interface (API)**.

Building Integration Hooks

An API is a programming mechanism that allows an application or system function to expose its capabilities (make them available) to other applications. Hence an API supports application-to-application communication. An API is a bit like a two-sided coin. One side faces outward, providing an interface to external applications. The other side reaches inward, hooking into the private capabilities of the application.

An API lets one program talk to another program

Most application systems provide a few built-in interfaces. Generally there's some type of human interface available, but it's hard to get another application to think and act like a human. Sometimes, particularly in the case of purchased applications, an application includes a set of APIs designed to support internal integration among its related modules. These APIs often support proprietary formats, and that makes it difficult to use them for external integration. Sometimes you're lucky, and the application provides an interface designed for external integration. But rarely will you find a comprehensive set of APIs that lets you do everything you want to do. At some point along the way, you'll probably have to build your own integration hooks and then expose them through an API. You can use Web services to build open, nonproprietary APIs.

Applications usually don't supply all the APIs you need

Building Integration Hooks

You can build an integration hook either by leveraging an existing interface or by modifying the application to create a completely new interface. These integration hooks are often called **application adapters**. Conceptually, an application adapter is similar to a power adapter. If you want to power an electrical appliance, you need an electrical outlet that matches the power plug on your appliance. If the power plug and the electrical outlet don't match, you can use a power adapter to make them work together. In some cases the power adapter acts as a pass-through, simply realigning the

An application adapter is like a power adapter

Figure 1-2: An application adapter acts as a go-between, resolving incompatibilities between application interfaces.

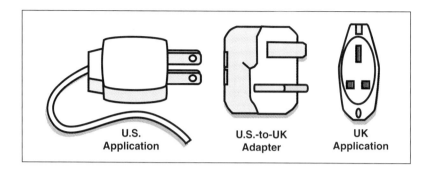

physical outlet configuration to allow the positive, negative, earth, and ground wires to connect. In other cases the power adapter actually modifies the voltage, switching between, for example, AC and DC power or 110 and 220 volts. An application adapter can work the same way. In some cases it simply realigns the programming interface. In other cases it adds additional processing. Figure 1-2 shows a conceptual overview of an application adapter.

An application adapter can act as a simple pass-through

If your application has internal APIs and if you have access to the proprietary formats used by these APIs, you can build an application adapter that makes these APIs accessible to outside applications. In this case the application adapter acts as a simple translator. Outside applications call the adapter using an open API. The adapter then translates the request into the proprietary API that's native to the application.

A screen scraping adapter modulates the interface by simulating human interaction

In some cases you may want to add business or navigation logic to the application adapter that either simplifies or adds value to the native application interface. For example, you can encapsulate a human interface using a technique known as **screen scraping**. Essentially you build an application that simulates human interaction. Outside applications call this screen scraper application, which initiates a dialog with the application through its native graphical user interface (GUI) or browser interface. This technique is the least invasive method for creating an interface to an existing application, but it is also the least efficient method, and it tends to generate the most errors and be the hardest to maintain. Imagine the maintenance headaches you'll get when you upgrade to the latest revision of a packaged application and you realize that the GUI has completely changed.

If an existing interface can't supply you with the integration hooks that you need, you can always build a custom API into your application. A custom API is new application code that you develop to support a particular business requirement. Obviously, a custom API requires more time and effort, and it is by far the most invasive integration technique, but it does exactly what you need it to do.

You can design custom-built APIs to do exactly what you need

Quite a few enterprise application integration[2] (**EAI**) vendors provide connectivity **frameworks** that can help you build application adapters for your applications. Adapter framework vendors include Attunity, GE Global eXchange Services, IONA, iWay Software, Software AG, TIBCO Software, webMethods, and many more. Traditionally these vendor frameworks have generated adapters that rely on the vendors' proprietary protocols. Most of these vendors are now adopting Web services so that the adapters can be more widely used.

EAI vendors provide application adapter frameworks

Exposing Interfaces Across the Network

So far we've talked about building integration hooks that reach into an application to access its information and business logic. An application adapter also needs to expose those integration hooks to the

Network APIs are created using communication middleware

---

[2] Although we touch on EAI in this book, we do not cover it in any depth. EAI solves a much larger problem than basic application integration. EAI focuses on extraction, aggregation, routing, and dissemination of information based on business rules. It tends to operate outside the production process. For the most part, this book focuses on direct application-to-application communication during the production process. To be clear, Web services don't replace EAI. Please see *Enterprise Application Integration*, by David S. Linthicum, ISBN 0-201-61583-5, for a thorough guide to EAI.

Chapter 1   The Application Integration Crisis

outside world through an open, network-enabled API. You normally create a network API using some type of communication middleware. Web services represent a new type of communication middleware.

Middleware provides easy access to complex system facilities

Middleware is a software package that sits between your application code and its underlying platform, providing easy access to core system facilities such as the network, storage, and processors. Middleware hides the complexities of the underlying facilities from the programmer and provides a consistent interface across various hardware and software environments. Middleware allows programmers to concentrate on solving business problems and not waste time trying to make the business application run properly on a particular machine. Middleware systems include file systems, database systems, application servers, transaction processing monitors, message brokers, and distributed computing systems. **Communication middleware** is middleware that lets applications talk to one another across the network.

Communication middleware hides the complexity of the network

There are many kinds of communication middleware, each offering slightly different features and capabilities, but the basic goal of all communication middleware is to allow applications to communicate while hiding the complexity associated with using the network. Figure 1-3 provides an overview of communication middleware functionality. The middleware performs all the work associated with establishing network connections, creating network messages, and transferring the messages on behalf of the applications. Because different machines and different programming languages use different formats to represent data, middleware often performs data translation.

Each middleware system uses specific protocols

Each type of communication middleware communicates in its own way. Each system supports a specific set of programming languages, operating systems, and network **protocols**. Most **traditional middleware** systems use a binary data format to represent

Exposing Interfaces Across the Network

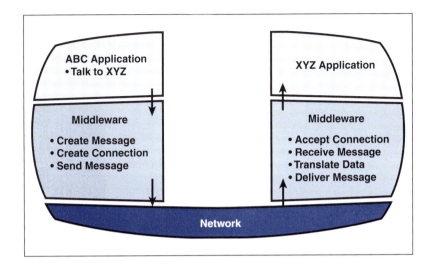

Figure 1-3:
Communication middleware performs all the work necessary to create and exchange messages over a network.

the information as it gets sent across the network. A **binary data format** is a compact way to represent information. Unfortunately, each middleware system uses a different binary data format, and this means that different types of middleware can't talk to each other. For the most part, two applications must both use the same type of middleware to communicate.

The tricky part is that it's hard to find one middleware solution that supports all your applications. Each middleware product supports a limited set of operating systems and programming languages. All these differences make it hard to support heterogeneous environments. Web services solve this problem by supporting any language on any platform.

Web services support any language on any platform

Middleware Styles

There are two fundamental styles of communication. Applications can communicate either by passing messages or by invoking functions. With traditional middleware, you use a different type of middleware product to perform these different types of communication. Web services support both styles of communication.

Applications communicate by passing messages or invoking functions

Chapter 1   The Application Integration Crisis

Message-oriented Middleware

MOM passes messages

Message-oriented middleware (MOM) uses an **asynchronous, peer**-based style of communication for passing messages. The two communicating applications act as equal peers. One application sends a message and then goes about its business. The other application receives and processes the message on its own schedule. The receiving application may send a response message back to the first application, but then again, it may not.

MOM is not pervasive

There are quite a few MOM middleware products, such as IBM WebSphereMQ, Microsoft MQ, Sonic Software SonicMQ, and TIBCO Rendezvous. Many of these products are available for a wide array of platforms, but these products aren't pervasive. With the exception of Microsoft MQ, you must license each product for each system on which it's deployed. License fees can get pretty steep if you need to deploy the middleware on all of your machines. Microsoft MQ is pervasive on Windows systems, but it isn't available for other platforms. More to the point, you can't use Microsoft MQ to talk to other platforms.

Each product communicates using proprietary protocols

One of the most frustrating things about MOM is that each product uses a proprietary communication protocol. Two applications using different MOM products cannot interoperate. The Java platform provides a standard programming interface to MOM products called the Java Message Service (**JMS**) API. This API lets a developer write an application that can work with almost any MOM product, but even so, the two applications that are communicating must use the same MOM product.

RPC-style Middleware

RPC-style middleware invokes functions

Function invocation middleware, also known a **remote procedure call** (**RPC**) middleware, uses a **synchronous, client/server**-based style of communication. With RPC-style communications, one application acts as a client, and the other acts as a server. The client calls the server and requests a specific action. The client always expects a response, and in most circumstances it sits idle until it gets one. When the server receives the request, it immediately performs the requested action, and when it is complete, the server sends back the response. Most developers find RPC-style middleware to be more intuitive and easier to use than MOM middleware.

RPC middleware products include Open Network Computing (**ONC**) **RPC**, Distributed Computing Environment (**DCE**) **RPC**, **Microsoft RPC**, Microsoft Distributed Component Object Model (**DCOM**), Object Management Group (OMG) Common Object Request Broker Architecture (**CORBA**), and Java Remote Method Invocation (**RMI**). Many RPC systems are formal industry standards, but, as with MOM products, you cannot use one RPC system to talk to a different RPC system. You must use the same type of system on both sides of the connection.[3]

Most RPC-style systems are based on standards, but they don't interoperate

The biggest challenge associated with RPC-style middleware is finding a single RPC system that supports all your programming languages on all your platforms at a reasonable cost. The Java platform provides built-in support for RMI and CORBA, and the Java platform is pervasive, but it supports only the Java programming language. All Microsoft Windows platforms include built-in support for Microsoft RPC and DCOM. These systems support virtually any programming language, but you almost never find them on non-Windows platforms. Most UNIX and Linux systems include built-in support for ONC, but you rarely find ONC on Windows, and for the most part it supports only C, C++, and Java. Although DCE is available for most platforms, it's rarely built in to the platform. You must license the technology separately. And, as with ONC, most DCE

It's hard to find a single RPC system that supports all your platforms

---

[3] It is possible to use a gateway or bridge to connect disparate systems. For example, you can use a COM/CORBA bridge to link DCOM applications with CORBA applications. This bridge translates the protocols during transmission.

Chapter 1   The Application Integration Crisis

implementations support only C, C++, and Java. Of all the RPC-style middleware systems, CORBA gives you the best language and platform coverage. CORBA can run on virtually every platform, and it supports virtually every programming language. But, as with DCE, it doesn't come with your platform. You must license the technology separately.[4] And, more to the point, although you can use CORBA with Visual Basic and other popular Windows languages, the Microsoft development tools don't provide integrated support for CORBA. Hence many developers view CORBA as hard to use.

Traditional Middleware Blues

Traditional middleware poses a number of challenges

Historically, most people use a mixture of MOM and RPC-style middleware to integrate their application systems. But there are a number of challenges associated with integrating your applications based on these traditional middleware technologies. I refer to these challenges as the Traditional Middleware Blues. I can summarize these challenges in two basic themes. The first theme relates to pervasiveness and heterogeneity. The second theme relates to the total cost of ownership associated with integration.

Pervasiveness and Heterogeneity

It's hard to find one middleware package that supports all your languages and platforms

From my description of the various middleware products, I'm sure you already have a sense of this first issue. Each middleware system uses a different communication protocol. For two applications to communicate, you must use the same type of middleware on both systems. This requirement is one of the most frustrating restrictions associated with using middleware. It's hard to find a single middleware package that supports all your languages and platforms. Very often you're forced to use multiple middleware packages to complete a single integration project.

[4]There are a number of open source CORBA implementations available.

Unfortunately, your systems don't necessarily come fully stocked with all these different flavors of middleware. Microsoft includes Microsoft MQ, Microsoft RPC, and DCOM with every Windows platform. Most Windows-based tools and applications provide native support for these technologies, but you can't use these middleware systems to talk to non-Windows applications. UNIX and Linux systems usually include ONC and Java RMI, but you can't use these systems to talk to popular Windows languages such as Visual Basic and PowerBuilder. You might consider using CORBA or a third-party MOM product to bridge the gap between these environments, but by comparison with the native Microsoft middleware, CORBA and MOM are fairly hard to use. You often need to send your developers to extensive training classes for them to become proficient with these technologies.

Windows middleware doesn't work with other platforms

And then there's the issue of licensing. Middleware isn't pervasive. If you intend to use a particular type of middleware in your applications, you need to make sure it's deployed on all the systems used by those applications. And that can cost you. Many middleware packages require a deployment license for every system that uses them. Your administrative staff must also bear the burden of ensuring that the required middleware is properly installed and running on all the systems that need it. Things can get tricky if you don't have administrative control over all the systems involved. You may not be able to dictate what type of middleware to use.

Middleware isn't pervasive—you must pay to make it available on each system

The good news is that Web services address these issues. Rather than rely on special protocols, Web services communicate using the **World Wide Web**. The **Web** is pervasive. All your systems provide native support for the Web. More to the point, all major vendors have endorsed Web services. You can find support for Web services on any platform—from embedded systems to mainframes. Microsoft provides native support for Web services in Windows. The Java platform also provides native support for Web services.

Web services are pervasive

Most development tools provide native support for Web services. Increasing numbers of software vendors are adding built-in support for Web services to their products. You don't need to buy runtime licenses for Web services for each of your systems. In short, Web services are pervasive.

Web services support heterogeneous integration

In addition to being pervasive, Web services can support any programming language. Web services communicate using the Extensible Markup Language (**XML**), a text-based protocol that all applications can understand. Web services tools are available for almost any programming language, including Visual Basic, JavaScript, Java, C++, COBOL, Smalltalk, Ada, Perl, Python, and many, many more. In short, Web services support heterogeneous integration.

Total Cost of Ownership

Development and maintenance cost much more than the middleware

Another serious issue associated with traditional middleware is the total cost of ownership. The cost of the middleware licenses is only a fraction of the total cost associated with an integration project. The heavy costs come from development and maintenance. Traditional middleware is fairly hard to use. Application integration based on traditional middleware generally requires high-priced expertise. Integration projects require experienced developers with both domain knowledge and middleware experience. In contrast, Web services are easier to use than traditional middleware.

Each integration hook increases the total cost of ownership for the application

Maintenance also carries a hefty price tag. Each integration hook dramatically increases the total cost of ownership for your applications. Most application adapters are written separately from the application logic. The developers who maintain the application must be aware of all APIs that have been built to access the application. They also must be aware of any impact a small change to the application might have on those APIs. If the change impacts the

APIs, developers must also make changes in every application that uses those APIs.

This maintenance nightmare stems from a concept called **tightly coupled** connections. A tightly coupled connection is a single-purpose connection designed to address the specific integration requirements of one set of applications. In most situations, RPC-style middleware systems, such as RPC, DCOM, CORBA, and RMI, produce tightly coupled connections. These systems define very exact specifications of how messages must be constructed and passed between the two communicating applications. As a result, tightly coupled connections limit the flexibility and reusability of application adapters.

Tightly coupled application connections limit flexibility and reusability

Quite frequently, you find yourself building a new integration interface each time you need to connect two applications. Either the existing integration hooks don't quite suit your needs, or the middleware is incompatible with the new required environment. Pretty soon you find yourself with hundreds of APIs to maintain.

Point-to-point connections cause a maintenance nightmare

The maintenance nightmare gets worse. Application integration causes dependencies between application systems, and these dependencies may not be adequately documented. When the time comes to upgrade the application to support a new business requirement, any change to the application may break the corresponding adapter.

Application adapters are brittle

Message-oriented systems generally don't suffer as much from tightly coupled connections. They typically use **loosely coupled** connections, meaning that there is a greater layer of abstraction between the application code and the adapter's message format. Two communicating applications must agree to the format of the message, but the application has a bit more flexibility in how it

Loosely coupled connections separate the application code from the message format

processes the message. If you modify the application, it doesn't necessarily force a change in the application interface. This is the primary reason people tend to use MOM technologies to implement EAI solutions, which require general-purpose interfaces.

MOM is harder to use than RPC-style middleware

So why not just use MOM? There is one reason: MOM is harder to use than RPC-style middleware. RPC-style middleware makes it easy for a developer to build a connection to a remote application. RPC-style middleware provides tools that generate all the communication code for an application. With MOM products, on the other hand, the developer must write the code that connects the application to the message. In addition, MOM is proprietary. You must use the same MOM product on every system throughout your environment. Systemwide MOM deployments can get very expensive. This issue becomes even more challenging as you start to venture outside your corporate boundaries, as discussed in the next section.

Web services support the loosely coupled features of MOM with the ease of use of RPC

Web services combine the advantages of MOM and RPC-style middleware. Web services support loosely coupled connections, and at the same time they support the ease of use of RPC-style middleware. Web services tools can generate all your communication code while still providing a high level of abstraction between the application code and the message format.

Extending Integration to Work Across the Internet

Integration also benefits your B2B processes

So far I've confined my discussion to the issues associated with internal application integration. But your business processes don't stop at your firewall. Integration benefits your B2B processes as much as it does your internal business processes. Supply chain management and demand chain management initiatives focus on streamlining interbusiness interactions. These initiatives require extensive application-to-application integration efforts.

Extending Integration to Work Across the Internet

Unfortunately, traditional middleware solutions aren't designed to support intercorporate communication across the Internet. Middleware messages are frequently blocked by **firewalls**. Firewalls inspect incoming messages and determine whether they may pass. Unfortunately, most firewalls can't interpret the binary formats used by traditional middleware, so they block the traffic. In addition, these middleware solutions rely on domain-based security, reliability, and transaction systems to ensure the integrity of the environment, and these domain-based systems don't effectively extend across the open Internet. It has become obvious that to effectively conduct business-to-business application integration, we need a new type of middleware that inherently supports the Internet.

Traditional middleware doesn't work across the Internet

Using the Internet as an Integration Platform

When we stop to consider the Internet, we realize that there's a totally pervasive distributed computing infrastructure just sitting there waiting to be used: the Web. Almost every computer in your organization has inherent support for the Web. Most Windows, Linux, UNIX, midrange, and mainframe servers include a Web server. If you don't have one, there are plenty of open source products to choose from. We'll talk a bit more about the Web in Chapters 2 and 3.

The Internet is pervasive

Unlike traditional middleware systems, Web systems typically communicate using text-based messages. Text is much bulkier than binary data, but you don't need special middleware products to convert the data into a proprietary binary format. Any application can communicate over the Web. As it turns out, firewalls are much happier dealing with text information than binary data. A firewall can inspect the information and apply security rules before allowing it to pass.

The Internet communicates using text, which all applications can understand

One of the most popular ways to represent data on the Internet is using XML, a universal, text-based, self-describing data format. Almost every computer in your organization has inherent support

XML is a universal data format

Chapter 1   The Application Integration Crisis

for XML. Any application, written in any language, running on any platform, can process XML data. We'll talk a bit more about XML in Chapter 3.

Web services rely on XML and the Web

So considering that we have this incredibly pervasive distributed computing infrastructure in place, doesn't it make sense to build a new integration platform based on it? The Web is pervasive. Any application can speak XML. This sounds like a great opportunity to create a totally pervasive middleware system. And, in fact, we did. Web services represent a new middleware integration platform built on XML and the Web.

Web services work with firewalls

Web services let applications communicate over the Internet. Web services can securely navigate their way through firewalls, and they rely on new Internet-based technologies to manage cross-domain security, transactions, and reliability.

Using Web Services for Integration

Web services solve the heterogeneous communication problem

Web services address the challenges associated with traditional middleware. Probably the most powerful feature of Web services is that they provide a common way for any application, written in any language, running on any platform, to talk to any other application. In this way, Web services solve the heterogeneous communication problem.

All major software vendors support Web services

As an added benefit, Web services technology is pervasive. You don't have to install a special software package on every one of your systems. Web services rely on standard Internet protocols, which are already resident on every Internet-enabled system. All major software vendors have bought into the idea of Web services. Operating systems, application servers, database systems, application systems, language platforms, and development tools now come prepackaged with Web services support.

One thing that's remarkable about Web services software is that it is much less expensive than most other middleware. Most vendors treat Web services as a new feature of their existing products, such as application servers and development tools. The primary impetus behind Web services is heterogeneous communication, so vendors can't develop lock-in strategies that led to high price tags. Also, the open source community has been deeply involved in the development of Web services technologies right from the beginning. These factors have kept software prices very low.

Web services are cheaper than traditional middleware

Best of all, Web services are easier to use than most traditional middleware, so development costs are lower. Developers with advanced skills in CORBA, RMI, DCOM, or MOM are expensive—if you can find them at all. Professional training classes often cost $500 or more per day. In contrast, Web services technology is much easier to use. Many developers are learning the technology on their own, knowing that these new skills have broad application and will make them more marketable. You can expect to find a large supply of talent at a reasonable price.

Web services are easier to use than traditional middleware

The cost savings also apply to long-term maintenance and total cost of ownership. Web services combine the ease of use of RPC-style middleware with the loose coupling of MOM. Application adapters built with Web services are much more flexible and adaptable than those built with traditional RPC-style middleware. These adapters are cheaper and easier to maintain.

Web services connections are flexible and easy to maintain

Web Services Have Tactical and Strategic Value

In case it isn't obvious by now, I'm recommending that you adopt Web services to help you battle the integration crisis. The arguments I've cited thus far give you a host of tactical reasons to consider this technology. Web services technology is cheap and easy,

The tactical advantages alone should convince you to try this technology

Chapter 1   The Application Integration Crisis

and it works with any application language on any platform. It works for both internal and external integration projects. It's a safe choice because all vendors support it, and they are committed to ensuring interoperability. You won't find yourself locked in to a proprietary solution. These tactical advantages, by themselves, should be enough to convince you to at least consider Web services for your next integration project.

Web services have the potential to finally deliver on the promise of reusability

Web services also have profound strategic value. This value stems from the concept of reusability. One of the most costly aspects of integration is that application adapters are rarely reusable. Each new point-to-point connection between applications causes an exponential increase in the total cost of ownership of your applications. Reusability has been an elusive goal for many generations of application development technology. Web services represent the latest generation of technology that tries to deliver reusability. And this generation is likely to be much more successful than previous generations, such as objects, components, and frameworks. A Web service is a larger piece of application functionality than objects or components. This larger granularity gives Web services the potential to finally deliver on the promise of reusability.

"Integratable" applications have a much lower cost of ownership

Web services aren't automatically reusable. You must put some thought into the design to ensure that more than one application can effectively use a service. So to gain the strategic value of Web services, you may need to make some changes in your application design process.[5] Even so, it is easier to design for reusability when you're working at the service granularity level than at the object or component level. It's relatively easy to build a general-purpose Web

---

[5] Reusable application design is beyond the scope of this book. Please see *Patterns of Enterprise Application Architecture*, by Martin Fowler et al., ISBN 0-321-12742-0, for a thorough discussion of application design patterns and architecture.

Web Services Have Tactical and Strategic Value

service application adapter for one of your legacy applications. After you have built this general-purpose adapter, the legacy application becomes "integratable." Any application can use the adapter to talk to the legacy application. At this point you have one adapter to maintain for this application rather than one for every application that wants to use it.

The real strategic value appears after you have created general-purpose adapters for all your application systems. When all your applications are integratable, you then have the ability to dynamically configure your systems to support your business. You can dynamically modify or manipulate your business process. You can dynamically aggregate data from multiple systems. You can dynamically use your data mining tools and analytics to discover new trends. You can turn your business into a dynamic enterprise, one that can respond to business drivers in real time.

Integratable applications let you respond to business needs in real time

2

Web Services Basics

If you ask five people to define Web services, you'll probably get at least six answers. Some people use the term "Web services" to describe applications that communicate with Simple Object Access Protocol (**SOAP**). (SOAP is an XML messaging protocol. We'll discuss it in detail in Chapter 3.) Other folks use the term to describe only the SOAP interface. Still other people vehemently object to the idea of constraining the definition to a specific technology such as SOAP. Some people use the term to describe any application that communicates over the Internet. Other people use the term to describe any Web-based application. Some people view Web services as anything that's accessible over the Web. And some people use the term to describe the **software-as-a-service** business model.

There's no one official definition of "Web services"

Given that there is no official consensus within the industry, I am establishing my own set of names and definitions. I want to give you a basic grounding to help you understand this technology, so my goal is to make things as simple and straightforward as possible.

For the purposes of this book I am defining my own terminology

What Is a Web Service?

The simplest and most basic definition that I can give you is that a Web service is an application that provides a **Web API**. As mentioned in Chapter 1, an API supports application-to-application communication. A Web API is an API that lets the applications communicate using XML and the Web.

A Web service is an application with a Web API

So here's the basic concept: Web services use the Web to perform application-to-application integration. A lot of the hype around Web services talks about dynamic assembly of Web-based software

Web services use the Web for application-to-application integration

services. It talks about the software-as-a-service business model. It talks about spontaneous discovery of new business partners. My advice is to ignore this hype. It's possible that at some point in the future some of these glossy images will become reality, but please don't let the science fiction stories distract you from reality or dissuade you from using this technology today to solve real business issues.

Why Web Services?

Web services help you integrate applications

Rather than "what?" I think the more important question is "why?" Why should you care about Web services? The answer is that Web services mitigate the application integration crisis. They help you integrate applications, and they do so at a significantly lower price point than any other integration technology.

XML and the Web solve the "Traditional Middleware Blues"

Web services represent a new form of middleware based on XML and the Web. XML and the Web help solve the challenges associated with traditional application-to-application integration, which I identified in Chapter 1 as the Traditional Middleware Blues. To summarize:

- Traditional middleware doesn't support heterogeneity.
- Traditional middleware doesn't work across the Internet.
- Traditional middleware isn't pervasive.
- Traditional middleware is hard to use.
- Traditional middleware is expensive.
- Traditional middleware maintenance costs are outrageous.
- Traditional middleware connections are hard to reuse.
- Traditional middleware connections are fragile.

Web services support heterogeneous interoperability

Web services address these issues. Web services are platform- and language-independent. You can develop a Web service using any language, and you can deploy it on any platform, from the tiniest device to the largest supercomputer. More to the point, any Web service can be accessed by any other application, regardless of either's language or platform. Web services communicate using XML and Web protocols, which are pervasive, work both internally and across the Internet, and support heterogeneous interoperability.

Web services simplify the process of making applications talk to each other. Simplification results in lower development cost, faster time to market, easier maintenance, and reduced total cost of ownership. The bottom line is this: Web services allow you to integrate your applications at a fraction of the cost of traditional middleware.

Web services are inexpensive

Traditional RPC-style middleware, such as RPC, CORBA, RMI, and DCOM, relies on tightly coupled connections. A tightly coupled connection is very brittle, and it can break if you make any modification to the application. Tightly coupled connections are the source of many a maintenance nightmare. In contrast, Web services support loosely coupled connections. Loose coupling minimizes the impact of changes to your applications. A Web service interface provides a layer of abstraction between the client and server. A change in one doesn't necessarily force a change in the other. The abstract interface also makes it easier to reuse a service in another application. Loose coupling reduces the cost of maintenance and increases reusability.

Web services are flexible and adaptable

Defining "Web" and "Service"

So let's dig a little deeper into our definition. Just what is a Web service? If we dissect the name, we can infer that a Web service has something to do with the Web and something to do with services. I like to say that a Web service is a service that lives on the Web. This definition doesn't help us very much, though, unless we know the meaning of the terms "Web" and "service." So let's start there.

A Web service is a service that lives on the Web

Chapter 2   Web Services Basics

The Web is a huge information space filled with interconnected resources

The Web is an immensely scalable information space filled with interconnected resources. The architecture for the Web has been developed and standardized by the World Wide Web Consortium (**W3C**). A **Web resource** is any type of named information object—such as a word processing document, a digital picture, a Web page, an e-mail account, or an application—that's accessible through the Web. All resources on the Web are connected via the Internet, and you access Web resources using standard Internet protocols. Any network-enabled application or device can access any resource in the Web. Right off the bat, you can see that the Web solves one of your integration challenges: The Web is pervasive and provides universal connectivity.

A service is an application that can be consumed by software

A **service** is an application that exposes its functionality through an application programming interface (API). In other words, a service is a resource that is designed to be consumed by software rather than by humans.

"Service" refers to the service-oriented architecture

The term "service" implies something special about the application design. It refers to something known as the **service-oriented architecture** (**SOA**). The SOA is the basic architecture used by most RPC-style middleware systems. Chapter 3 talks about the SOA in detail.

An interface hides the complexities of the internal system

One of the most important features of the SOA is the separation of interface from implementation. A service exposes its functionality through an interface, and that interface hides the inner workings of the application. A client application doesn't need to understand how the service actually performs its work. All it needs to understand is how to use the interface. To give you an analogy, let's look at a car. A car is a complicated machine, but the car provides a set of interfaces that's relatively simple to use. To start a car, you don't need to know how an internal combustion engine

Defining "Web" and "Service"

works, or even how the starter motor works. You only need to know how to use the interface that the car supplies to start it: Turn the key.

A Web service possesses the characteristics of both a Web resource and a service. It is an application that exposes its functionality through an API, and it is a Web resource that is designed to be consumed by software rather than by a human sitting at a browser.

A Web service is both a Web resource and a service

Understanding the concept of a service is key to understanding Web services. A service is a piece of software that does work for other software. In most circumstances, a service runs on a server, waiting for an application to call it and ask it to do some work. In many cases services don't provide any type of human interface, and the only way to access the service is through its API.

A service is software that does work for other software

A service can perform system functions or business application functions. For example, a file service can create, find, save, or delete a file. A stock quote service can retrieve the current ask and bid prices of an equity.

A service can perform system or business functions

All client/server technologies rely on this basic concept of a service. A service is the business or system application that plays the part of the server in a client/server relationship. Print servers, file servers, database servers, Web servers, and **application servers** are all examples of service-oriented systems.

A service plays the role of server in a client/server relationship

Any business application that exposes its capabilities through an API is a service. Business application services often run in an application server. An application server manages and coordinates the utilization of all resources available in a shared, multiprocessing environment, enabling optimized performance, scalability, reliability, and availability.

Application services often run in an application server

Chapter 2   Web Services Basics

Figure 2-1: A service can be shared by many different applications.

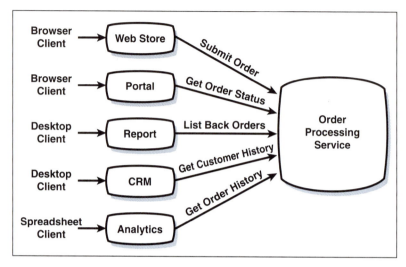

A service is a shared resource

You often need this type of scalability because many different users can share a single service. A service is a shared resource. One reason you might want to design a business application as a service is to consolidate your efforts and reduce duplicated work. If there is a particular piece of functionality that many of your applications need to perform, you should build this functionality as a service rather than reimplement the functionality in each application.

One service can support many applications

For example, as shown in Figure 2-1, it's much simpler and easier to manage and maintain your order processing system if you have only one application service that actually processes orders. This one service can support all the different ways that you offer to place orders, inquire about order status, and generate reports about orders.

Building Services

You use middleware to create your network API

To let clients access a service over the network, you must build a network API for the service. You generally use some type of communication middleware to create a network API. You can use a traditional middleware technology, such as RPC, DCOM, CORBA, RMI, or MOM, but all these technologies suffer from the Traditional

Middleware Blues. If you want to make your services available to heterogeneous users across multiple systems (including the Internet) at a reasonable cost, you should use middleware technology that supports these requirements.

Web services represent a new type of middleware that relies on the Web. The Web resolves the pervasive aspects of the Traditional Middleware Blues.[1] The Web is pervasive. The Web is free. The Web is completely vendor-, platform-, and language-independent. The Web uses the Internet as its native communication protocol. Web services support easy integration, flexibility, and service reusability.

Web services are Web-based middleware

Web Evolution

The Web was originally created to support interactive communication. People use the Web to communicate with other people and to access information. You use e-mail and instant messaging to converse with friends and colleagues. You use a browser to access information.

The Web was designed for interactive communication

In the early days of the Web, a **Web site** was simply a set of static pages that were stored in files. You could view only the text and pictures contained in these files. To change what users saw, a Web site operator had to edit the files. Soon we realized that we could also use the Web to access dynamic information. When you link to a dynamic page, the **Web server** doesn't merely display a file. Instead it calls an application that dynamically generates and renders the requested information. The introduction of this technique marked the point when the Web evolved to allow people to talk to applications.

A dynamic Web site allows people to talk to applications

---

[1] The other Traditional Middleware Blues tend to be a function of tightly coupled connections. Web services solve these issues using XML. Chapter 3 discusses XML.

Chapter 2   Web Services Basics

Web services allow applications to talk to applications

Web services represent the next step in the Web's evolution because they allow applications to talk to applications. Web-based application-to-application integration allows us to exploit the universal connectivity and immense scalability of the Web, and it supports a much richer set of usage models than do human-oriented applications.

Web sites support humans; Web services support software

Figure 2-2 summarizes the differences between a Web *site* and a Web *service*. A Web site represents a group of Web resources that are designed to be accessed by humans, and a Web service represents a group of Web resources that are designed to be accessed by applications.

A service interface must be structured and unambiguous

The interfaces to these two types of applications are fundamentally different. A Web site supports human clients who have a tremendous capacity to interpret the meaning of information. The site returns information as a Hypertext Markup Language (**HTML**) page—a string of text containing formatting information, often including graphics, clickable buttons, and links. A human interprets this information based on visual layout and physical association. In contrast, an application can't interpret information this way. An

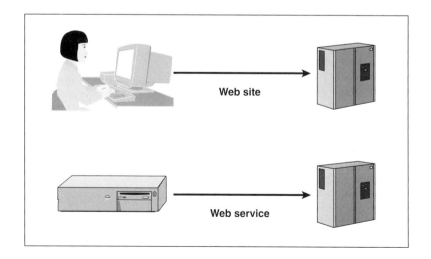

Figure 2-2: A Web site is designed to be accessed by humans. A Web service is designed to be accessed by applications.

34

application needs unambiguous information. It needs to know what programmatic functions are available, and it needs to know how to structure and interpret the data being exchanged. A Web API defines these programmatic functions and data structures in a completely unambiguous way.

Defining Characteristics of Web Services

A Web service exhibits the following defining characteristics:

- A Web service is a Web resource. You access a Web service using platform-independent and language-neutral Web protocols, such as HTTP. These Web protocols ensure easy integration of heterogeneous environments.
- A Web service provides an interface—a Web API—that can be called from another program. This application-to-application programming interface can be invoked from any type of application. The Web API provides access to the application logic that implements the service.
- A Web service is typically registered and can be located through a Web service **registry**. A registry enables service consumers to find services that match their needs. These service consumers may be humans or other applications.
- Web services support loosely coupled connections between systems. Web services communicate by passing XML messages to each other via a Web API, which adds a layer of abstraction to the environment that makes the connections flexible and adaptable.

A Web service is a Web resource that provides an API

Understanding the Scope of Web Services

So now that we have the basic definition down, let's go back to the big picture. How do you build Web services? What do you need to run Web services? How do you use Web services? Obviously this

Web services concepts can be divided into four layers

Chapter 2 Web Services Basics

topic covers a lot of territory. Figure 2-3 divides the scope of our discussion into four basic concepts: XML and **Web services technologies**, **Web services infrastructure**, **Web services**, and **Web services application templates**. Each layer builds on the layers below it.

XML and Web services technologies provide the foundation for Web services

The bottom layer in Figure 2-3 comprises XML and Web services technologies. These technologies provide the foundation for Web services. Don't worry about all the acronyms used in this illustration. We'll take a closer look at these technologies in Chapters 3–5. (If you can't wait, you can find definitions for the acronyms in the Glossary.)

Infrastructure refers to products that implement Web services technologies

The next layer in Figure 2-3 represents Web services infrastructure: products that implement the XML and Web services technologies. You use these products to build, deploy, manage, and use Web services. Chapters 8 and 9 will take a closer look at Web services infrastructure.

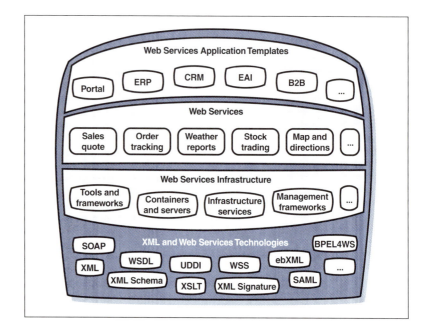

Figure 2-3: Web services concepts can be divided into four logical layers: XML and Web services technologies, Web services infrastructure, Web services, and Web services application templates.

36

Web Services Business Models

A Web service represents an information resource or business process that you have made available to other applications through a Web API. In particular, it is a resource that supports application-to-application communication using Web services infrastructure. You can turn any piece of application code into a Web service. A Web service can do whatever you've programmed it to do. Figure 2-3 lists five sample Web services: sales quote, order tracking, weather reports, stock trading, and map and directions.

Web services are applications that communicate using Web services infrastructure

Web services application templates represent the kinds of applications and initiatives for which Web services technology offers substantial benefits. The list of templates in Figure 2-3 is by no means exhaustive, but it identifies some of the more popular uses of Web services, such as portals, enterprise resource planning, customer relationship management, enterprise application integration initiatives, and business-to-business integration. We'll discuss a number of real-life Web services applications in this chapter and in Chapter 7.

Application templates represent systems that benefit from Web services

Web Services Business Models

You may have noticed that I didn't list software-as-a-service as a Web services application template. That's because software-as-a-service isn't an application. It's a business model in which you license subscription rights to access hosted software rather than license the rights to deploy the software in your own organization. For example, Salesforce.com uses the software-as-a-service business model. Salesforce.com hosts a CRM system, and users pay a monthly subscription fee to use the software.

Web services is not a business model

A lot of the early hype about Web services led many people to equate Web services with the software-as-a-service business model. The hype projects a blue-sky vision of being able to dynamically discover, assemble, and consume Internet-based software services.

Many people equate Web services with software-as-a-service

Chapter 2 Web Services Basics

But IDC predicts that the realization of this vision is at least 10 years away. I view that prediction as optimistic.

Web services should support your existing business models

My point is that, except in a few rare circumstances, you don't sell a Web service. Instead you sell some other type of product or service, and you use Web services to help you do that. Only in very rare circumstances are Web services the focus of their own business model. Without a viable business model, it's hard to create a business case for Web services. For example, let's look at Google.

Google

Google's business model is based on advertising

Google is the world's leading Web search company. Google provides a public search engine that contains an index of more than three billion Web pages. The normal interface to this search engine is a human-oriented browser interface. The business model that supports this public service is advertising. Users can access the service for free in exchange for viewing a few ads. Google collects revenues from the businesses that place the ads.

The Google Web service provides an API to the search engine

Google also provides a Web service interface to this public search engine. It calls this Web service the Google Web APIs. You can use these Web APIs to query the Google search engine from an application rather than from a browser. The results of the search are returned as structured data so that the requesting application can process the information.

Google is encouraging users to create innovative applications using these Web APIs

As of the time of this writing, this Web service is still in an experimental stage. Google is encouraging developers to use their imagination to create new and interesting applications using the Google Web APIs. Here are three examples:

- ❑ Subject monitoring: issue regularly scheduled Web searches to find any new information on a particular subject

Web Services Business Models

- Market research: issue regularly scheduled Web searches and analyze the difference in the amount of information available on the subject over time
- Plagiarism search: search for phrases from a piece of writing to ensure that it is original material

Researchers and developers may be excited about the Google Web APIs, but it's hard to figure out what benefit Google will gain from this Web service other than goodwill. The Google Web APIs undermine Google's normal business model. The Google Web APIs don't constitute a new service. Instead they simply provide a programmatic interface to Google's public Web search engine. The Web APIs are free. Users are required to register, and they are limited to 1,000 queries per day per user, but users of the Google Web APIs don't receive the Google advertisements.

The Google Web APIs undermine Google's normal business model

The cost of an individual Google search is minuscule. Google views it as a reasonable investment to give away a few million searches in exchange for the generation of goodwill. But in general, I wouldn't recommend that you follow Google's example. Web services should be designed to support your existing business model. They should provide a new or improved mechanism to sell or use an existing product or service.

Web services should support your existing business models

Kinko's

For example, let's look at Kinko's, the world's leading provider of document solutions and business services. Kinko's has offered a browser-based utility for quite a while that allows you to send documents from your PC directly to Kinko's for printing. Now Kinko's wants to use Web services to make the process even more seamless. Kinko's plans to roll out a "File, Print . . . Kinko's" Web service in mid-2003. This Web service allows you to send a print job to Kinko's over the Internet directly from any Microsoft Office

"File, Print . . . Kinko's" will allow you to send a print job to Kinko's directly from your Office application

Chapter 2   Web Services Basics

application. The service will require you to install a small add-in to Office, which will supply the client interface to the Kinko's Web service. After you've installed this add-in, "Kinko's" will appear in your list of printers when you select File and Print . . . from the Office menu. When you select the Kinko's print service, Office will launch Kinko's client interface, which then presents you with an easy-to-use dialog box to guide you through the process of submitting a print job. The dialog box will help you find a convenient Kinko's location, select options such as stapling and binding, and specify payment, notification, and delivery methods.

You can send the print job to any Kinko's anywhere in the world

Suppose you're sitting in your hotel room writing a proposal in Microsoft Word. When you're finished, you select File, Print . . . Kinko's. The hotel's high-speed Internet connection sends the print job to a Kinko's in another city, and the proposal is delivered directly to your client. Kinko's will even send you a notification when the job is complete.

Kinko's Web service supports the company's core business model

The "File, Print . . . Kinko's" Web service doesn't compete with the company's core business model. It enhances it by providing another way for users to submit print jobs. And it provides a level of convenience that many users will certainly appreciate.

Amazon

Amazon provides a Web API to support its marketing affiliates

Amazon also uses Web services to enhance its core business model. Amazon's business model is based on online retail sales. Amazon is renowned for the features of its online catalog, which provides the primary consumer sales interface. The catalog is designed to be viewed by a human sitting at a browser. Amazon also wants to make this catalog available to applications so that its 800,000 marketing affiliates can more easily sell products for Amazon. So Amazon created a Web API for its catalog. Before it offered this Web API, it was quite difficult to access the Amazon

Web Services Business Models

catalog from an application. You needed to build a screen scraping application that simulated a human sitting at a browser.

The new Amazon Web API allows Amazon's marketing affiliates to easily incorporate Amazon content and features into their Web sites. Many of Amazon's most popular search facilities—such as keyword search, ISBN search, and even "Listmania!"—are available through the Web service. Now consumers can buy products from Amazon transparently through the affiliate sites. The affiliate Web site uses the Amazon Web service to search Amazon's catalog and display the results on its own site, including features such as Amazon reviews and book ratings. This free Web service is a win-win situation for both the affiliates and Amazon. Each time a consumer makes an Amazon purchase through the affiliate site, the affiliate earns a 15% referral fee. Meanwhile Amazon expects to see a boost in product sales.

Amazon hopes its Web service will boost book sales

UPS

UPS also uses Web services to promote sales. UPS provides a set of Web APIs called UPS OnLine Tools. Businesses can use these APIs to connect their applications directly to the UPS logistics system to add integrated shipping, tracking, and related functionality. UPS OnLine Tools are available at no charge, and UPS provides free e-mail support. As with Amazon, this Web service offers a win-win situation. Customers appreciate the way this Web service can streamline their logistics process; UPS can expect to see an increase in UPS shipments.

UPS OnLine Tools streamline the logistics process

T-Mobile

Sometimes Web services can help enable a new business model. T-Mobile International, a division of Deutsche Telekom, is one of the world's leading international mobile communication providers. One of its service offerings, T-Mobile Online, provides a wireless Web portal for more than three million T-Mobile customers in

T-Mobile uses Web services to enable a new business model

Chapter 2   Web Services Basics

Austria, the Czech Republic, Germany, and the United Kingdom. As with most wireless plans, the business model is based on consumer usage.

T-Mobile needs interesting content to attract users

When first planning T-Mobile Online, T-Mobile realized that to promote consumer usage it needed to provide interesting content on the portal. Recruiting content providers was critical to the success of this new venture. T-Mobile needed to make sure that it was as easy as possible for content providers to join the network.

The content providers need consumer info and billing services

One of the biggest challenges T-Mobile faced was figuring out a way to give the content providers access to information about individual consumers. Providers need this information to furnish customized, localized, useful content. Another challenge was devising an affordable micro-payment system to ensure that the content providers got paid for their services.

Web services ensure easy content integration

Given that each content provider might have a completely different IT infrastructure, T-Mobile elected to use Web services. All consumer information and billing services are made available to the content providers as Web services, as shown in Figure 2-4. The Web services ensure that content providers can quickly, easily, and inexpensively integrate their content into the T-Mobile portal.

Web services enable this m-commerce business model

This venture has been very successful. T-Mobile Online has enlisted more than 200 content providers to make the wireless Web interesting and appealing to T-Mobile consumers. Through T-Mobile Online, these content providers provide services such as e-mail, Short Message Service (SMS) messaging, news, sports scores, restaurant recommendations, directions, stock trading, banking, ticket purchases, gambling, and more. T-Mobile doesn't charge either its consumers or the content providers for these Web services. Instead T-Mobile makes money from the increased airtime

Web Services Business Models

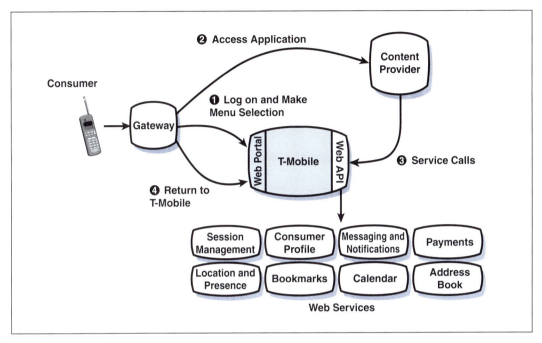

Figure 2-4: T-Mobile Web services maintain user session information, automatically capture and manage billing and payment services, and allow content providers to obtain information about consumers.

the consumers use to access these third-party offerings. The Web services aren't the focus of the business model, but it wouldn't work without them.

Internal Integration

In the examples I've cited so far, I've talked only about external integration applications. One key theme that permeates all these examples is that Web services can make it easier for your customers or partners to do business with you. Anything that simplifies business integration is a valuable commodity. Another recurring theme is that Web services do not themselves define a business model. Instead, they support existing business models, and in some circumstances they enable a new business model.

Web services can make it easier for your customers and partners to do business with you

Chapter 2   Web Services Basics

Web services lower the cost of application integration

Although the external applications are interesting, most production applications based on Web services are internal application projects. As with external Web services, internal Web services should support your core business model. You can use them to improve and optimize your internal application systems to make your business processes work better. The first and foremost reason you should be exploring Web services is that they can dramatically lower the cost of application integration.

Merrill Lynch saved more than 96% on a project with Web services

Merrill Lynch completed an internal application integration project in 2002. The idea was to build an integration bus to provide access to mainframe-based Customer Information Control System (CICS) applications. An integration bus is a common pathway that multiple applications can use to communicate. The original estimated cost for the project based on message-oriented middleware was $800,000. Then the company switched to Web services technology. Rather than purchase software licenses for the MOM technology on a host of different platforms and then build a bunch of adapters to allow the various client applications to use the MOM middleware, Merrill Lynch developed a small SOAP gateway for the CICS environment for only $30,000. Now any client environment can access the CICS environment using SOAP, and Merrill Lynch doesn't need any special software or any special adapters on any of its systems.

Executive Summary

A Web service is an application that provides a Web API

The simplest definition of a Web service is an application that provides a Web API. The Web API exposes the functionality of the application to other applications. The Web API relies on Web services technology to manage communications. Web services technology is pervasive, vendor-independent, language-neutral, and very low-cost.

Executive Summary

The purpose of a Web API is to enable application integration. More specifically, a Web API lets you integrate heterogeneous applications. You can use Web services to achieve many different goals. You can use them to implement internal point-to-point application integration projects. You can use them to consolidate your development efforts and reduce redundant applications. You can use them to implement a general-purpose integration bus for your internal application systems. And you can use them to make it easier for your partners and your customers to do business with you.

A Web API enables application integration

Web services do not represent a new business model. Instead Web services are a technology that you can use to build systems to support a business model.

Web services should support your core business model

IT departments are being asked to do more with less. There's less money in the budget to buy software, and there are fewer people to do the work. Nearly every application development project involves some level of application integration. It just makes sense to reduce the cost and simplify the process of doing integration. Web services are an obvious choice.

Web services let you do more with less

3

Web Services Technologies

Web services offer many valuable benefits. They support heterogeneous application integration at a fraction of the cost of other methods. They are simpler to build and easier to maintain than traditional middleware, and they can make your IT systems more flexible and adaptable. They also allow you to reuse application functionality, reducing development and administration costs.

Web services support low-cost, heterogeneous interoperability

Web services derive these benefits from their underlying Web technologies and standards. In particular, they derive these benefits from the Web, XML, and the SOA. In this chapter we will dig into these technologies and examine why they produce these benefits.

Web services leverage the Web, XML, and SOA

First let's get a bit more specific with our definition: A Web service is service-oriented application that communicates over the Web using XML messages. Looking at this definition, we can see that Web services represent the convergence of three core technologies:

A Web service is a service-oriented application that communicates over the Web using XML messages

- ❏ The Web. A Web service is a Web resource. It communicates over the Internet using standard Web protocols. Leveraging the Web yields universal connectivity and pervasiveness.
- ❏ XML. XML is a language for electronic documents and messages. It provides a universal, self-describing data format that can be interpreted, processed, and transformed by any application running on any platform. Leveraging XML yields heterogeneous platform support and tremendous application flexibility.
- ❏ SOA. The SOA describes a set of common practices for service-based applications. Most RPC-based middleware technologies rely on the SOA. The SOA defines mechanisms for describing services, advertising and discovering services,

Chapter 3   Web Services Technologies

and communicating with services. Leveraging the SOA yields developer productivity and runtime efficiencies.

The Web

The Web is an interconnected global information system

The Web offers universal connectivity. It is a vast, interconnected information system that relies on the Internet to support global communications. The Internet is a completely pervasive, highly reliable communications infrastructure. The Internet relies on two critical technologies: **TCP/IP** (Transmission Control Protocol/Internet Protocol) and **DNS** (Domain Name System). TCP/IP is a pervasive network protocol that is platform- and language-neutral. DNS maps an abstract network address, such as www.bowlight.net, to a physical TCP/IP network location, such as 192.168.1.1. Together, these two technologies support the largest and most scalable network on earth.

URIs allow us to identify, access, and share resources

The Web consists of resources and links. A resource is any type of named information object, such as a word processing document, a digital picture, a Web page, an e-mail account, or an application. The most fundamental concept that defines the Web is the **Uniform Resource Identifier** (**URI**). A URI is a compact, formatted name that identifies a resource. We use this name to identify, reference, access, and share a Web resource.

A URL is a URI that maps to a physical network address

A URI can take many forms. Some URIs are used simply as a name, and others can be resolved to a specific application running on a computer at a particular TCP/IP network address. A URI that is simply a name is called a **Uniform Resource Name** (**URN**). It doesn't point anywhere. For example, I could create a URI to represent myself, such as urn:AnneThomasManes. This URI doesn't resolve to a TCP/IP address. It is simply a name. A URI that does resolve to a physical network address is called a **Uniform Resource Locator** (**URL**). At runtime the Internet can use DNS to map a URL to a physical network address. When one resource refers to another via its URL, it forms a link. These links create the interconnections that constitute the Web.

Users interact with a Web resource using some type of Web application protocol. The Web can support many types of applications, such as Web browsing, e-mail, file transfer, terminal emulation, and network management. There are a number of Web application protocols, such as **HTTP**, Simple Mail Transfer Protocol (**SMTP**), and File Transfer Protocol (**FTP**), that support these different types of applications. Each application protocol supports different semantics and behaviors. For example, HTTP supports a request/response behavior, and SMTP supports a one-way messaging behavior. Table 3-1 shows the application protocols used for some popular Internet applications.

HTTP, SMTP, and FTP are Web application protocols

Table 3-1: Internet Application Protocols

Internet Application	Application Protocol
Web browsing	Hypertext Transfer Protocol (HTTP)
E-mail	Simple Mail Transfer Protocol (SMTP)
File transfer	File Transfer Protocol (FTP)

The first part of a URL, called a **URI scheme**, often indicates the application protocol used to access the resource. Table 3-2 shows three URLs, each supporting a different protocol.

A URI indicates which protocol is used to interact with the resource

Table 3-2: Three URI Schemes

URI Scheme (Boldface)	Resource
http://www.bowlight.net/index.html	A Web page
mailto:atm@bowlight.net	An e-mail mailbox
ftp://ftp.bowlight.net/atmbio.pdf	A file

Chapter 3   Web Services Technologies

The Web Versus Other Networks

Web services communicate using the Internet

Web services use the Web as a communications infrastructure. The Web supports universal connectivity. A Web service is a Web resource, so it is identified, referenced, and accessed by its URL. Web services rely on the Internet to map the URL to a physical network address at runtime.

Traditional middleware technologies predate the Web

Traditional middleware technologies were designed before the introduction of the Web, so they don't rely on the Internet for communications. In fact, these technologies were designed to work over a variety of network technologies, such as TCP/IP, DECnet, and System Network Architecture (SNA). At the time these technologies were developed, network independence was considered a feature. More important, these technologies were designed to support communications between applications within a single corporation. These technologies are not particularly suited for intercorporate communications. Most companies use a firewall to restrict external access to corporate systems. This means that unless instructed otherwise, a firewall blocks traditional middleware traffic.

Web services work well with firewalls

Unlike traditional middleware systems, Web services generally communicate using standard Web protocols, such as HTTP and SMTP. These protocols are designed to work over the Internet, and they work very well with standard firewalls. Moreover, these protocols are ubiquitous. Most systems include support for these protocols, and you don't need to pay license fees to use them.

XML

All Web services speak the same language: XML

A Web service can be developed using any programming language and can be deployed on any platform. In addition, a Web service can be accessed by an application written in any programming language running on any platform. Although the Web supports universal connectivity, the Web by itself doesn't resolve the issue of heterogeneous communication. Different programming languages use different formats to represent data. Web services support heterogeneous communication because they all use the same data format: XML.

XML is the secret sauce that gives Web services their power and flexibility. When you exchange information between two heterogeneous systems, you need to convey this information using a data format that both applications can understand. Web services communicate by passing XML messages, and XML is the Web's universal language. Every programming language and every platform can understand XML.

XML is the secret sauce

XML is a language for electronic documents. An **XML document** is a structured way to represent information. An XML document is a hierarchy of **XML elements**. An element represents a distinct piece of information in the document. For example, an element can represent someone's name. Furthermore, each element can be structured into subelements. For example, a name element can have three subelements that represent first name, middle initial, and last name. As mentioned in Chapter 2, applications must work with unambiguous structured data, such as XML.

XML is used to create electronic documents

XML is a **markup language**. You structure your document using **tags**, which provide a label and a container for each element. A tag is a word or set of characters encased in pointy brackets—for example, <name>. An element has a start tag and an end tag; the end tag begins with a forward slash. The element content sits between the start and end tags. For example, a name element would look like this: <name>Anne</name>.

XML is a markup language

You can think of an XML document as an electronic form containing a set of labeled fields. Each element represents a field. The tags

An XML document is like an electronic form

Chapter 3   Web Services Technologies

Figure 3-1: In an XML document, each element sits within a set of tags. The elements are structured in a hierarchy.

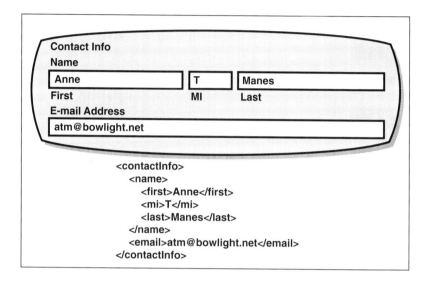

provide the label for each field. Figure 3-1 compares a printed form and the XML that represents the form electronically.

HTML specifies formatting information

Some markup languages, such as HTML, use the markup tags to specify formatting information. These tags indicate that certain pieces of text should be formatted with a particular font, at a particular size, in a particular color. They indicate that text should be formatted into paragraphs, bulleted lists, tables, and so on. A browser uses these tags to determine how to display the HTML page. The set of tags defined in the HTML standard is called the HTML **vocabulary**. A vocabulary defines the set of tags that can be used in a specific type of electronic document, such as an HTML page.

HTML doesn't provide enough structure for an application

Although HTML is an excellent vocabulary for Web browsers, it's not particularly useful for application-to-application communication. An application doesn't care about fonts and colors. Instead it needs unambiguous information. For example, it needs to know that one particular bit of information represents a name, and another bit of information represents an e-mail address.

XML

Unlike HTML, XML doesn't define formatting information. Instead it uses tags to define each bit of information in the document. An application can navigate its way through the tags and find the information it needs. Another important feature of XML is that it doesn't define a limited vocabulary. The "X" in XML stands for "extensible." XML is what's known as a **meta-markup language**: a language that you can use to define your own vocabulary. You can create your own tags to describe the contents of your specific documents. For example, you can create a tag called `<contactInfo>` and use it to represent contact information in an electronic document. HTML doesn't give you the ability to create your own tags. You can use only the tags defined in the HTML vocabulary.

You can use XML to create your own vocabularies

XML Schema

You can define the structure, semantics, and constraints of a particular type of XML document using the W3C standard known as **XML Schema**. For example, you might create a schema to define the structure of a purchase order document. This schema would specify which elements are required or permitted in a purchase order document, the order and hierarchy of the elements, and any constraints on the number of occurrences of each element.

XML Schema defines the structure of a document

A schema makes it easier for an application to process the contents of a document. First of all, the application needs to know what structure to expect. In many cases it also needs to know what kind of data it's working with. For example, it needs to know whether a particular element contains simple text, an integer, a decimal number, or a value representing a date. XML Schema allows you to specify each element's **datatype**.

A schema makes it easier to process a document

Applications can be picky about data structures. If an application receives a document that doesn't match the expected structure, it may cause an error. You can avoid these errors by validating the document against its schema at runtime. The validation process

You can validate an XML document against a schema

Chapter 3   Web Services Technologies

compares the document structure with the rules defined by the schema and identifies any discrepancies. If an application receives a document that it determines to be invalid, it can reject the document, or it can try to modify the document to make it valid. In this way, it may be possible to fix an error in transit and continue execution.

XSLT

You can transform an XML document into a different structure using XSLT

One of the reasons XML is such a flexible data representation format is that you can transform documents. Extensible Stylesheet Language Transformations (**XSLT**) is a language for transforming an XML document into a different structure. You use XSLT to create a **style sheet**. A style sheet provides instructions on how to modify or restructure a document. For example, you can change the name of element tags, reorder the sequence or hierarchy of the elements, and add or remove elements.

XSLT enables flexibility

Transformability makes XML flexible and adaptable. You can use XML and XSLT to build automatic application adapters. For example, if you receive a purchase order document that doesn't quite match the structure required by your application, you can use a style sheet to transform it into the structure you need. You can use a style sheet to merge information from multiple documents into a single document or vice versa. You can also use a style sheet to transform a proprietary format used by one of your internal applications into a standard format used by the rest of your industry.

You can transform XML into other types of documents

You can also use a style sheet to transform an XML document into a different type of document, such as an HTML page, a Wireless Markup Language (**WML**) card deck, or a **VoiceXML** file. WML is an XML-based markup language that can be displayed in a Wireless Application Protocol (WAP) browser on a mobile handset. VoiceXML is an XML-based markup language that represents

XML

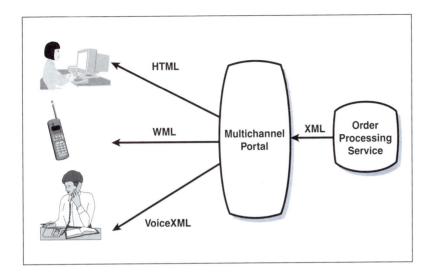

Figure 3-2: A multichannel portal application can take XML content from a Web service and use XSLT to transform it into the appropriate format for the device being served.

spoken text. You can build an automated interactive voice response (IVR) interface using VoiceXML.

XML's transformability is one of the reasons Web services work well for building portals. As shown in Figure 3-2, backend Web services deliver content to the portal in XML format. The portal presentation logic, called a **portlet**, can transform the content as needed to work with the portal user interface, which might be a frame within a browser, a portable handset, or a standard telephone (using voice generation and voice recognition software).

XML supports multichannel portal applications

XML Versus Other Data Representations

Web services communicate by exchanging XML messages. In contrast, traditional middleware technologies encode their data using a binary format, and each middleware system uses a different one. ONC uses the External Data Representation (XDR). CORBA uses the Common Data Representation (CDR). DCOM uses the Native Data Representation (NDR). Java RMI sends data as serialized Java objects. These different data representations mean that these middleware systems can't talk to each other. Web services

Traditional middleware systems use data representations that only they can understand

Chapter 3 Web Services Technologies

are different. Web services use XML. Any programming language on any platform can interpret XML, and this gives Web services complete heterogeneous support.

Traditional middleware systems don't let you define or validate document structures

XML Schema gives you the ability to define standard XML document templates. For example, you can define the format of your corporate purchase order document using XML Schema. Or you can adopt a standard purchase order format defined by an industry group such as RosettaNet. Any XML document can be validated to determine whether it conforms to a particular schema. Traditional middleware systems don't have the capacity to define and validate document structures.

Traditional middleware systems don't let you transform messages in transit

XSLT makes it easy to transform messages during processing. Validation and transformation during processing gives Web services tremendous flexibility. In traditional middleware technologies, if a message doesn't exactly match the expected format, the communication process fails. With Web services, on the other hand, the client or service can validate a message, and, if it doesn't match the expected format, the application can transform the message into an acceptable format.

XML helps you deal with multiple versions of a service

This feature is particularly helpful if you must deal with multiple versions of a service. Suppose that you want to upgrade a deployed service, and you have a number of clients already using the service. Your new upgrade adds support for a "frequent customer" program. To take advantage of the program, the client must add a frequent customer number to the purchase order. This means that you need to add a new element to the schema for your purchase order, and you need to change your API. In a traditional RPC-based middleware environment, this kind of change would break all your existing clients. But not so in a Web services environment. You can arrange to let your upgraded Web service support clients using both the old API and the new API. When you receive a request based on the old API, you can validate it and automatically transform it so that it matches the new API.

XML resolves the Traditional Middleware Blues associated with tightly coupled connections. Traditional RPC-based middleware, such as RPC, RMI, CORBA, and DCOM, relies on tightly coupled connections, resulting in inflexible and brittle applications. Any change you make to the service may cause all connections to break. Message-oriented middleware (MOM) doesn't suffer from this problem. It uses loosely coupled connections, meaning that there is a greater layer of abstraction between the application and the message format. But MOM doesn't do as much work for the application as RPC-based middleware does, so MOM is harder to use.

XML solves the Traditional Middleware Blues associated with tightly coupled connections

Web services support the ease of use of RPC-based middleware, and they support loosely coupled connections as MOM does. Web services don't require an exact match between client and service. The system can transform messages in transit to keep the applications up and running. XML makes Web services flexible and adaptable.

Web services are loosely coupled and easy to use

SOA

The service-oriented architecture (SOA) describes a set of well-established patterns that help a client application connect to a service. These patterns represent mechanisms used to describe a service, to advertise and discover a service, and to communicate with a service. RPC-based middleware systems, such as RPC, CORBA, DCOM, and RMI, rely on these SOA patterns. Web services also rely on these patterns. These patterns are very familiar to most programmers.

SOA defines a set of patterns to connect a client to a server

Figure 3-3: SOA describes patterns used to describe a service (via a contract published by the service provider), to advertise and discover a service (via a service broker), and to communicate with a service (via protocols defined in the service contract).

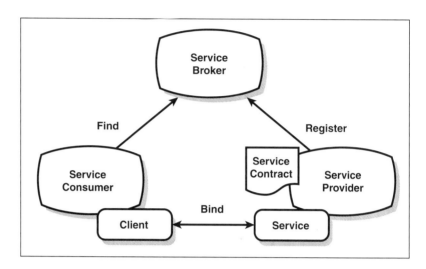

The three SOA roles are the provider, consumer, and broker

Figure 3-3 depicts the conceptual roles, artifacts, and operations of the SOA. The three basic roles in the SOA are the **service provider**, the **service consumer**, and the **service broker**. The service provider supplies the service, the service consumer uses the service, and the service broker facilitates the advertising and discovery process.

The three SOA artifacts are the client, service, and service contract

The three basic artifacts in the SOA are the **client**, the **service**, and the **service contract**. The client is the code that the service consumer uses to access the service; the service is the code that supplies the service; and the service contract describes the API that the client uses to access the service.

The three SOA operations are register, find, and bind

The three basic operations in the SOA are **register**, **find**, and **bind**. When a service provider makes a service available, it describes the service by publishing a service contract. The service provider then registers the service with a service broker. A service consumer queries the service broker to find a compatible service. The service broker gives the service consumer directions on how to find the service and its service contract. The service consumer uses the contract to bind the client to the service, at which point the client and service can communicate.

WSDL, UDDI, and SOAP

Web services rely on these SOA patterns. Although Web services can be developed using any XML-based language and communications protocol, the industry is converging on a core set of technologies to enable language and platform independence and to ensure multi-vendor interoperability. The standard technologies for implementing the SOA patterns with Web services are **Web Services Description Language** (**WSDL**), **Universal Description, Discovery & Integration** (**UDDI**), and **Simple Object Access Protocol** (**SOAP**).

Web services rely on the SOA patterns

WSDL, UDDI, and SOAP

WSDL, UDDI, and SOAP are the three core technologies most often used to implement Web services. WSDL provides a mechanism to describe a Web service. UDDI provides a mechanism to advertise and discover a Web service. And SOAP provides a mechanism for clients and services to communicate. Figure 3-4 shows these technologies mapped to the SOA.

WSDL, UDDI, and SOAP support the SOA functions

The primary advantage of using Web services rather than traditional SOA-compliant middleware is that WSDL, UDDI, and SOAP are much more flexible than other systems. They support any language on any platform, and they don't require you to install

Web services are more flexible than traditional SOA middleware

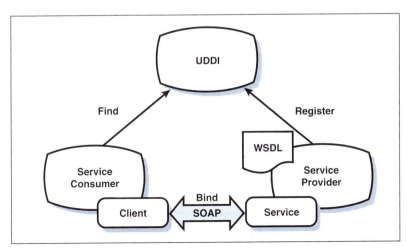

Figure 3-4: In the Web services architecture, you use WSDL to describe a service, UDDI to advertise and discover a service, and SOAP to communicate with the service.

specialized, homogeneous software on every client and server machine. Web services are simpler, less expensive, and more pervasive than traditional SOA-based middleware.

Description (WSDL)

WSDL describes a Web service

WSDL is an XML language that describes a Web service. You use WSDL to create a Web service contract. A WSDL document describes *what* functionality a Web service offers, *how* it communicates, and *where* to find it. You can separate the various parts of a Web service description into multiple documents to provide more flexibility and to increase reusability.

The what *part describes the service interface*

The *what* part of a WSDL document describes the **abstract interface** of a Web service. This interface description specifies which operations the service supports, and it defines the format of the messages that must be exchanged to perform the operation.

The interface description defines a Web service type

This interface description essentially defines an abstract **Web service type**. A **type** is an abstract representation of a thing. The concept is similar to that of a car model. I drive a Volkswagen Cabriolet. The car model, Volkswagen Cabriolet, is an abstract type of car. The car in my garage is one particular **implementation** of that type of car. There are many other Volkswagen Cabriolet implementations in the world. A Web service type is called a **portType**. As with car models, you can have multiple implementations of a particular portType. All these implementations support the same abstract interface and do essentially the same thing, but they are supplied by different service providers.

The how *part describes how to encode and transfer messages*

The *how* part of a WSDL document maps an abstract interface to a concrete set of protocols. This mapping is called a **binding**. The binding specifies the technical details of how to communicate with a service. It indicates how the input and output messages defined in the abstract interface should be packaged into a message. It

WSDL, UDDI, and SOAP

indicates how the message should be structured and how the data should be **encoded**; it indicates which schema defines the message format; and it indicates which Web application protocol should be used to transfer the message.

The *where* part of a WSDL document describes a specific **Web service implementation**. A Web service implementation can support one or more portTypes, each with one or more bindings. Each portType binding is called a **port**. Each port specifies an **endpoint**, which is the URL used to access the service. A business might offer multiple endpoints to a particular service, each implementing a different binding to support multiple protocols.

The where *part specifies the URL of a specific service implementation*

A WSDL document containing all three parts describes everything that you need to call a specific Web service implementation. This file can be compiled into application code, which a client application can use to invoke the Web service, as shown in Figure 3-5. This generated application code is called a client **proxy**. The proxy represents the Web service to the client application. The client application calls the client proxy, and the proxy constructs the messages and manages the communication on behalf of the client application.

WSDL compiles into a proxy client

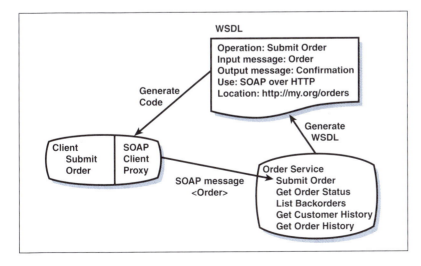

Figure 3-5: A WSDL document can be compiled into a client proxy, which automatically manages the SOAP message exchange at runtime.

61

Chapter 3   Web Services Technologies

An application can use a WSDL document at runtime to perform dynamic integration

A WSDL document can also be interpreted at runtime, permitting much more dynamic integration. At development time a developer can compile only the WSDL *what* part to create an abstract programming interface, which the client application can use to invoke any Web service that implements the portType. At runtime the application retrieves an implementation WSDL file and generates a **dynamic proxy** to bind to the specific Web service implementation. This process is known as **dynamic binding**.

A dynamic proxy allows a single client application to talk to multiple Web service providers

For example, as shown in Figure 3-6, suppose you have a procurement application that can place orders with any of your contracted suppliers. Let's assume that all your suppliers support the same procurement abstract interface (as defined by a portType), which accepts your purchase order as input and returns a confirmation. Each of your suppliers uses a slightly different protocol binding, and each Web service is accessed through a different URL. At runtime, your procurement application selects a specific supplier and dynamically generates the proxy code

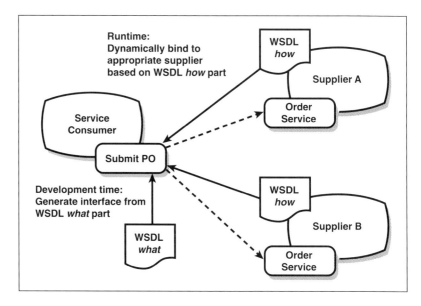

Figure 3-6: A single client application can interpret WSDL at runtime to dynamically bind to multiple implementations of the same service type.

62

WSDL, UDDI, and SOAP

needed to talk to that specific Web service based on the supplier's WSDL file.

WSDL Versus Other Description Languages

Most traditional SOA systems use an **interface definition language** (**IDL**) to describe the service contract. IDL describes the **signature** of a service. This signature describes the procedures or methods that the service offers, and it specifies the order of the input and output parameters required for each method. Different IDL languages are used for ONC, DCE, CORBA, and DCOM. Java RMI is slightly different. Rather than use a separate IDL language, Java RMI simply uses Java to describe the service signature. To some degree IDL is comparable to the WSDL *what* part. The major difference between IDL and a WSDL portType, though, is that portTypes are abstract, and IDL is specific and concrete.

Most SOA systems use IDL to describe service APIs

An IDL-defined signature represents a very tightly coupled connection. The order of the parameters in the input and output messages in the signature is critical. The input and output messages must exactly match the signature, or else the communication will fail.

A signature is a very tightly coupled connection

Unlike WSDL, RMI and IDL systems do not specify information about *how* to communicate with the service. Traditional middleware systems support only one set of communication protocols. It's assumed that you will use the protocols defined by the middleware, so there's no need to specify a *how* part. In contrast, Web services let you use different protocols based on the specific requirements of your application or network.

Traditional middleware systems support only one set of communication protocols

Unlike WSDL, RMI and IDL systems do not specify information about *where* to find a service. Traditional middleware systems do not use a URL to identify, reference, and access a service. Instead traditional middleware systems rely on their advertising and

Traditional middleware systems don't use URLs to locate services

Chapter 3   Web Services Technologies

discovery system to keep track of the location of the service. Each middleware system uses a different advertising and discovery service. DCOM systems use the NT Registry, CORBA systems use the CORBA Naming Service, DCE systems use the Cell Directory Service, and RMI systems use either the Java Naming and Directory Interface (JNDI) or the RMI registry.

Traditional middleware systems have great difficulty working across corporate boundaries

In all these traditional middleware systems, the client must query the advertising and discovery service at runtime to obtain the location of the service before the client can bind to the service. The reason for this overhead is that the service does not have an abstract address such as a URL. A client must reference the service by its physical network address, and the physical network address may change each time a service is started. Because these systems don't use a URL to identify a service, it's somewhat difficult to make these systems work across the Internet.

Web services are designed to work across the Internet

Web services are designed to work across the Internet. Each Web service is identified, referenced, and accessed by its URL, and this address is resolved at runtime using native Internet services (DNS). A Web service client doesn't need to query the advertising and discovery service at runtime if it already knows the URL of the service, and the URL is specified in the WSDL *where* part. Web services usually communicate using Web application protocols, and these protocols work well with firewalls. Even so, Web services can communicate using any type of protocol. A service provider might make the same service available via multiple protocols to support different client requirements. The WSDL *how* part describes the protocols that can be used to access the service.

From my perspective, I'd say that the most important difference between WSDL and traditional middleware description languages is that WSDL allows you to specify the interface definition separately from the implementation definition *in the service contract*. Although

WSDL, UDDI, and SOAP

all SOA-based middleware systems support the separation of interface from implementation, none of the traditional middleware systems lets you define that separation in the service contract. By defining the *what* part separately from the *how* and *where* parts, WSDL allows an application to dynamically bind to a different service each time you use it. No other middleware system supports this level of dynamic interaction.

Traditional middleware systems can't separate interface from implementation in the service contract

Advertising and Discovery (UDDI)

UDDI provides a mechanism to advertise and discover Web services. UDDI is a registry for Web services, and UDDI is itself a Web service. The primary difference between a UDDI registry and other registries and directories is that UDDI provides a mechanism to categorize businesses and services using any number of **taxonomies**. These taxonomies help service consumers find a particular service that matches their requirements. You can use UDDI on a very large scale, such as the entire Internet, or on a smaller scale, such as within a private business community or within your enterprise. Chapter 4 talks more about these options.

UDDI is an advertising and discovery service

A UDDI registry manages information about service types and service providers. The service type registrations represent abstract services and industry standards. The service provider registrations specify information about a business and the specific services it provides.

UDDI manages information about service types and service providers

A service type represents an abstract service that can be offered by one or more service providers. It is comparable to a WSDL portType. Programmers, businesses, industry groups, and standards bodies can define service types, and each service type can be categorized using any number of descriptive taxonomies. Consumers can search the registry using these taxonomies to find service types that match their requirements, and they can search for service providers that support these service types.

A service type is comparable to a WSDL portType

Chapter 3   Web Services Technologies

A tModel points to the specification that defines a reusable resource

A service type is defined by a UDDI registry entry called a **tModel**, which stands for "technical model." A tModel represents an abstract and reusable resource, and it provides a pointer to the specification (for example, a WSDL file) that describes the resource. You should use a tModel to register the abstract interface (the WSDL *what* part) of a Web service and use additional tModels to register each of the bindings (the WSDL *how* part) available for the Web service. You should not use a tModel to represent a specific implementation of a service. A specific service implementation is associated with the service provider that provides it.

A service provider registers the services that it offers

A service provider registers its business and all the services that it offers. Conceptually, the service provider registration can be thought of as containing white pages, yellow pages, and green pages information.

The white pages supply basic identity and contact information

The white pages information includes basic identity information for the business, such as the name of the business, the business address, contact information, and business identifiers such as a D-U-N-S number or Thomas Register supplier identifier. These identifiers provide some assurance to the service consumer that the provider is an established business.

The yellow pages categorize the business and services with taxonomies

The yellow pages information includes categorization information for the business and its services. UDDI allows you to categorize a business or service using any number of taxonomies. UDDI provides built-in support for a number of standard international taxonomies, such as the United Nations Standard Products and Services Codes system (UNSPSC), the North American Industry Classification System (NAICS), and the ISO 3166 Country Codes standard. UDDI also allows you to define your own taxonomies to support more focused categorization. Service consumers can search for businesses or services using any combination of built-in and custom taxonomies.

The green pages information provides access to the technical specifications that describe a service implementation. The technical specification information is maintained in a UDDI registry entry called a binding template. A binding template represents an endpoint of a service implementation. The binding template references its technical specifications through a set of tModels. It points to the tModels that represent the WSDL portType and the WSDL binding that the service implements. The binding template also specifies the access point for the service implementation. A service consumer can use the binding template to retrieve all the information needed to access the Web service.

The green pages provide binding details for a service implementation

This registration model might seem complicated, but it offers tremendous power and flexibility in terms of service advertisement and discovery. In particular, it supports the concept of industry standard service types. A number of vertical industry groups, such as ACORD, OMA, OTA, and RosettaNet, are defining XML-based standards for electronic business for their particular industries. These standards can be registered as tModels in UDDI. Businesses can indicate that they support these industry standards by referencing these tModels. Potential consumers can quickly and easily find businesses that support the standards by searching for services that implement the tModels.

UDDI makes it easy to find service implementations that support industry standards

Figure 3-7 provides an overview of the information in a UDDI registry, and it shows the relationship between the UDDI entries and the types of WSDL descriptions. In this diagram, an industry standards group has defined a standard for an Order service. This standard is registered in the UDDI registry as a tModel. The tModel points to the WSDL portType definition (the *what* part) that defines the industry standard. Companies A and B provide Order services that implement the industry standard. Each company registers its business (represented by a business entity) and the service it offers (represented by a business service). Each company also registers

UDDI allows a service provider to associate its service with an established industry standard

Chapter 3 Web Services Technologies

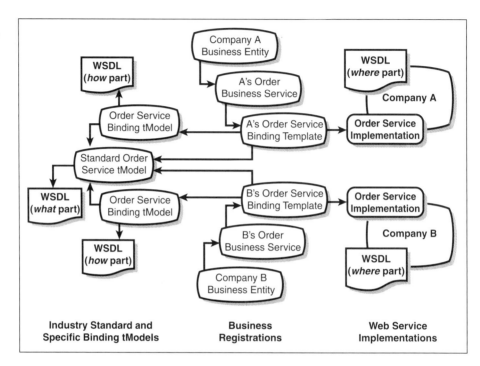

Figure 3-7: An overview of the information in a UDDI registry.

technical specification information for its particular implementation of the Order service (represented by a binding tModel, which points to the WSDL *how* part). The company then uses a binding template to associate the business service with the industry standard tModel and the specific binding tModel. The binding template also points to the service implementation access point.

Users can search UDDI by service type or by service provider

When looking for a Web service, a service consumer queries the UDDI registry searching for a business that offers the type of service desired. Users can search the registry for services by service type or by service provider, and queries can be qualified using the taxonomies.

UDDI is used most often at development time

For the most part, a UDDI registry is used at development time to locate available services that can be used to implement a solution. A developer queries the registry using a browser interface, using human intellect to qualify and select an appropriate service from all the potential services registered in the UDDI registry. The developer uses the UDDI registry to find a specific service implementation and to retrieve the service access point and its WSDL description. The developer then uses the WSDL file to generate the appropriate communication code needed for the client application.

A UDDI registry can also be used at runtime. A UDDI registry is itself a Web service, and applications can access the UDDI registry using SOAP messages. A developer can program the application to query a UDDI registry to look for a service that implements a particular service type, locate the implementation WSDL file, and generate a dynamic proxy to perform the communication.

UDDI can also be used at runtime

UDDI Versus Other Discovery Systems

Traditional SOA systems don't use URLs to reference services, and they don't use DNS to resolve the network address. Instead they use their advertising and discovery systems as a naming service to resolve network addresses at runtime. These systems don't rely on the Internet to enable communication.

Traditional SOA systems don't rely on URLs and DNS

Web services rely on the native features of the Internet (URLs, DNS, and TCP/IP) to enable communication. You don't need to use UDDI at runtime to obtain the physical address of a service. UDDI is an optional service used to help match service consumers with service providers. It is used primarily to categorize services. It is also used to publish corporate or industry standard service types and schemas and to indicate that services conform to those standards.

UDDI was designed to facilitate the use of standards

Traditional SOA systems don't use their advertising and discovery services to categorize services. Instead these systems assume that the client knows which service it wants to use. Only CORBA provides something somewhat comparable to UDDI. CORBA defines an optional service called a Trader, which helps match clients to

Traditional SOA systems don't categorize services using taxonomies

Chapter 3   Web Services Technologies

services. The Trader service allows you to define arbitrary properties about a service. These properties could be used to implement taxonomies, but the Trader doesn't allow you to search based on these taxonomies. You must search based on a service signature. You can use the properties only to qualify the search.

Traditional SOA systems don't support service types

From my perspective, the most important difference between UDDI and traditional middleware discovery mechanisms is UDDI's ability to characterize services by their service types. Traditional SOA discovery systems don't support the concept of service types. Only UDDI provides a mechanism to publish standard service types, to indicate that a service conforms to the standard, and to search for services based on those service types. This feature perfectly complements the dynamic binding features of WSDL to support dynamic interaction.

Communication (SOAP)

SOAP allows one application to send an XML message to another application

Simple Object Access Protocol (**SOAP**) is an **XML protocol** used to communicate with Web services. SOAP provides a simple, consistent, and extensible mechanism that allows one application to send an XML message to another application.

SOAP provides a container for an XML message

SOAP provides an envelope for an XML message. Just as you put a letter into an envelope to send it through the postal service, you put an XML message into an envelope to send it across the network. The **SOAP envelope** provides a container for the XML message.

A SOAP message can be sent over any transport protocol

You can think of a SOAP envelope as being similar to a transportation shipping container. A shipping container can be carried by a variety of transport systems, such as boat, rail, and truck. A SOAP envelope can also be carried by a variety of transport systems. In this case we're talking about communication protocols. The most common way to transfer SOAP messages is to use HTTP, although you can also transfer messages using other Web protocols, such as

WSDL, UDDI, and SOAP

SMTP and FTP, or using non-Web protocols such as IBM WebSphereMQ or a JMS implementation. You can select the transport protocol based on the requirements of your specific application.

A SOAP message consists of two parts, as shown in Figure 3-8. The **SOAP header** contains directive information, and the **SOAP body** contains the message payload.

A SOAP message contains a header and a body

The SOAP header includes system-level information most often used to manage or secure the message. The SOAP header can include information such as security credentials, transaction context, message correlation information, session identifiers, or management information. If no system-level information is required, the SOAP header can be omitted.

The SOAP header contains directive information

The SOAP body contains the message payload—the information that is being sent to the target application. In the example shown in Figure 3-8, the payload is a purchase order.

The SOAP body contains the message payload

The WSDL description associated with the Web service defines the structure of the SOAP message. The contents of the message payload should conform to the input and output messages defined in the WSDL *what* part. The WSDL *how* part defines how the messages should be packaged in the SOAP envelope, and it defines the

The WSDL description defines the format of the SOAP message

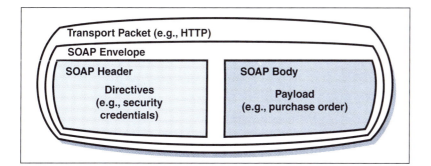

Figure 3-8: A SOAP message contains a header and a body and is packaged in a transport packet.

71

Chapter 3   Web Services Technologies

information that should be included in the SOAP header. The WSDL *how* part also specifies which transport protocol should be used to transfer the message.

A SOAP message can be routed through any number of SOAP intermediaries

A SOAP message can be transferred directly from the **SOAP sender** to the **SOAP receiver**, or it can be routed through any number of **SOAP intermediaries**. A SOAP intermediary can perform a variety of functions, such as auditing or logging a message, storing the message for reliability, checking security credentials, encrypting or decrypting the message, validating the payload, transforming the payload, or routing the message. A SOAP intermediary can operate transparently to the SOAP senders and receivers.

Document-style supports a more loosely coupled approach

SOAP supports two ways to structure messages: document-style and RPC-style. **Document-style** SOAP messaging supports very loosely coupled communications between two applications. The SOAP sender sends a message, and the SOAP receiver determines what to do with it. The SOAP sender doesn't really need to know anything about the implementation of the service other than the format of the message and the access point URL. It is entirely up to the SOAP receiver to determine, based on the contents of the message, how to process it. The formats of the document input and output messages are defined by XML Schema definitions, which can be defined in the Web service's WSDL document or in a separate schema. Formatting a SOAP message according to a specified schema is called **literal encoding**.

RPC-style supports a more tightly coupled approach

A more tightly coupled communication scheme uses the **SOAP RPC convention**. An **RPC-style** input message simulates an RPC invocation. It specifies the name of the procedure to be invoked, and it contains a set of input parameters. An RPC-style output message simulates an RPC response. It contains the return value and any output parameters of the procedure. You can literally define the format of the RPC input and output messages using XML

Schema, or you can dynamically construct the messages using a data model called **SOAP encoding**. This SOAP encoding data model is designed to make it easy to map complex object-oriented data structures to XML.

The advantage of using document or RPC messages structured using a literal XML Schema definition is that the messages can be validated using the schema. RPC messages constructed using SOAP encoding cannot be validated because there is no schema that describes the structure. The advantage of using SOAP encoding is that it provides a simpler and more efficient method to represent and transfer object-oriented data in XML, but it limits your ability to validate messages in transit. SOAP encoding has also been a source of interoperability issues.

SOAP encoding is more convenient, but it reduces flexibility

Extending SOAP

SOAP provides a built-in extension mechanism that allows you to add advanced middleware functionality to the basic communication environment. As mentioned earlier, you can pass directive or control information in a SOAP header. Either your SOAP runtime server or an intermediary can automatically process these directives. You can use this extension mechanism to add automatic middleware functionality, such as security, auditing, transactions, reliable delivery, load balancing, asynchronous communications, long-term conversations, and version control.

You can add extended middleware functionality to SOAP using SOAP headers and intermediaries

Securing SOAP Messages

For example, let's take a look at how you can use SOAP headers to support security. Quite a few people have the mistaken impression that SOAP isn't secure. In fact, it's easy to add security to SOAP messages. The simplest way to implement security is to use a secure communication protocol, such as Secure Sockets Layer/Transport Layer Security (**SSL/TLS**). Most SOAP implementations provide support for the Hypertext Transfer Protocol Secure

You can secure your SOAP messages

(**HTTPS**) protocol, which runs over SSL/TLS. HTTPS automatically encrypts the SOAP messages before sending them across the network.

SOAP headers give you fine security control

In some cases, encryption of network traffic may not provide you with sufficient protection. Perhaps you need to control access to sensitive services, or perhaps you need to provide a **digital signature** with a message. In these circumstances, you must apply security at the application layer rather than at the network layer. SOAP permits you to do so using SOAP headers.

Security includes authentication, authorization, confidentiality, integrity, and nonrepudiation

Security is an expansive topic, so let's start with some basic groundwork. There are five functions that fall under this topic:

- **Authentication** is the process that you use to verify a user's or an application's identity. There are a number of mechanisms that you might use for authentication, such as digital certificates or a login process.
- **Authorization** is the process that you use to determine whether an authenticated entity has permission to perform a particular action or function. You may want to define access control policies for all services at a given location, for individual services, or for specific operations in a service.
- **Confidentiality** prevents unauthorized access to the contents of the message. You usually use encryption to ensure confidentiality.
- **Integrity** prevents unauthorized modification of the message. You usually use encryption to ensure message integrity.
- **Nonrepudiation** provides proof that a particular user or application sent a message. A digital signature provides proof that the signed data were sent from a specific authenticated identity. All or part of a message can be signed.

WSDL, UDDI, and SOAP

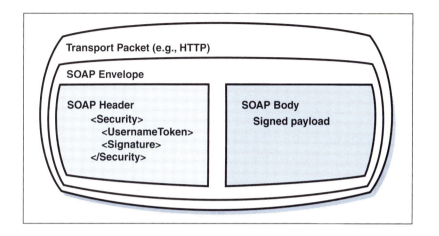

Figure 3-9: The contents of the SOAP body in this secured SOAP message have been digitally signed. The SOAP header contains authentication information and the digital signature.

You can secure your SOAP communications by including security information in the SOAP header. Figure 3-9 shows a secured SOAP message. In this example, we're signing the contents of the SOAP body, and we're passing authentication information and the digital signature in the SOAP header.

You can pass your identity and a digital signature in a SOAP header

You can send either login information (user ID and password) within the SOAP header, or you can send a security **token**. If you send login information, you want to make sure that you encrypt the message. A security token is an encrypted value that represents security information, such as your identity. If you use a security token you don't need to encrypt the message just to protect your identity information. You can get a security token from an authentication authority, such as a **single sign-on** service or a certificate authority. Examples of security tokens are digital certificates and **Kerberos** tickets. There is an Organization for the Advancement of Structured Information Standards (**OASIS**) standard called the Security Assertions Markup Language (**SAML**), which defines a way for you to exchange security information in XML, enabling an XML-based single sign-on facility. You can use a SAML authentication assertion as a security token.

You can identify the user by sending a user ID and password or a security token

75

Chapter 3 Web Services Technologies

A SOAP header processor implements the security functionality

You can set up your Web services environment to automatically manage security on behalf of your applications. You normally implement the security functionality in a **SOAP header processor**, which gets called automatically by the SOAP runtime system. Alternatively you can implement security by routing your messages through one or more security intermediaries. Either way, your security processors can perform functions such as authenticating the user, mapping the user's credentials to a known role in your security system, verifying that the user is entitled to perform the requested operation, encrypting or decrypting the contents of the message, and validating a digital signature. These security processors may be supplied for you by your Web services platform, or they may be additional services that you install to augment your environment.

SOAP Versus Other Communication Systems

Traditional SOA systems require special software on every machine

Most traditional SOA systems aren't designed to work over the Internet. At the time these systems were being developed, TCP/IP had not yet been adopted as the universal network protocol. At that time many companies still used other network protocols, such as DECnet, SNA, and Internetwork Packet Exchange (IPX), as the corporate backbone, and systems such as DCE and CORBA were designed to run across any of these types of networks. These systems use a dedicated application protocol that can run across any of these networks. Unfortunately, this application protocol must be installed on every client or server that wants to engage in the conversation. In contrast, SOAP doesn't require a specific application protocol. It can use pervasive Web protocols, such as HTTP and SMTP, so you don't need to install special networking software on every machine.

Traditional SOA systems encode messages using a binary format that cannot be validated or transformed

Traditional SOA systems encode the message data in a binary format that can be interpreted only by that specific middleware system. These binary formats are opaque to firewalls, and intermediaries cannot validate or transform the messages in transit. In contrast, SOAP encodes messages using XML. SOAP messages can be

Other Web Service Technologies

interpreted by any application written in any language running on any platform. Firewalls can inspect the XML to determine whether the requests may pass. Intermediaries can validate and transform the messages in transit, making SOAP much more flexible and adaptable than any other SOA communication system.

Traditional SOA systems aren't as extensible as SOAP is. As a SOAP user, you can include additional control information in a SOAP header to add any kind of middleware functionality to your system. Other SOA systems may provide additional middleware functionality, but you can use only the services provided. You don't have the ability to extend the environment any way you'd like.

Traditional SOA systems aren't as extensible as SOAP

Other Web Service Technologies

Although WSDL, UDDI, and SOAP have emerged as the predominant Web services technologies, you can also build Web services using other technologies. There are a number of XML protocols that predate SOAP, and quite a few of the earliest Web services were built using these technologies. Also a number of industries developed XML-based messaging standards before SOAP appeared on the scene.

You can use other XML-based technologies to build Web services

One of the earliest XML-based B2B integration systems is RosettaNet. RosettaNet is a subsidiary of the Uniform Code Council (UCC), a nonprofit standards organization. The RosettaNet standards were developed by representatives of the semiconductor industry to define standard XML formats to support integrated supply chains. RosettaNet has since been extended and adapted to support other industries beyond semiconductor manufacturing, and it has gained wide adoption.

RosettaNet supports Web services

Companies such as Macromedia and webMethods were some of the early innovators in the area of XML protocols. They developed proprietary XML protocols that are still used widely. Although they

Early proprietary XML protocol formats are still in use

77

Chapter 3   Web Services Technologies

still support these early protocols, these companies have since embraced SOAP and now also provide products based on what have become the de facto standard Web services technologies: SOAP, WSDL, and UDDI.

XML-RPC has a loyal following

One of the most popular XML protocols is XML-RPC, which is actually an early offshoot of the original SOAP project sponsored by Microsoft, DevelopMentor, and Userland. XML-RPC is a simpler variant of SOAP. Numerous open source implementations of XML-RPC are available, and the protocol still has a loyal following.

ebXML

ebXML is a comprehensive XML framework for B2B integration

At the same time that Microsoft, IBM, and their friends were developing SOAP, two standards organizations joined forces to develop a new set of international standards for electronic business. The Electronic Business using Extensible Markup Language (**ebXML**) project was a joint effort of the United Nations Centre for Trade Facilitation and Electronic Business (UN/CEFACT) and OASIS. The ebXML framework defines a comprehensive set of standards for business-to-business integration.

ebXML is designed for B2B applications only

One primary distinction between the ebXML framework and the SOAP/WSDL/UDDI architecture is that ebXML is designed specifically to support B2B integration. It includes built-in support for security and reliability that may not be necessary for in-house, lightweight, or device-based integration projects. The SOAP/WSDL/UDDI architecture provides a general-purpose Web services infrastructure that can support a wide variety of applications. SOAP can be used for internal application projects as well as B2B integration projects. SOAP can also be used in very small systems, such as a personal digital assistant (PDA) or mobile handset, for personal application integration.

Other Web Service Technologies

The ebXML messaging system is based on SOAP, but beyond this basic level, the ebXML framework diverges from what has become the de facto standard for Web services. The ebXML Message Service (**ebMS**) protocol extends SOAP by adding support for attachments, security, and reliability. Other SOAP systems can't communicate with ebMS systems without knowledge of the ebMS SOAP extensions. The ebXML message payload is generally conveyed as an attachment rather than within the SOAP body, and ebXML doesn't provide a service description language on a par with WSDL.

Although based on SOAP, ebXML diverges from the classic SOAP-based Web services architecture

Instead ebXML provides a number of description systems that allow you to describe and negotiate business relationships. The ebXML Collaboration Protocol Profile and Agreement (**CPPA**) specification provides a mechanism for specifying the details of how you support B2B integration. Your CPPA descriptions generally refer to a Business Process Specification Schema (**BPSS**), which describes a choreographed interchange of messages that must be exchanged to complete a specific business transaction. The ebXML framework also uses a different advertising and discovery service called the **ebXML Registry and Repository**. This service offers capabilities similar to those of UDDI, including support for industry standard service types and categorization through flexible taxonomies. Unlike UDDI, the ebXML Registry and Repository also provides a repository that can manage and maintain XML schemata, CPPA descriptions, BPSS specifications, and other metadata. UDDI doesn't provide a repository. You must store WSDL descriptions and XML Schema definitions in an external file, repository, or content management system.

ebXML supports detailed features for negotiating and executing business relationships electronically

The ebXML project was completed in April 2001, and the resulting specifications were transferred to OASIS and UN/CEFACT for long-term management. Even though the ebXML specifications are formal industry standards, ebXML has been slow to attract wide industry adoption. From a vendor perspective, the project's

The ebXML specs are official standards, but ebXML lacks IBM and Microsoft endorsement

Chapter 3 Web Services Technologies

strongest support comes from Sun Microsystems. On the flip side, IBM has been noncommittal, and Microsoft has been dismissive of ebXML. Even so, ebXML has won endorsement from a number of powerful industry groups, including the Open Application Group, the OpenTravel Alliance, and RosettaNet. A handful of large software vendors, such as Commerce One, Documentum, PeopleSoft, and Sterling Commerce, as well as a few software startups, such as Bind Systems, Killdara, and XML Global, are developing products that support ebXML.

DealerSphere provides a data exchange platform for car dealers

One of the most interesting ebXML-based projects is a data exchange platform for automotive retailers called DealerSphere, a joint project of EDS, Killdara, The Cobalt Group, and Sun Microsystems. DealerSphere proposes to create a standard, Web-enabled "data broker" that will facilitate B2B information exchange. DealerSphere will define a standard data and transaction interface that promises to enable seamless integration with popular dealer management systems.

Executive Summary

Let's review some basic concepts

We've covered a lot of ground in this chapter. (I'm sure you'll be pleased to hear that the rest of the book isn't quite as technical as this chapter.) Let's spend a moment reviewing some of the basic concepts.

Web services represent the convergence of the Web, XML, and the SOA

A Web service is service-oriented application that communicates over the Web using XML messages. Web services represent the convergence of three core technologies: the Web, XML, and the SOA.

The Web is pervasive and provides universal connectivity

The Web provides the basic infrastructure that supports Web services. The Web helps solve the Traditional Middleware Blues associated with lack of pervasiveness. The Web is pervasive and provides universal connectivity. It is free and unencumbered as well as completely platform-independent.

Executive Summary

Web services communicate using XML. XML helps solve the Traditional Middleware Blues associated with lack of heterogeneous interoperability and high total cost of ownership. XML is the *lingua franca* of the Web. Any application, written in any language, running on any platform, can understand XML. In addition, XML is flexible and adaptable. You can validate and transform XML in transit. XML helps ensure that Web services are loosely coupled, reducing maintenance costs and increasing reusability.

XML supports heterogeneous integration

The SOA is the most common architecture used to support application-to-application integration. It's the foundation for most RPC-based middleware systems, including DCOM, CORBA, RPC, and RMI. The SOA is familiar and intuitive to your developers.

The SOA supports application-to-application integration

The SOA specifies mechanisms for describing services, advertising and discovering services, and communicating with services. The most common technologies used to implement these functions in Web services are WSDL, UDDI, and SOAP. Figure 3-10 shows these three technologies working together.

Most people use WSDL, UDDI, and SOAP to implement Web services

WSDL is an XML language for describing Web services. A WSDL document describes *what* a service does, *how* it communicates, and

WSDL describes a Web service

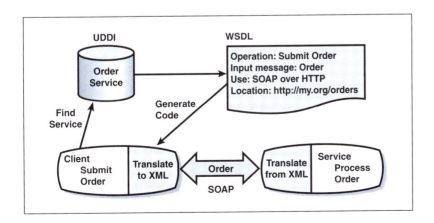

Figure 3-10: A client finds a service and its WSDL via UDDI. It uses the WSDL to generate a proxy. The client uses the proxy to talk to the service.

Chapter 3 Web Services Technologies

where to find it. You can compile a WSDL document and generate a client proxy, which contains all the code you need to communicate with the service.

UDDI is a Web service registry

UDDI facilitates the advertising and discovery process. It is a Web service registry. A service provider uses UDDI to advertise its business and services. When you register a service you can categorize it using a variety of taxonomies. These taxonomies make it easier for service consumers to find services that match their specific requirements. You can also associate your service with the industry standards that you support. A service consumer uses UDDI to find a service and its WSDL description. The consumer can search by business, by taxonomy, by service type, or by a combination of factors.

SOAP is an XML protocol

SOAP is an XML protocol that Web services use to communicate. SOAP provides a simple, consistent, and extensible mechanism that allows one application to send an XML message to another application. The WSDL description associated with the Web service defines the structure of the XML message.

Web services support heterogeneous, low-cost, flexible integration

Together, these technologies implement an extensible, lightweight SOA-based infrastructure. The SOA has evolved over the past 15 years to support high performance, scalability, reliability, and availability. But most SOA-based systems suffer from the Traditional Middleware Blues. They don't support heterogeneity. They don't work across the Internet. They rely on tightly coupled connections. They're expensive to use and even more expensive to maintain. Web services take all the best features of the SOA and combine them with the Web and XML. The result is an architecture that eliminates the Traditional Middleware Blues. Web services support heterogeneous, low-cost, flexible integration.

4

Standardizing Web Services Technologies

Although you can build Web services with other technologies, SOAP, WSDL, and UDDI have become the de facto standards for Web services. For the remainder of this book I will focus on these technologies and their derivatives. SOAP, WSDL, and UDDI are the most widely accepted Web services technologies, and products supporting these technologies are available from dozens of vendors. Surprisingly, though, the SOAP-related technologies were not developed by an accredited standards organization. For the most part, these technologies were developed by IBM and Microsoft.

SOAP, WSDL, and UDDI did not start out as official standards

Considering how much has been accomplished based on these de facto standards, you might wonder whether it really matters if these specifications have some official seal of approval. But it does. For one reason, the existing specifications contain a number of ambiguities and inconsistencies that make it difficult to ensure interoperability among multiple **SOAP implementations**.[1] Second, these specifications address only basic Web services communication, and they don't provide standard facilities to support advanced functionality, such as security, transactions, and reliable delivery. Third, the intellectual property contained in the specifications is currently owned by the companies that wrote the specifications. Although Microsoft, IBM, and the other copyright holders are not likely to attempt to extract royalty fees from the people using SOAP, WSDL, or UDDI, they do have the right to do so. I,

It would be better if these technologies were standardized

---

[1] A SOAP implementation is a product that implements the SOAP specification. We discuss these products in Chapter 8.

Chapter 4 Standardizing Web Services Technologies

for one, would feel much more comfortable if this intellectual property were placed in the public domain.

A formal standardization effort promotes the development of open, interoperable technologies

Standards provide benefits to the industry at large by enabling consistency, interoperability, and vendor independence. Standards also enable a vibrant third-party market for software accessories and software applications. Moreover, a formal standardization effort promotes the development of open, interoperable technologies. A standards organization also provides a venue that gives any interested party, large or small, vendor or customer, an equal footing in the development of these technologies.

The History of SOAP

SOAP was developed by DevelopMentor, IBM, Lotus, Microsoft, and Userland

SOAP originated as a joint project started in 1998 by representatives from Microsoft, DevelopMentor, and Userland. Partway through the development process, Dave Winer of Userland published a simpler variation of SOAP called XML-RPC, which still has a strong following. Microsoft et al. published the SOAP 1.0 specification in late 1999. SOAP certainly wasn't the first XML messaging protocol, but because it offered an interesting, extensible design and had Microsoft's weight behind it, SOAP attracted more attention than previous XML messaging protocols. But at this point most people still viewed SOAP as a Microsoft-centric technology. In an effort to establish vendor-neutral credibility, Microsoft recruited representatives from IBM and Lotus to join the effort. These five companies then published the SOAP 1.1 specification in April 2000. The authors jointly submitted this specification to the W3C, garnering support from six other companies in the process. The W3C subsequently published the specification as a **W3C Note**. Although a W3C Note doesn't imply any endorsement from the W3C, publication of the Note lent significant credibility to the specification.

The History of SOAP

In May 2000, IBM released the first implementation of the SOAP specification, an open source implementation for the Java language called SOAP4J. IBM submitted this implementation to the Apache Software Foundation, and it then became known as Apache SOAP. Shortly afterward, Microsoft produced a Windows-based SOAP implementation for Visual Basic and Visual C++ called the Microsoft SOAP Toolkit. Then in July 2000 Microsoft launched the **.NET** initiative, much of which is based on Web services and SOAP. SOAP rapidly became a major force in the industry.

IBM released the first SOAP implementation, followed shortly by Microsoft

A number of other companies and individuals released independent SOAP implementations over the next few months, including Systinet's IdooXoap, Simon Fell's PocketSoap, and Paul Kulchenko's SOAP::Lite. These implementations support Java, Visual Basic, and Perl, respectively. By the end of 2000 there were more than 20 SOAP implementations available, supporting a multitude of programming languages. Other companies and individuals have since jumped on board, and by the end of 2002 there were more than 90 SOAP implementations.

A number of independent SOAP implementations soon began to appear

Challenges with SOAP 1.1

Although SOAP 1.1 has enormous industry support and many implementations are available, SOAP users have uncovered significant interoperability issues. SOAP is designed to be vendor-neutral, but not all vendors interpret the specification in the same way. Some aspects of the specification are inaccurate, incomplete, contradictory, or open to interpretation. For one thing, the SOAP specification doesn't specify how application languages interface with SOAP. Although it is easy to get a Java client using Apache SOAP to talk to a Java server using Apache SOAP, or to get a Visual Basic client using Microsoft SOAP to talk to a Visual Basic server using Microsoft SOAP, it can be difficult to get a Java client using Apache SOAP to talk to a Visual Basic server using Microsoft SOAP or vice versa.

SOAP 1.1 has experienced serious interoperability issues

Chapter 4 Standardizing Web Services Technologies

The SOAP vendors organized the informal SOAPbuilders group to resolve these issues

In 2001 many of the SOAP vendors joined together to create an informal group known as **SOAPbuilders**. The group has created a series of test suites that SOAP implementers can use to identify and resolve interoperability issues. The group communicates using an e-mail discussion group, and the members meet once per quarter for face-to-face "interop-athons."

Most SOAP implementations now support simple interoperability

Through the SOAPbuilders' efforts, the SOAP vendors have dramatically improved many of the interoperability problems, and most implementations now support seamless interoperability as long as you keep your messages simple. But as soon as message structures become more complex, interoperability can still be very challenging.

More formal efforts are required

More formal efforts are necessary to achieve seamless interoperability in a realistic business setting. Two formal efforts are under way: the Web Services Interoperability Organization (**WS-I**) and the formal standardization of Web services technologies.

WS-I

WS-I promotes Web services interoperability

In February 2002, Accenture, BEA, Fujitsu, HP, IBM, Intel, Microsoft, Oracle, and SAP launched the WS-I organization. WS-I's charter is to promote Web services interoperability across platforms, operating systems, and programming languages. Obviously the industry liked the idea of a formal venue for this work, because within a week more than 60 organizations had joined the consortium. The organization caused a bit of a flap at first because the founding members had not invited Sun to participate. Eventually everyone's feathers were smoothed out, and by late 2002, membership had grown to more than 150 companies, including Sun.

WS-I is defining profiles and guidelines for interoperability

WS-I is defining a set of profiles and guidelines for Web services. The primary focus of current WS-I efforts is to enable interoperability. The profiles will help your IT organization understand what level of interoperability it can expect from various Web services technologies. The guidelines will help your developers build interoperable Web services. As long as you adhere to these guidelines, you can reasonably assume that any Web services you build can be accessed by service consumers using any platform language or tool. WS-I is also developing tools and test suites that you will be able to use to verify that your Web services comply with the guidelines.

WS-I's first deliverable is the **WS-I Basic Profile**. A draft of this document was first published in October 2002 and updated in April 2003.[2] It defines a profile based on the SOAP 1.1, WSDL 1.1, and UDDI 2.0 specifications, and it defines a set of constraints that you must follow to ensure interoperability using these technologies. If you build your Web services within the constraints defined by the Basic Profile, then you can claim conformance with the profile. Many vendors have pledged to implement support for the profile, something that also improves your chances for interoperability.

The Basic Profile defines constraints that ensure interoperability

WS-I chose to address the interoperability issue by reducing the number of permitted options. SOAP and WSDL give you a fair amount of latitude in how you construct messages and describe services. Although this latitude gives you quite a bit of flexibility, it also makes it much more difficult to ensure interoperability. The WS-I Basic Profile reduces the number of options defined in the specifications. WS-I based its decisions on real world use cases and scenarios for Web services.

WS-I specifications improve interoperability by reducing options

WS-I doesn't position itself as a standards body. WS-I is not developing new technologies. Instead it is focused on making the current technologies work better. In the course of its work, though, it has identified some of the most troublesome aspects of the current

WS-I's focus is current technology, not new technology

---

[2] Obviously this information will become quite dated in a short period of time. Please visit http://www.bowlight.net for periodic updates.

specifications and is feeding this information into the formal standardization efforts.

W3C and OASIS

The W3C launched an activity in September 2000 to standardize SOAP

The formal standardization efforts are happening at the W3C and OASIS. In September 2000 the W3C launched the XML Protocol Activity to define a standard based on SOAP 1.1. More than 140 representatives from more than 65 W3C member companies have participated in the development of this standard XML protocol, now called SOAP 1.2.

SOAP 1.2 corrects the inaccuracies, omissions, contradictions, and ambiguities in SOAP 1.1

SOAP 1.2 is a formal standard,[3] developed using an open, collaborative process. It is quite similar to the SOAP 1.1 specification, but it corrects many of the inaccuracies, omissions, contradictions, and ambiguities that appear in SOAP 1.1. The XML Protocol Working Group published a **W3C Candidate Recommendation** in December 2002, followed by a **W3C Proposed Recommendation** in May 2003. I expect the final **W3C Recommendation** to be approved in the second or third quarter of 2003. A number of SOAP implementations provide preliminary support for SOAP 1.2, including Apache Axis, BEA WebLogic Server, Microsoft .NET, SOAP::Lite, Systinet WASP, TIBCO Web Services SDK, and WhiteMesa Server.

The History of WSDL

Originally IBM and Microsoft had different description languages

In the early days of SOAP, IBM and Microsoft each developed a unique language to describe Web services for its SOAP toolkit. Developers using these early toolkits would define their services

---

[3] I refer to SOAP 1.2 as a formal standard, although I should point out that W3C and OASIS are not formal international standards organizations. They are vendor consortia. For practical purposes, though, the industry views their works as formal standards.

The History of WSDL

using these languages and then would compile the definitions to generate the SOAP communications routines for client and service applications. IBM's definition language was called Network Accessible Service Specification Language (**NASSL**). Microsoft's language was called SOAP Contract Language (**SCL**). Both languages performed essentially the same function, but they used two different XML vocabularies to represent information about the Web service contract, such as the method names and the input and output messages. There was no way to use a NASSL definition from the IBM toolkit to generate a client with the Microsoft toolkit, and no way to use an SCL definition from the Microsoft toolkit to generate a client with the IBM toolkit. It quickly became apparent that a common description language was needed to enable integration across multi-vendor implementations.

Following the successful collaboration that produced the SOAP 1.1 specification, IBM and Microsoft again joined forces to merge NASSL and SCL and develop a common description language. In September 2000, they published a unified description language called WSDL.

They joined efforts and produced WSDL

Over the next few months, IBM and Microsoft corrected a few inconsistencies in the original WSDL specification and then submitted the WSDL 1.1 specification to the W3C. The authors managed to recruit 23 other co-submitters, making it the largest submission team in the history of the W3C. The specification was published as a W3C Note in March 2001, and the industry adopted WSDL 1.1 with as much gusto as it had SOAP 1.1. In short order most SOAP implementations added support for WSDL.

The W3C published WSDL 1.1 as a W3C Note in March 2001

Challenges with WSDL 1.1

But just as with SOAP 1.1, the WSDL 1.1 specification was never put through the rigorous analysis and review of a formal standardization process. It also contains a number of ambiguities and inconsistencies that contribute to the interoperability issues.

WSDL 1.1 also contains ambiguities and inconsistencies

Chapter 4   Standardizing Web Services Technologies

WS-I tries to clarify these ambiguities

The WS-I profiles and guidelines make an effort to clarify the meaning of many of the ambiguities in WSDL, but they don't resolve the underlying issue that the WSDL specification needs improvements. Moreover, these improvements should occur under the auspices of an accredited standards body.

The W3C launched the Web Services Activity in March 2002

In March 2002, the W3C stepped up its efforts in Web services technologies. It launched a major Web Services activity consisting of multiple working groups and a coordination group. The XML Protocol Working Group was moved into this activity, and two other working groups were formed, including the Web Services Description Working Group and the Web Services Architecture Working Group. The Web Services Coordination Group acts as a liaison with related W3C activities, such as the XML Activity, the XML Signature Activity, the Semantic Web Activity, and the W3C Technical Architecture Group, as well as with other standards organizations such as the Internet Engineering Task Force (**IETF**) and OASIS.

WS-Desc is working on the next version of WSDL

The Web Services Description Working Group (WS-Desc) is working on a new and improved description language called WSDL 1.2. More than 40 representatives from more than 30 W3C member companies are contributing to this effort. The WS-Desc group published its third **W3C Working Draft** in March 2003. Based on current discussions, I anticipate that WSDL 1.2 will be quite different from WSDL 1.1. I expect the final version of the WSDL 1.2 specification to be published in late 2003 or early 2004.

WS-Arch is defining a reference architecture for Web services

The Web Services Architecture Working Group (WS-Arch) is defining a **reference architecture** for Web services.[4] This architecture defines the various functional components and technologies that are or might be required to implement applications based on Web services technologies. Examples of some of these functional

[4] My architectural descriptions in Chapter 3 are based on WS-Arch discussions.

components are message exchange, service description, service publishing and discovery, security, reliability, and choreography. More than 80 representatives from more than 50 W3C member companies have contributed to this effort. The group published its first Working Draft of the architecture in November 2002.

Some of the functional components identified in the Web Services Architecture are in the process of being standardized by other W3C working groups. For example, the XML Protocol group is developing a standard for message exchange (SOAP 1.2), and the WS-Desc group is developing a standard for service description (WSDL 1.2). Some functional components are in the process of being standardized by other standards organizations. For example, the OASIS UDDI Specification Technical Committee (UDDI-spec) is standardizing a method for service publishing and discovery (UDDI V2 and UDDI V3), and the OASIS Web Services Security Technical Committee is defining standards for security.[5] As part of the architectural definition process, the WS-Arch team is identifying functional areas that require standardization and is making recommendations for further working groups.

WS-Arch identifies components that need to be standardized

The first such group was formed in January 2003. At the request of the WS-Arch team, the W3C launched another working group within the Web Services Activity. The Web Services Choreography Working Group (WS-Chor) is developing a **choreography** language for creating composite services and for defining choreographed interchanges among multiple Web services.[6] The WS-Chor team may base its work on Web Services Choreography Interface (**WSCI**), a choreography language developed by BEA, Intalio, SAP, and Sun, which was contributed to W3C and published as a W3C Note in August 2002. Although BEA, IBM, and Microsoft have

WS-Chor is developing a choreography language for composite Web services

---

[5] We'll dig a little deeper into security in Chapter 5.
[6] We'll dig a little deeper into choreography in Chapter 5.

Chapter 4 Standardizing Web Services Technologies

also developed a choreography language called Business Process Execution Language for Web Services (**BPEL4WS**), the WS-Chor team isn't using this specification as a source of input. Instead, the BPEL4WS authors launched a competing standardization effort at OASIS in April 2003 called Web Services Business Process Execution Language (WS-BPEL).

The History of UDDI

UDDI.org developed the UDDI specifications

UDDI is a more complex technology than either SOAP or WSDL, so for this effort IBM and Microsoft invited the leading software and service vendors to participate in an informal consortium called **UDDI.org**. Ariba, IBM, and Microsoft published a draft of the UDDI 1.0 specification and launched UDDI.org in September 2000. The three founders then invited Accenture, Commerce One, Compaq, Equifax, Fujitsu, Hewlett-Packard, i2 Technologies, Intel, Oracle, SAP, Sun Microsystems, and VeriSign to join the UDDI Working Group. Representatives from these companies met once a month for approximately two years to work on the UDDI specifications. In addition to the core working group, more than 300 other companies joined the UDDI Advisory Group, providing input for the specification requirements and commenting on preliminary specifications.

UDDI 1.0 has limited value

The original UDDI 1.0 specification has very limited value. Its most blatant limitation is that it provides integrated support for only three industry taxonomies, and it makes no provision to support custom taxonomies. It also has no complex query facilities.

UDDI 2.0 adds support for custom taxonomies

UDDI.org published the UDDI 2.0 specification in June 2001. This version adds support for custom taxonomies, making UDDI much more interesting and valuable. This version also adds support for business relationships, and it greatly enhances query capabilities.

The History of UDDI

The UDDI 3.0 specification was published in July 2002. This version adds more enhanced query facilities, internationalization support, security, subscription and notification services, and interregistry relationships. Following the publication of UDDI 3.0, UDDI.org submitted the specification to OASIS for formal standardization and shut the doors on the informal consortium. All subsequent work on the specifications now occurs at OASIS. The UDDI-spec committee published the UDDI V2 and V3 specifications as **OASIS Committee Specifications** in September 2002. The UDDI V2 specification was approved as an **OASIS Standard** in April 2003. The UDDI V3 specification requires a bit more work. It should become a formal OASIS standard in the second half of 2003.

The UDDI specifications are now managed by OASIS

UDDI Business Registry

Loosely associated with UDDI.org is a formal business partnership called the **UDDI Operators Council**. The members operate a public UDDI registry called the **UDDI Business Registry** (**UBR**). The public registry is available free of charge for anyone to advertise and discover public Web services.

The UDDI Operators Council operates a public UDDI registry

The UBR was launched in September 2000 at the same time that UDDI.org was established. Initially the members of the UDDI Operators Council were Ariba, IBM, and Microsoft, the three founding members of UDDI.org. Ariba dropped out of the partnership in May 2001. Hewlett-Packard quickly stepped forward to take Ariba's place, and SAP and NTT joined the partnership in late 2001. Following the acquisition of Compaq, though, Hewlett-Packard decided to scale back its investments in Web services middleware and withdrew from the partnership. At the time of this writing, IBM, Microsoft, NTT, and SAP operated the UBR, implementing the UDDI 2.0 specification.

IBM, Microsoft, NTT, and SAP are the current members of the UDDI Operators Council

Each member of the UDDI Operators Council operates a **UBR node**. All nodes within the UBR contain identical information. All

All UBR nodes contain identical information

data registered in one node is replicated to all the other nodes within about an hour.

Anyone can register a service or service type in the UBR

Any individual, business, or industry group can register services and service types in the UBR. Before you register any information, though, you must become a registered publication user of the registry node. Publication registration is free, but you must establish your credentials with the UBR node operator. Each UBR node operator uses a different mechanism to set up credentials. After you register information in a specific UBR node, that node becomes the custodian of the registration. Any subsequent modifications made to the registration must be made through the same UBR node. If for some reason you become dissatisfied with your UBR node operator, you can request that custody of your registration be transferred to a different operator.

All information in the UBR is available to the general public

Anyone can query the UBR. You must be a registered query user, but the query credentialing process is much more relaxed than the publication credentialing process. Anyone with a valid e-mail address can query the UBR. All information in the UBR is available to the general public. Thus you shouldn't register any information in the UBR that you don't want to publish to the entire world.

The UBR has not been popular with the industry

Although UDDI.org at first touted the UBR as "a core element of the infrastructure that supports Web services," it has not been a big hit with the industry. Very few businesses have registered services in the public registry. The UBR has been a victim of its own hype. It has been promoted as, among other things, the ultimate comparison shopping agent. One of the most hyped UDDI scenarios says that you can use the UBR to find a supplier that will give you the lowest price with the best delivery options. Unfortunately, this scenario depends on a lot of assumptions that just aren't real. The UBR can help you find a supplier that provides the goods you want, but it doesn't give you a facility to compare prices.

When you get past the unrealistic hype and look at UDDI for what it is, you soon realize that UDDI does in fact play an important role in Web services technology. Although you can easily develop and deploy Web services without UDDI, after you've deployed a few you'll find you need UDDI to help manage your environment. UDDI's value increases as the number of your Web services increases.

UDDI helps you manage your Web services

Private UDDI Registries

UDDI plays a much more valuable role in a private setting. A business or business community can set up a private UDDI registry to advertise and discover Web services within a secure and controlled environment. You can use a private UDDI registry to publish Web services within your own organization or to a select set of customers or business partners.

A private UDDI registry gives you added security and control

For example, you can use a private UDDI registry to help manage your corporate software assets. As departments and business units in your organization build reusable Web APIs for their application systems, you need a way to let other departments and business units know about the APIs. You can set up an internal private UDDI registry, and each time a developer deploys a new Web service for internal use, this Web service can be registered and categorized in the internal registry. You can set up your own custom taxonomies to indicate information such as the owning department, release version numbers, and internal charge-back policies. These custom taxonomies provide the real value of private UDDI.

An internal UDDI can help you manage your software assets

Another popular way to use a private UDDI registry is to control redundant application functionality. The U.S. Navy manages tens of thousands of applications, and currently it's not uncommon to find multiple applications that perform essentially the same function. In an effort to reduce redundant systems, the Navy is establishing a process using UDDI that identifies duplicative applications before they are deployed.

The U.S. Navy uses UDDI to control redundant applications

Chapter 4   Standardizing Web Services Technologies

UDDI supports the Navy's portal architecture

All Navy application systems are accessed through a portal. Users can customize their portal layouts to view various applications in different sections or frames within the browser. A Navy application runs within one of these frames. An application consists of a portlet and a set of backend services. The portlet contains the presentation logic that displays the application interface in the frame. The backend services perform the actual application logic. A backend service might be a locally resident service, or it might be a remote function implemented by either the Navy or some other organization. For example, the portlet might call out to an FAA service to obtain a weather report. To add a new application to the portal, you must configure the portlet and register the backend services in UDDI. Registration requires comprehensive analysis and assessment of each new application to justify its purpose and determine its value. This process enables the Navy to identify duplicative applications and select best-of-breed solutions. Additionally, it allows developers to identify existing applications and Web services that can be leveraged to provide content for additional business processes in new applications.

UDDI makes it easier to set up extranet operations

A private UDDI registry can also simplify your extranet operations. Let's say, for example, that you would like to allow your distributors to place orders or submit forecasts electronically. You can do so by creating a set of Web services with simple Web APIs that can support any type of client application. But how do you tell your distributors about these APIs? You could assign one or more of your employees the task of contacting each of your distributors and locating the specific person responsible for developing the client interfaces and then relaying information about the location of the WSDL descriptions for each of your Web services. Or you could exploit the benefits of UDDI and register these services in your private extranet UDDI registry, letting your distributors know that the services are now available. Each distributor can then query the extranet UDDI registry to find the needed information.

A private UDDI registry is an invaluable asset in a Web services-based electronic marketplace. An e-marketplace brings together buyers and sellers and facilitates e-procurement. Generally you must be a member to use the marketplace facilities, and the registration process requires some level of due diligence to ensure the integrity of the member companies. By joining the marketplace, you get an instant, qualified list of buyers and suppliers. All that's left to do is to build the interfaces into your application systems to let you engage in electronic business. If the definitions of those interfaces are registered in a private UDDI registry, it makes it that much easier for you to integrate your systems.

A private UDDI registry is indispensable to an e-marketplace

Programming Standards for Web Services

Unlike other middleware systems, SOAP, WSDL, and UDDI do not define programming standards. These specifications simply define the communication protocols in terms of XML. They don't indicate how an application program written in, say, Java or Visual Basic should interact with Web services. The specifics of how applications interact with SOAP and WSDL have been left as an exercise to the application community.

SOAP, WSDL, and UDDI don't specify how application languages should work with them

Any application language can parse (syntactically analyze) and process XML, so, at a minimum, you can simply construct XML messages within your application, package them in a SOAP envelope, and exchange them with other applications. But such manual processing isn't conducive to developer productivity, and it doesn't exploit the fact that WSDL is machine-readable and therefore can be compiled into application code.

Working with SOAP, WSDL, and UDDI via an XML parser isn't as productive as using SOAP tools

Most SOAP implementations provide tools that automatically generate the code necessary for your applications to send and receive SOAP messages. For the most part, you'll find that these tools can be used only with their associated SOAP implementation. Although

Although the technology is standard, each SOAP tool is different

Chapter 4 Standardizing Web Services Technologies

the technology is standard, the way you use it isn't. This situation threatens to limit the potential long-term market for third-party software accessories and business applications. Standard programming interfaces can open up this market.

Microsoft can define its own standards for the Visual Studio languages

Microsoft has the ability to define its own standard programming interfaces for its development tools. The .NET framework provides a set of standard Web services class libraries and frameworks for the C# language, and Visual Studio .NET supplies visual tools and services for C#, Visual Basic, and the other .NET languages. The Microsoft SOAP Toolkit provides comparable tools for earlier versions of Visual Studio.

Other proprietary language vendors can define their own SOAP standards, too

Similarly, other proprietary language vendors, such as Borland and Sybase, can develop their own standards for integrating SOAP with their languages. Borland has developed SOAP tools for C++Builder, Delphi, and Kylix, and Sybase is developing SOAP tools for PowerBuilder.

No one vendor can establish standards for the Java community

Java poses a slightly more challenging situation, though. No one vendor can establish standards for the Java community. More than two dozen SOAP implementations for Java are on the market, and until recently each of them provided its own programming interfaces and class libraries. Having a multitude of Java APIs for SOAP doesn't impact the capabilities of SOAP, but it does impact the productivity of your developers and the amount of vendor lock-in you experience. The concept of "Write Once, Run Anywhere" and cross-vendor portability are pretty much out of reach if you have different APIs for every SOAP implementation for Java.

Java standards must be developed through the JCP

In an effort to stave off industry fracture, the Java community has come together to define a set of standard Java APIs for Web services through the **Java Community Process** (**JCP**). In 2002, the JCP

Programming Standards for Web Services

delivered five standard Java API specifications for Web services. More specifications are in development.

Java Standards for SOAP

There are many different levels at which an application might like to work with SOAP. A lot of Java developers prefer to work strictly with Java constructs and not worry about parsing or manipulating XML. Other developers might prefer to work directly with the XML documents. And at times you may need to work directly with the SOAP constructs. Therefore the JCP has created three Java APIs for working with SOAP.

There are three Java APIs for working with SOAP

The Java APIs for XML based RPC (**JAX-RPC**) is a WSDL-aware, Java-centric, RPC-style programming interface that makes SOAP look and feel a lot like RMI. Although the name suggests otherwise, JAX-RPC can be used for both RPC-style and document-style Web services. A JAX-RPC tool provides a **WSDL compiler** that generates the code that maps the Web service's XML data structures to native Java objects. At runtime, JAX-RPC automatically performs all data translations between Java and XML, and it automatically constructs and interprets the SOAP messages according to the definitions in the WSDL description.

JAX-RPC makes SOAP transparent to the Java developer

JAX-RPC provides full support for all the dynamic features associated with SOAP and WSDL. A JAX-RPC client application can use a development-time precompiled client proxy to access a specific service implementation. It can also select an implementation of a given service type at runtime, and JAX-RPC will generate a dynamic binding.

JAX-RPC supports both static and dynamic binding

The Java API for XML Messaging (**JAXM**) is an XML-centric, message-oriented programming interface that doesn't rely on WSDL. You would use this API if you have an XML document, such as a purchase order, and you simply want to send it to another application.

JAXM is an XML-centric API

Chapter 4   Standardizing Web Services Technologies

JAXM hides the mechanics of SOAP messaging. JAXM uses a profile that defines a template for the SOAP message structure, and it automatically constructs the SOAP envelope, SOAP header, and SOAP body based on this template. The Java application simply adds the XML payload to the message.

JAXM doesn't support WSDL

JAXM is designed to be used with document-style SOAP messages rather than RPC-style messages, although a developer could use JAXM to build RPC-style messages. One of the primary distinctions between JAXM and JAX-RPC is that JAXM does not support WSDL. JAXM provides no facilities to automatically map Java objects to XML structures. Thus it's up to the developer to define the appropriate mappings and to ensure that the SOAP messages conform to the WSDL description.

JAXM was originally designed to support ebXML

JAXM was initially designed as an API for the ebXML Message Service (ebMS). When the ebXML initiative adopted SOAP 1.1 as its underlying XML protocol, the JAXM effort expanded its scope to also support SOAP messaging. When you're using the ebMS you usually send the message payload as an attachment to the SOAP message rather than within the SOAP body. An ebMS SOAP header holds security and reliability information about the message, and the SOAP body contains a manifest of the attachments to the message. An ebMS JAXM profile can automatically generate this basic SOAP message structure, and then the application adds the message payload as an attachment. The WSDL specification doesn't indicate how to specify the contents of an attachment, so WSDL doesn't play as important a role in this situation.

SAAJ gives the developer direct access to the SOAP envelope

The SOAP with Attachments API for Java (**SAAJ**) provides a low-level programming interface that allows Java applications to work directly with the constructs of the SOAP message. SAAJ is used by both JAXM and JAX-RPC, so even when using these APIs, a developer can always drop down into the SAAJ API to access the SOAP envelope.

Programming Standards for Web Services

Java Standards for WSDL

Under most circumstances, a Java application doesn't need to interact directly with a WSDL document. Usually a Java application uses JAX-RPC to interact with a SOAP service, and JAX-RPC manages all the WSDL manipulation for the application. The primary exception to this rule is an application that wants to dynamically discover and use a service, and hence it has no access to the WSDL document at development time. In this circumstance, the application needs access to the WSDL file at runtime.

Generally an application doesn't need to interact directly with a WSDL document

For this situation, developers can use the Java API for WSDL (**JWSDL**), which is an API that allows a Java application to create, inspect, and manipulate a WSDL document. SOAP tools use JWSDL to compile a WSDL document into a SOAP communication routine. SOAP runtime systems use JWSDL to generate dynamic bindings. Java applications can use JWSDL to dynamically interpret the operations and messages supported by a service.

JWSDL lets you create, inspect, and manipulate a WSDL document

Java Standards for UDDI

A UDDI registry is a Web service, so the standard way for an application to speak to UDDI is to send it SOAP messages. The Web service interfaces (there are two: inquiry and publish) are described by WSDL documents. So any application that can speak SOAP can access a UDDI registry. For example, a Java client application can use JAX-RPC to communicate with a UDDI service. Even so, the UDDI data model is fairly complex, and it's helpful to have a dedicated Java API that understands UDDI tModels, binding templates, and categorization schemes and automatically constructs valid UDDI SOAP messages for you.

UDDI has a standard SOAP API

Most UDDI vendors provide UDDI client APIs with their products. You can use any UDDI client API to talk to any UDDI registry as long as they both conform to the UDDI specifications. One of the most popular UDDI client APIs in the Java community is **UDDI4J**.

UDDI4J is a popular open source UDDI client API

This API was first developed by IBM in 2001 and then released as open source. UDDI4J provides a direct mapping of the UDDI SOAP operations and data structures to Java methods and classes. For someone who's familiar with the UDDI data model, this API is very intuitive.

JAXR provides a common interface to both UDDI and ebXML registries

Despite UDDI4J's popularity, it is not the standard Java API for UDDI. The Java API for XML Registries (**JAXR**) is an API for both UDDI and the ebXML registry. This dual-purpose API is quite an achievement, given that the data structures in UDDI are different from those in ebXML. The JAXR data model is based on the ebXML data model, which is a bit more generic than the UDDI data model. The JAXR data model is business-oriented, and the API streamlines a number of operations.

You should try both JAXR and UDDI4J to determine which you like better

One side effect of this higher-level data model is that JAXR's object names don't match the UDDI element names. For example, JAXR uses terminology such as "Concept" rather than "tModel," and "ClassificationScheme" in place of "categoryBag." For developers who are accustomed to UDDI terminology, the JAXR API takes a bit of getting used to. Some of your developers may prefer to work with a more UDDI-centric API. I suggest that you try both and determine which one you like better. If you plan to use both registries, you should definitely use the JAXR API.

Executive Summary: Status Check

IBM and Microsoft started the Web services phenomenon

The basic Web services technologies—SOAP, WSDL, and UDDI—did not start out as formal industry standards. IBM, Microsoft, and a few invited friends are responsible for launching this new approach to application integration. Now these technologies are well on the way to formal status. Table 4-1 summarizes the status of these standardization efforts.

Executive Summary: Status Check

Table 4-1: Summary of Standardization Efforts

Specification	Group	Status	Estimated Completion
SOAP 1.2	W3C	Proposed Recommendation: May 2003	W3C Recommendation: Q2/Q3 2003
WSDL 1.2	W3C	Working Draft: March 2003	W3C Recommendation: Q4 2003/Q1 2004
UDDI 2.0	OASIS	OASIS Specification: May 2003	OASIS Specification: April 2003
UDDI 3.0	OASIS	Committee Specification: September 2002	OASIS Specification: Q4 2003

You may have noticed an interesting trend in the Web services standardization process. Nearly every technology advancement has been developed by a small number of companies working together to solve a problem. These companies publish a specification to the general public, and, if it gains traction, the authors submit the specification to W3C or OASIS. Shortly afterward, a working group or technical committee is created to develop a formal standard based on the submission. This process has proved to work quite successfully and is responsible for the rapid advancement of Web services technology.

Most standards efforts are based on vendor-developed contributions

5

Advanced Web Services Standards

SOAP, WSDL, and UDDI form the core foundation for the Web services architecture, but these technologies provide only the most basic functionality. As mentioned in Chapter 3, SOAP gives you a powerful extension mechanism via SOAP headers. You can use SOAP extensions to add advanced middleware functionality, such as security, management, and transactions, to the environment.

SOAP extensions support security and other functions

When extending SOAP, people can devise their own SOAP header structures and their own intermediaries to process them, but if you'd like to make your extra middleware services interoperable it's helpful to have standards for these SOAP extensions. Standard SOAP extensions ensure cross-vendor and cross-business interoperability.

Standards ensure interoperability

Web Services Security Standardization Efforts

Security has been a big concern for SOAP users from the beginning, and the industry has made excellent progress in defining security standards for XML and Web services. As mentioned in Chapter 3, the simplest way to make SOAP secure is to encrypt your network traffic using HTTPS and SSL/TLS. But network-based security is rather crude. It doesn't offer very much control at the application level. For fine security control, you must implement security at the application level, something that requires a different set of security standards.

The industry has made excellent progress in defining security standards

Chapter 5   Advanced Web Services Standards

Web services security standards build on existing security standards

Security is a broad subject, and many groups are working on various aspects of XML and Web services security standards. (Remarkably, there's almost no overlap across the various efforts.) The purpose of these new standards is not to replace existing security standards but instead to provide an XML-based abstraction layer that enables Web services to transparently use a variety of security technologies for confidentiality, integrity, nonrepudiation, authentication, and authorization.[1]

W3C and OASIS are working on XML and Web services security standards

The National Institute of Standards and Technologies (**NIST**) and the IETF manage most of the low-level security standards associated with data **encryption** and digital signatures. The W3C and OASIS are building XML and Web services security standards based on the core NIST and IETF work. The W3C manages the XML standards associated with encryption, digital signatures, and **key management**. OASIS manages most of the efforts focused on security information exchange, access control, and SOAP message protection. Figure 5-1 shows the responsibilities of these groups.

Figure 5-1: IEFT, W3C, and OASIS share responsibility for developing Web services security standards.

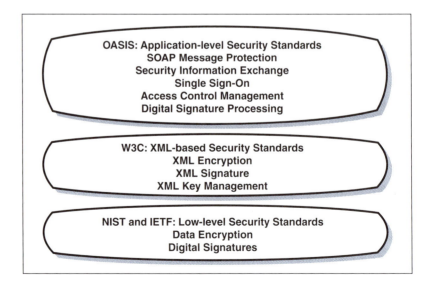

[1] See Chapter 3 for a description of these security functions.

106

Confidentiality and Integrity

Let's start by talking about data confidentiality and integrity. Confidentiality protects the contents of a message from unauthorized access. Integrity ensures that the contents of the message have not been changed in transit. Encryption is the most common mechanism used to ensure the confidentiality and integrity of data. You can use SSL/TLS to encrypt your messages during transport, but network-level encryption is an all-or-nothing approach. You might need to route a message through a number of intermediaries on its way to its final destination. If you're using network-level encryption, the message will get decrypted at each stop along the way. If you want to make sure that a particular piece of information is kept confidential, you must encrypt it at the application level so that only the intended recipient can see it. XML encryption standards let you encrypt all or part of an XML message.

Encryption provides data integrity and confidentiality

Encryption

Encryption uses a string of characters called a key to mathematically encode and decode data. The two most common types of encryption are **symmetric encryption** (single key) and **asymmetric encryption** (public key). In symmetric key encryption, a message is encrypted and decrypted using the same key, which must be confidentially exchanged in a separate transmission. In asymmetric key encryption, a message is encrypted and decrypted using two keys (one public, one private). If the message is encrypted with the public key, it can be decrypted only with the private key. Similarly, if the message is encrypted with the private key, it can be decrypted only with the public key.

There are two types of encryption

NIST manages most low-level encryption standards. IETF controls the standards for SSL/TLS and HTTPS, which are the technologies used to encrypt messages at the network level. To implement encryption at the SOAP level, we need additional standards designed specifically to work with XML data.

NIST and IETF manage the low-level encryption standards

Chapter 5 Advanced Web Services Standards

XML Encryption defines processing instructions to encrypt and decrypt XML and a syntax to represent encrypted data

The W3C formed the **XML Encryption** Activity in January 2001 to develop a standard to support XML encryption. The resulting XML Encryption W3C Recommendation was approved in December 2002. This standard defines a process for encrypting and decrypting all or part of an XML document. It also defines an XML syntax for representing encrypted content in an XML document and an XML syntax for representing the information needed to decrypt the content.

Digital Signatures

Digital signatures support data integrity and nonrepudiation

A digital signature uses encryption technology to support data integrity and nonrepudiation. A digital signature provides proof that a particular person (the signatory) sent a piece of information (the signed data). Digital signatures rely on public key cryptography. You create a digital signature by using your private key to apply a signing encryption algorithm to the data being signed. The signing algorithm does not modify the data, but it does produce a unique value, which is the digital signature. The receiver verifies the signature by applying a verification encryption algorithm to the same data, but this time using the signatory's public key. The generated value should match the digital signature. If the signed data have been tampered with in any way during transport, the signatures won't match. Because only the signatory has access to the private key, the receiver is assured that the signed data did in fact come from that person and that the data have not been altered in any way.

XML Signature defines a syntax to represent signatures in XML

As with encryption, NIST and IETF are responsible for the low-level digital signature standards. The issue at hand is how to make digital signatures work with XML data and how to represent a digital signature in XML. An XML document often contains a lot of **white space**—blanks and line feeds that have no semantic meaning. Because the encryption process becomes invalid if even one character within a document has changed, it's necessary to transform an

Web Services Security Standardization Efforts

XML document into **canonical** form (which removes all white space) before signing the data.[2] Hence XML signatures require a little extra processing. The W3C XML Digital Signatures Activity has been working with the IETF xmldsig working group to define the necessary technologies needed to sign XML data. These two groups jointly produced the W3C **XML Signature** Recommendations in February 2002. These standards define an XML syntax to represent signed data in XML and a set of processing instructions to canonicalize XML, sign data, and interpret signatures.

Managing Keys and Processing Signatures

Now that you have an inkling of the way digital signatures work, you're probably wondering how an application might go about acquiring encryption keys and creating and verifying a digital signature. Every public key infrastructure (**PKI**) system provides APIs that you can use to manage keys and process signatures. Unfortunately, these APIs are fairly difficult to use, and they require you to deploy special PKI client code on each system that wants to process signatures.

You normally use PKI APIs to manage encryption keys and process signatures

You probably don't want to write key management and signature processing code in every one of your applications. It is much more convenient to encapsulate this code into a centralized, reusable **trust service** that can perform this complex processing on behalf of your applications. A trust service is a Web service that provides security functions for your applications. Any client or application can access these services using simple SOAP requests. If you use trust services, you no longer need to deploy PKI client software on all your systems.

A trust service is a Web service that provides centralized security processing

---

[2] Canonicalization involves a number of other functions in addition to removing white space. If you have a burning desire to learn all about XML encryption and XML signature, I recommend *Secure XML*, by Donald Eastlake and Kitty Niles, ISBN 0201756056.

Chapter 5   Advanced Web Services Standards

XKMS defines a set of trust services that help you register, manage, and obtain encryption keys

The W3C XML Key Management Activity, which was formed in December 2001, is developing specifications for a set of trust services that can manage the registration and distribution of public keys. These Web services are described using WSDL and are accessed using SOAP. They completely hide the complexity of using PKI APIs from your applications. The group published the first Working Draft of the XML Key Management Specification (**XKMS**) in March 2002. This draft is based on the XKMS specification developed by Microsoft, VeriSign, and webMethods. The authors and seven other companies submitted the specification in March 2001.

OASIS DSS is defining trust services for XML signatures

The OASIS Digital Signature Services (**DSS**) Technical Committee, which was formed in December 2002, is developing specifications for a set of trust services that can create and verify XML signatures. These Web services will also be described using WSDL and accessed using SOAP, and they hide the complexities of the PKI signature processing APIs.

Authentication and Authorization

Authentication and authorization protect your systems from unauthorized access

Another important part of security is authentication and authorization. Authentication verifies the identity of a user or application. Authorization determines whether or not a user has permission to perform a particular action. These two security functions protect your systems from unauthorized access.

If you rely on network-based authentication you may lose track of the original caller

There are many ways to accomplish authentication. As with encryption, you can rely on the network to manage authentication. HTTP supports two mechanisms for passing a user ID and password with the message; one mechanism uses clear text, and the other uses encryption. But again, as with network-based encryption, HTTP-based authentication is rather crude. If the request passes through multiple intermediaries or if the request accesses multiple services, you may lose track of the identity of the original caller.

A more flexible and reliable way to manage authentication is to set up some type of authentication authority. A user goes to the authentication authority, provides some proof of identity, and in return receives a security token that represents an assertion by the authority of the user's identity. Examples of an authentication authority include a directory service, a certificate authority, or a single sign-on service. Users prove their identity by passing an authentication challenge (user ID password or biometric) or via their private key. Security tokens include X.509 certificates, Kerberos tickets, and XML tokens. You can use these security tokens to pass authentication information in subsequent SOAP requests.

A security token represents a decision made by a security authority

Expressing and Exchanging Security Information in XML

A number of groups at OASIS are working on XML-based authentication and authorization standards. These groups are defining XML vocabularies that allow you to express and exchange security information using XML.

OASIS sponsors many security activities

The OASIS XML Common Biometric Format (**XCBF**) Technical Committee has defined an XML vocabulary for representing and exchanging biometric information in XML. You can use this biometric information to create an XCBF security token, which you can use for authentication and identification purposes. XCBF was approved as an OASIS Committee Specification in January 2003.

XCBF represents biometric information

The OASIS Security Assertions Markup Language (SAML) standard defines an XML syntax for representing security assertions. OASIS formed the XML-Based Security Services Technical Committee

SAML defines authentication and authorization assertions

Chapter 5   Advanced Web Services Standards

(SSTC) in December 2000, and the specification was approved as a formal OASIS Standard in November 2002. SAML supports three types of security assertions:

- Authentication. An authentication assertion states that a particular authentication authority has authenticated the subject of the assertion (either a human or a digital entity such as a computer or application) at a particular time, and this assertion is valid for a specified period of time.
- Authorization. An authorization assertion states that a particular authorization authority has granted or denied permission for the subject of the assertion to access a particular resource within a specified period of time.
- Attributes. An attribute assertion provides qualifying information about either an authentication or an authorization assertion. For example, an authorization assertion might say that Joe Cool is authorized to submit purchase orders to Acme Parts, and an attribute assertion indicates that his spending limit is $5000.

SAML can support any type of security authority

SAML defines a set of Web APIs that you use to obtain these assertions from a trust service that makes authentication or authorization decisions. SAML doesn't specify which authorities can be used to obtain these assertions. In fact, SAML is designed to support any type of security authority. After the authority has made its assertion, SAML gives you the means to exchange that security information with other systems.

Single Sign-on

SAML supports single sign-on

SAML also provides a mechanism to support an XML-based single sign-on service. A single sign-on service allows a user to log in once with a recognized security authority and then use the returned login credentials to access multiple resources for some predefined period of time. You can sign on to a SAML authentication authority and use the returned SAML assertion as an authentication token on subsequent SOAP requests. SAML allows you to authenticate yourself once and access many different Web services within your security domain within the allotted timeframe.

The **Liberty** Alliance Project is developing a set of standards that allow you to use a SAML authentication assertion across multiple security domains. The Liberty Alliance Project is a consortium of more than 150 technology and consumer organizations working to develop open specifications for **federated identity**. The founding members include American Express, AOL, Bell Canada, France Telecom, GM, HP, MasterCard, Nokia, NTT DoCoMo, Openwave, RSA Security, Sony, Sun, and Vodafone.

Liberty lets SAML work across multiple security domains

The Liberty federated identity infrastructure allows you to create a **circle of trust** with your business partners. Although each member of the circle maintains and protects unique user account information, you can use a single federated identity credential as proof of authentication with all members of the circle. Each member maps the credential to the private user identity known by that system.

Liberty allows you to create a circle of trust

For example, let's say that you would like to make some travel reservations, and you'd like to pay for your airline tickets using frequent flyer miles. If you're like me, you have a decent stash of frequent flyer miles with most of the airlines, so you have a choice of carriers. Wouldn't it be nice if you could use an online travel agent to see what your options are and then book the flight directly? Unfortunately, as of this writing you need to book these tickets directly through the airline. Your frequent flyer information is owned and managed by each airline. The airline requires that you perform a login before you can access your frequent flyer account to purchase tickets. And no doubt you have a different user ID and password with each airline. Currently, there is no way for the online travel agent to log in with the airline on your behalf. The identity you have with the travel agent is different from the

Without Liberty, you need a different identity for each company

Chapter 5 Advanced Web Services Standards

identities you have with the airlines, and the online travel agent doesn't know all the user IDs and passwords you use to authenticate yourself with the airlines (and you really don't want the agent to know that information).

A Liberty federated identity maps to multiple account identities

With Liberty, all these travel-related companies can create a circle of trust to support federated identification. A Liberty federated identity is a single identity that can map to multiple account identities within the circle of trust. When you log in to a Liberty single sign-on service, you obtain a SAML authentication assertion that represents your federated identity credential. As you interact with each of the circle members, this credential maps to the specific account ID that you maintain with each company.

Liberty allows the partners to interact on your behalf while protecting your privacy

This means that you will be able to use an online travel agent to book a flight using your frequent flier miles. You'll be able log in to your travel agent site using your federated identity. The travel agent site can then use that identity to conduct transactions on your behalf (with your permission) with the various airlines. All the while, Liberty doesn't permit the partners to share your personal information, so it protects your privacy.

Liberty products are available now

The Liberty Alliance Project is a private consortium that operates like a formal standards body. The Liberty V1.1 specifications were published in January 2003. I expect the next version of the specifications to be released in the first half of 2003. Liberty-based products are or soon will be available from a number of directory and identity service companies, including Cavio, Communicator, Entrust, NeuStar, Novell, Oblix, OneName, Phaos, RSA Security, Sun, and WaveSet.

Authorization

XACML defines a policy-centric access control system

After you prove your identity to a system, it can determine whether you're authorized to access or use a particular resource. OASIS has a two technical committees working on specifications for authorization. The XML Access Control Markup Language (**XACML**) takes a policy-centric approach to authorization, which is typically used to control access to application functions and enterprise data. XACML defines a language for defining access policies and rules. These policies may apply to multiple resources or services. A user must obtain permission from an authorization authority to gain access to these resources and services. At runtime the authorization authority evaluates the policies to determine whether access is permitted. The results of the authorization decision are formatted into a SAML authorization assertion. XACML was approved as a formal OASIS Standard in February 2003.

The Extensible Rights Markup Language (**XrML**) takes a content-centric approach to access control, which is typically used to control access to content and multimedia. It uses a digital rights methodology. It defines an XML language for specifying access rights and permissions, permitting you to say who can view a particular resource and under what conditions. Access rights must be defined for each protected resource. The Rights Language Technical Committee was formed in May 2002. XrML is based on a specification submitted by Content Guard, which maintains rights to the intellectual property.

XrML defines a content-centric access control system

Using XML Security in Web Services

We've talked a lot about basic security technologies and discussed how to represent security information in XML, but we have yet to mention how to use these technologies with Web services. This is where the OASIS Web Services Security (**WSS**) effort comes into play. IBM, Microsoft, and VeriSign developed the **WS-Security** specification and submitted it to OASIS in July 2002. The OASIS WSS technical committee was formed in September 2002 to standardize this specification and to explore future requirements for securing Web services.

WSS focuses on using XML security with Web services

Chapter 5 Advanced Web Services Standards

WS-Security is a standard SOAP extension that specifies how to pass security information in SOAP headers

WS-Security, a SOAP extension specification, defines a standard way to represent security information in a SOAP message. WS-Security allows you to pass security tokens for authentication and authorization in a SOAP header. It provides a mechanism that allows you to digitally sign all or part of a SOAP message and to pass the signature in a SOAP header. It also provides a mechanism that allows you to encrypt all or part of a SOAP message. And it provides a way to pass information in a SOAP header about the encryption keys needed to decrypt the message or verify a digital signature.

WSS has defined bindings for many security tokens

WSS has published a series of working draft specifications. As of this writing, the most recent draft was published in March 2003. In addition the team has defined bindings for a variety of security tokens, including a simple username, SAML, XCBF, XrML, X.509 certificates, and Kerberos tickets.

SOAP header processors build and process the WS-Security header

Pulling all these standards together, you have very fine-grained security control over your SOAP messages. Figure 5-2 shows how you can use SOAP header processors and a variety of trust services to simplify SOAP security. SOAP header processors automatically manage the security process on behalf of both the client and service applications. You should have no problem with interoperability because the format of the WS-Security security header is standard.

The header processor on the client side creates the WS-Security header

In this example, the client first calls a SAML-compliant single sign-on service to log in and obtain a token containing a SAML authentication assertion. The SOAP header processor creates a WS-Security SOAP header and places the SAML token into the header. It then calls a DSS service to sign the message payload. It places the resulting digital signature and information about the user's public key in the SOAP header and sends the message on its way.

At the receiving end, the SOAP header processor uses the key information to obtain the client's public key from an XKMS service. The

Web Services Management Standardization Efforts

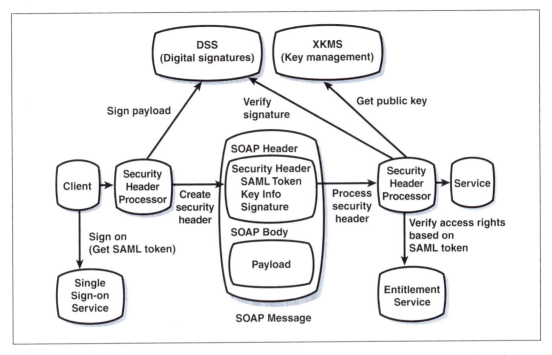

Figure 5-2: SOAP header processors automatically manage security on behalf of the client and service applications. The SOAP header processors use trust services to manage digital signatures, encryption keys, and authentication and authorization decisions.

SOAP header processor then calls the DSS service, which uses the public key to verify the signature. The SOAP header processor also calls an entitlement service to verify the client's access rights to the service based on the SAML token.

The header processor on the service side verifies the signature and access rights

Web Services Management Standardization Efforts

Distributed application systems impose serious management challenges. If one application component goes down, it may impact a number of application systems. If an application system isn't working properly, how do you identify the one component that's actually causing the problem? After you've identified the problem, what can you do to fix it and to avoid it in the future?

Distributed application systems are hard to manage

Chapter 5   Advanced Web Services Standards

Management includes monitoring and control activities

There are two distinct management activities. One activity focuses on reporting, and the other focuses on control. The purpose of the reporting activity is to help you monitor systems to understand what is going on. The purpose of controlling activities is to configure systems and solve any problems that might arise. By and large it's easy to develop standards for management reporting. It's much more difficult to convince vendors to agree on standards for control.

Most people use a management framework to monitor distributed systems

Most people use a systems management framework, such as BMC Patrol, CA Unicenter, HP OpenView, and IBM Tivoli, to monitor their production systems. These management frameworks consist of a set of monitoring agents and a central management coordinator. The agents collect information about the various nodes, devices, networks, and applications throughout your system, and they send the information to the central manager, which aggregates the information into a management console.

A management console provides a global view of the environment

This management console gives system administrators a global view of the situation. When systems don't perform within specified parameters, the central manager issues an alert, highlighting the problem on the console. The system administrators can then issue commands to the various agents to adjust the system. Each agent interacts with the component that it's managing through some type of instrumentation API. This instrumentation API lets the agent observe what's going on and potentially adjust the object's runtime configuration. A separate agent is required for each type of managed component.

Proprietary protocols lock you into a single management vendor

When these system management frameworks first appeared, each system used proprietary communication protocols. These proprietary protocols made it impossible for different frameworks to communicate, and therefore you could use only the agents supplied by the framework provider. If the framework provider didn't supply an agent for the device or application you needed, you couldn't manage that component through the framework. Over the past decade, a number of organizations have come together to develop management standards that would enable interoperability across multi-vendor agents and frameworks.

To enable an open management framework, a number of standards are required. You need the following:

- A standard protocol that the agents use to report information to the central manager
- A standard format for the management information
- A standard command API that the central console can use to give instructions to the agents to manage a particular resource

You need standard protocols, formats, and APIs to support interoperability

The first and most critical standard is IETF Simple Network Management Protocol (**SNMP**). SNMP is the standard protocol used by agents to report information to the central manager. SNMP was first developed in 1988 and standardized in 1990. Almost everyone has adopted SNMP for all reporting activities. But SNMP addresses only the first requirement.

Agents communicate with the central manager using SNMP

The Distributed Management Task Force (**DMTF**) is trying to address the other two requirements. DMTF develops standards that build on SNMP to provide a vendor-neutral, Internet-based management infrastructure for both reporting and control. The DMTF Common Information Model (**CIM**) defines a common management data model that is independent of any particular management framework. This data model defines the structure and format of management information.

CIM defines a common management data model

CIM also defines a standard set of control commands called CIM Operations, which are used to give instructions to the management agents. The CIM specifications enable interoperability

CIM Operations defines standard control commands

Chapter 5 Advanced Web Services Standards

among multiple management frameworks so that you are no longer forced to buy your entire management solution from a single vendor. When using CIM, you can obtain specialized management agents from third parties to monitor components of your environment that aren't supported by the core framework.

WBEM defines CIM in terms of XML

The CIM specifications have been available since 1998. The data model is specified in Unified Modeling Language (**UML**), a standard, object-oriented modeling language defined by OMG. The DMTF Web-Based Enterprise Management (**WBEM**) initiative extends CIM one step further by bringing it more in line with the Web. The xmlCIM specification defines CIM in terms of XML. The CIM Operations over HTTP specification defines a transport mechanism that allows you to send CIM commands to the agents over HTTP.

Vendors have been slow to adopt CIM and WBEM

Although the interoperability characteristics of CIM seem quite appealing, vendors of system management frameworks have been slow to fully adopt CIM and WBEM. Of course if they did, they would relinquish the lock-in features of their frameworks.

WBEM doesn't do quite enough to manage Web services

Although WBEM is based on XML, it does not define instrumentation APIs for Web services. More to the point, the CIM data model doesn't really define the right type of management elements needed to represent distributed application components and the relationships that might exist among multiple components that collaborate to complete a transaction.

Most management frameworks don't understand how to manage a distributed application

Most management systems focus on monitoring and managing individual network elements, such as nodes, routers, and switches. More recently these systems have also been extended to let you manage software servers such as database systems, Web servers, and application servers. But very few management systems understand how to manage individual application components running

Web Services Management Standardization Efforts

within these software servers. Nor do they understand the relationships and dependencies that exist among software components running in different environments. A management framework can manage all the individual systems that host the various components of a distributed application, but it really doesn't understand how to view a distributed application system as a single entity.

For the moment you must rely on separate management tools supplied by the application server vendors. These tools allow you to manage the individual application components running within the server. But in most circumstances, even these tools don't give you a holistic view of the composite application system. To facilitate runtime management of Web services, a more comprehensive model is required.

Application server management tools control individual application components

One promising approach is described in a specification developed by HP and webMethods. The Open Management Interface (**OMI**) takes a different track from that of WBEM—one that attempts to enable application management rather than element management. OMI does not build on CIM. Instead it defines a new management data model and a new set of management interfaces. The OMI data model represents individual application elements *and* the relationships among them. The OMI data model recognizes dependencies among multiple resources, and hence it gives you a holistic view of a composite application system.

OMI gives you a holistic view of a composite application

OMI defines a set of Web APIs, implemented using SOAP and WSDL, for managing resources such as Web services. In this model, every managed resource supports a management API. An OMI-compliant management framework uses this API to manage the resource. In other words, OMI uses Web services to manage Web services. Although OMI looks promising, as of this writing none of the big vendors of system management frameworks has released

OMI manages Web services using Web services

Chapter 5 Advanced Web Services Standards

products that use it. My guess is that they are waiting for some kind of formal endorsement from a standards group.

OASIS is developing a management framework for Web services

At the time of this writing, the most interesting standardization effort is the OASIS Web Services Distributed Management (**WSDM**) Technical Committee. This group was formed in February 2003. Its charter is to define a management framework that uses Web services architecture and technology to monitor and control distributed resources, such as Web services. This group will leverage a variety of standards and specifications, including SNMP, CIM, WBEM, and OMI. The goal is to produce a specification by January 2004.

Transactions, Orchestration, and Choreography

Dynamic assembly is still far off, but we're making progress

One area that has been the focus of a lot of Web services hype is Web service assembly and business process automation. Quite a few people have painted rosy pictures of users dynamically assembling Web services into complex business transactions. I think dynamic assembly of services is still far off in the future, but at least we're working in the right direction.

Business process automation can improve operational efficiency

Business process automation has always been a popular effort. That's because multistep processes are notorious as a sinkhole of inefficiency. If you can find a way to automate these processes, you have the opportunity to reduce costs, improve quality, and increase efficiency. Application integration is at the heart of any business process automation project. Given that Web services make it easier to integrate applications, it's only natural that people would try to use this technology to implement business process automation.

There is very little consensus within the industry

Many view it as a critical priority to develop standards to support Web service assembly. Unfortunately there is very little consensus in the industry as to what approach to take, how much to standardize, or even what to call it. Is it **orchestration** or choreography? Are the two terms interchangeable, or do they have different meanings? Does Web services assembly require a new loosely coupled distributed transaction protocol?

Transactions

One of the most challenging aspects of business process automation is the management of long-running, loosely coupled, asynchronous transactions. Traditional transaction middleware assumes that communications are synchronous and tightly coupled. Given that multistep business processes may span minutes, days, or even weeks, traditional transaction middleware may not be applicable to the job.

Traditional transaction middleware often isn't applicable

The OASIS Business Transactions Technical Committee has developed the Business Transaction Protocol (**BTP**) specification. BTP defines an XML-based transaction coordination system that supports asynchronous, loosely coupled, long-term transactions. BTP supports the concept of **atomic transactions** (in which all tasks within a transaction must complete successfully or else the entire transaction must be reset) and **cohesive transactions** (in which a certain set of tasks within a transaction must complete successfully or else the entire transaction must be reset).

BTP supports loosely coupled transactions

BTP can coordinate transactions for Web services based on SOAP, ebXML, or any other XML protocol. The BTP specification was approved as an OASIS Committee Specification in May 2002 but thus far has not won the endorsement of strategic vendors such as IBM and Microsoft. As a result it has received little attention.

BTP is applicable to SOAP, ebXML, and other XML protocols

Many people in the industry think that a new loosely coupled distributed transaction coordination system is not really required—at least not for the majority of applications. Most applications can get by using existing transaction services, such as those supplied with database systems, application servers, and workflow

WS-Coordination and WS-Transaction can enable interoperability across existing transaction systems

Chapter 5 Advanced Web Services Standards

engines. Rather than build a new transaction coordination system, the goal is to provide an XML-based abstraction layer that enables Web services to transparently use existing transaction systems, and to enable interoperability across disparate environments. To this end BEA Systems, IBM, and Microsoft published two specifications called **WS-Coordination** and **WS-Transaction** in August 2002.

WS-Coordination defines a framework for coordinating a distributed activity

WS-Coordination defines a coordination framework that allows multiple participants to reach agreement on the outcome of a distributed activity. It defines a set of Web APIs and protocols that allow a Web service to create a coordinated activity and to propagate information about that activity, known as **context**, to other Web services.

The coordination framework defines standard APIs for an underlying transaction system

The coordination framework assumes that there is some type of transaction management system that will coordinate the activity. For example, you could use a J2EE-based transaction manager or a BTP-compliant transaction coordinator. WS-Coordination defines a set of standard control APIs for conversing with the transaction management system. Normally you would use a set of SOAP header processors to manage the distributed activity on behalf of the application programs.

The transaction context is exchanged using SOAP headers

Figure 5-3 shows an overview of the framework. In this diagram, the client initiates the activity. The client-side coordination header processor uses the WS-Coordination APIs to create a coordinated activity and to obtain context information. The header processor takes the context and puts it into a SOAP header in the request message. The receiving header processor on the server side uses the context information to enroll the service as a participant in the coordinated activity. The transaction management system uses its own transaction protocol to coordinate the activity.

Transactions, Orchestration, and Choreography

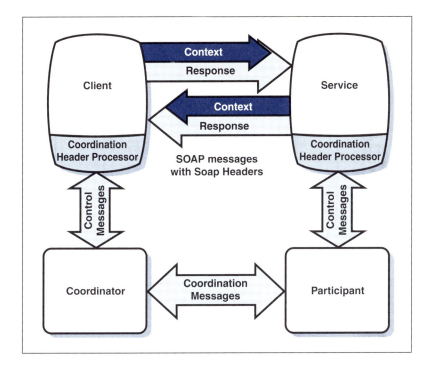

Figure 5-3: The coordination framework works by propagating context between participants in the distributed activity.

To act as coordinator for the activity, a transaction service must provide support for the WS-Coordination Web APIs. WS-Coordination can support a variety of types of transaction coordination, such as atomic transactions, cohesive transactions, and loosely coupled business activities. The specific protocols used to implement the various types of transaction coordination are defined separately. WS-Transaction defines the specific protocols used to implement atomic transactions and loosely coupled business activities.

A transaction service must add support for the WS-Coordination Web APIs

WS-Coordination and WS-Transaction are not direct competitors to BTP. WS-Coordination defines a common Web API that allows Web services to register a transaction with a transaction coordinator, but it does not define the actual transaction coordinator. It can be used with any transaction coordinator. BTP defines a new standard for a transaction coordinator. A BTP-compliant transaction coordinator

WS-Coordination and BTP could work together

could support the WS-Coordination Web APIs and act as the Web service transaction coordinator.

WS-Coordination and WS-Transaction are for review and evaluation only

Currently, the WS-Coordination and WS-Transaction specifications are not industry standards. According to the document status section of the specifications, they are intended for review and evaluation only. As of this writing, they have not been submitted to a standards organization, and there are no other specifications on the horizon that appear to compete with these two. Given the backing of BEA, IBM, and Microsoft, I expect these specifications to form the basis for future Web services transaction coordination standards.

Orchestration and Choreography

Orchestration and choreography are much more contentious

The next area of contention—orchestration and choreography—doesn't have quite as clear a resolution. Five proposals are competing in this area, including solutions from ebXML, a joint effort lead by Sun, a new effort at the W3C, the Business Process Management Initiative (**BPMI**), and the BEA/IBM/Microsoft triumvirate.

People can't even agree on the meaning of the terms

The first point of contention is in the definition of the terms. Some people use the terms "choreography" and "orchestration" interchangeably. Others view choreography as a description of service interactions (without workflow), and orchestration as the controlled execution of service interactions (with workflow).

EbXML BPSS defines a business collaboration for ebXML applications

The ebXML solution focuses on the lighter-weight choreography approach. The ebXML Business Process Specification Schema (BPSS) defines a framework for defining dual-party or multiparty business collaborations. Business collaboration is defined as a choreographed exchange of business documents among two or more business parties that results in an electronic commerce transaction.

BPSS does not describe the actions that must be executed by the various business parties. It simply defines the messages that must

Transactions, Orchestration, and Choreography

be exchanged according to a defined pattern of collaboration. BPSS relies on the Web services that take part in the exchange to coordinate the transaction. It does not assume that there is a central coordinator, nor does it require a transaction protocol. One limitation associated with BPSS is that it relies on other ebXML infrastructure components—including ebMS and CPPA—and it does not work with SOAP or WSDL. EbXML BPSS was published in July 2002.

BPSS relies on the ebXML infrastructure

The second contender in this space is the Web Services Choreography Interface (WSCI) specification. WSCI was jointly developed by BEA, Intalio, SAP, and Sun. It was published in June 2002 and submitted to W3C in August 2002.

Sun and friends contributed WSCI to W3C

WSCI is based on the SOAP and WSDL infrastructure. As with BPSS, WSCI describes Web service composition in terms of message exchange patterns. It makes no assumptions about the internals of a particular application that processes a message, and it does not define a business process execution language.

WSCI defines a business process as a set of message exchange patterns

WSCI describes a message exchange in terms of sequencing rules, message correlation, exception handling, and transactions. Unlike BPSS, which describes collaboration participants in terms of business roles, WSCI describes the exchange as an interaction of Web services. Each message exchange is described as a prescribed sequence of invocations of WSDL operations. In fact, WSCI is an extension to WSDL. A WSCI process is defined within a WSDL document. WSCI doesn't attempt to prescribe who or what is responsible for ensuring that the process gets executed as prescribed. For example, a business process engine or another Web service could coordinate the process.

WSCI extends WSDL

In January 2003, the W3C formed the WS-Chor working group to develop a formal standard for choreography. Its charter is to develop a language for creating composite services and

W3C formed a working group to address choreography

Chapter 5   Advanced Web Services Standards

for defining choreographed interchanges among multiple Web services. The charter requires that the language build on WSDL. It is beyond the scope of this group to define a business process modeling language. Although the group is free to develop a completely new language, it will use the WSCI specification as formal input for consideration.

BPMI and BPEL4WS focus on workflow

You'll notice that these first three proposals don't address the workflow aspect of business process coordination. The last two efforts focus on standards for business process engines: BPMI and the BEA/IBM/Microsoft triumvirate.

BPMI develops BPM standards

BPMI is a nonprofit consortium dedicated to the development of business process management (BPM) standards. The founding members include Aventail, Black Pearl, Blaze Software, Bowstreet, Cap Gemini Ernst & Young, Computer Sciences Corporation, Cyclone Commerce, DataChannel, Entricom, Intalio, Ontology.Org, S1 Corporation, Versata, VerticalNet, Verve, and XMLFund. Membership has grown to more than 80 software and service companies, including key players such as BEA, BMC, Commerce One, EDS, IBM, SAP, and Sun. In November 2002 BPMI published a Web services-based standard for business process engines.

BPML defines an execution engine that can manage a WSCI choreography

The BPMI Business Process Modeling Language (**BPML**) is an XML vocabulary for modeling business processes. BPML relies on WSDL and WSCI to describe Web service interactions. It defines an execution language that specifies the runtime semantics of interactions, and it defines an abstract execution model to manage the orchestration of those interactions. BPML assumes the use of a transactional business process engine. A number of vendors, including Intalio, SeeBeyond, and Versata, plan to release products based on BPML.

The last proposal is from the BEA/IBM/Microsoft triumvirate. In conjunction with the WS-Coordination and WS-Transaction specifica-

Transactions, Orchestration, and Choreography

tions, these three vendors published a BPM language called the Business Process Execution Language for Web Services. BPEL4WS is an execution language designed to support workflow-oriented orchestration based on a SOAP and WSDL infrastructure. BPEL4WS represents a convergence of the ideas in Microsoft's **XLANG** and IBM's Web Services Flow Language (**WSFL**) specifications. It provides a language that describes business processes and business interaction protocols. Following a similar vein as WSDL, BPEL4WS allows you to describe abstract versus executable business processes. An abstract process can be thought of as a process type, which can be implemented by multiple services. An executable process is an implementation of an abstract process that can be executed by a business process engine. BPEL4WS is based on SOAP, and it defines interactions between Web services as described by a WSDL operation.

BPEL4WS represents the convergence of XLANG and WSFL

At the time of this writing, it appears that there is division among the vendors. In a controversial move in March 2003, the BPEL4WS authors spurned the W3C WS-Chor effort. Microsoft representatives attended the first WS-Chor meeting and left partway through, saying that the effort didn't match their plans. A month later the BPEL4WS authors launched a competing effort at OASIS. The OASIS WS-BPEL Technical Committee will develop a BPM standard based on BPEL4WS.

WS-Chor and WS-BPEL are competing standards efforts

Perhaps I'm being too harsh by saying the efforts are competing. After all, WS-Chor focuses on choreography, and WS-BPEL addresses orchestration, but I think it's unlikely that the two efforts will end up being complementary. WS-BPEL will be a superset of WS-Chor, and you can be sure that the WS-BPEL team won't wait for the WS-Chor team to define choreography standards for them. The OASIS team already has a working specification. My prediction is that WS-BPEL will eclipse all other efforts. BPSS will maintain the ebXML niche, but BPMI will kowtow and adopt WS-BPEL. And

WS-BPEL is the likely winner

Chapter 5 Advanced Web Services Standards

WS-Chor will fade into obscurity as it haggles over requirements. WS-BPEL has already garnered product support. IBM provides a preliminary implementation of a BPEL4WS process engine, called BPWS4J, available through alphaWorks. Collaxa and Momentum provide commercial products that support BPEL4WS. And since the launch of WS-BPEL, many BPM companies have expressed support for the effort.

Reliability

Reliability supports loosely coupled transactions

Reliability is another area of contention. "Reliability," also known as **reliable message delivery**, refers to the ability to guarantee the proper delivery of messages, in the right sequence, within an acceptable time frame. Reliability is often associated with transactions and choreography because it provides a foundation for loosely coupled, asynchronous transaction coordination.

Many SOAP implementations support reliability at the transport layer

A number of SOAP implementations support reliable messaging at the transport layer by using a reliable transport protocol, such as a message queuing service. Although this approach is effective, it limits your options. It forces you to use a specific transport, which may not be available on all platforms. An application-layer reliability specification allows you to implement reliable message delivery using any transport protocol, including HTTP. At the time of this writing, two reliability proposals are competing for dominance. One proposal is in development at OASIS. The other proposal comes from BEA, IBM, Microsoft, and TIBCO.

WS-RM defines reliability at the application layer

In January 2003 Fujitsu, Hitachi, NEC, Oracle, Sonic Software, and Sun published a specification for message reliability called WS-Reliability. This specification defines a SOAP extension to support guaranteed delivery of messages with guaranteed message ordering and no duplicates. The authors submitted the specification to OASIS in February 2003, coinciding with the launch of the Web Services Reliable Messaging (**WS-RM**) Technical Committee. The group intends to produce a specification by September 2003.

In March 2003 BEA, IBM, Microsoft, and TIBCO published a competing set of reliability specifications called WS-ReliableMessaging and WS-Addressing. These SOAP extensions address essentially the same requirements as WS-Reliability, although they do so in a different way.

The big boys published a competing proposal

For discussion purposes, I refer to the OASIS proposal as WS-RM(1) and the other proposal as WS-RM(2). One important distinction between the two proposals relates to asynchronicity. WS-RM(1) ties asynchronous messaging to reliability. WS-RM(2) defines asynchronous messaging in a separate specification, WS-Addressing. By separating asynchronicity from reliability, WS-RM(2) is more flexible and extensible.

WS-RM(2) separates asynchronicity from reliability

Although I think WS-RM(2) is a better specification, I don't think the industry needs two competing reliability specifications. What's most aggravating about this situation is that the rift appears to be entirely political. The OASIS team members have established a timeline that precludes any extensive discussions about requirements or redesign. It appears as if their goal is to standardize the WS-Reliability specification as quickly as possible. For their part, the authors of the second proposal don't seem particularly interested in working with the OASIS team. As of this writing, no one from BEA, IBM, Microsoft, or Tibco has joined the OASIS effort, nor have the authors submitted the specifications to a standards group. It would be better for the industry if the two teams joined forces to develop a single set of specifications that draws the best features from both proposals.

The best solution would be consolidation

Chapter 5 Advanced Web Services Standards

Portlets and Interactive Applications

Web services can simplify the integration of applications into portals

One other area of high interest is that of portlets and interactive applications. One of the most obvious places to use Web services is as a content provider for a portal. Portals provide a convenient, personalized interface to numerous applications. But to make an application available to a portal, you must implement an interface between the portal and the application. This interface, known as a portlet, consists of presentation logic that tells the portal how to access and display the content. Normally, a separate portlet is required for each portal application. Web services technology provides an opportunity to devise a standard mechanism to simplify the integration of remote applications and content into portals.

WSRP defines a specification for pluggable portlets

Two OASIS technical committees are working together to do just that. The Web Services Interactive Applications (**WSIA**) Technical Committee and the Web Services for Remote Portals (**WSRP**) Technical Committee are jointly developing the WSRP specification for "pluggable portlets." WSRP defines a generic adapter that enables any WSRP-compliant portal to consume and display any WSRP-compliant Web service, without the need to develop a specific portlet for each service. This specification allows portal administrators to add new content to a portal with only a few clicks of a mouse.

A WSRP service must implement the WSRP Web APIs

The generic portal adapter talks to a WSRP service through a set of standard Web APIs, which are defined using standard WSDL. All WSRP services must implement these WSRP Web APIs.

A WSRP service supplies its own interactive presentation logic

A WSRP service must also supply its own interactive presentation logic as part of its Web API. Because it supplies its own presentation logic, no application-specific portlet is required. A WSRP-compliant portal accesses the WSRP service using the generic WSRP portlet

Other Advanced Efforts

adapter. The WSRP service returns a response containing a presentation markup fragment that can be displayed in a browser.

The WSRP service can generate the appropriate markup fragment for many types of display or listening devices, such as desktops, mobile handsets, PDAs, or telephones. The WSIA technical committee is designing the presentation aspect of the joint WSRP specification.

A WSRP service can support multiple client formats

WSRP makes portals much more dynamic than ever before. WSRP allows users to gain access to new content dynamically. Users don't have to wait for an administrator to configure new content into the portal. Instead you can dynamically discover new content through a service registry, such as UDDI. Using a registry browser, a user can query the registry and select the service, and the portal can dynamically configure the service at runtime using WSRP.

WSRP enables dynamic access to new content providers

The WSLA and WSRP committees published the WSRP 1.0 Committee Specification in April 2003 and initiated the review process to promote the specification to full OASIS standard status. I expect WSRP to be approved as a formal standard by June 2003.

WSRP should be approved by mid-2003

Other Advanced Efforts

As you can see, quite a bit of activity is going on to develop advanced Web services standards. Even so, a number of areas are yet to be addressed by formal standards groups. The W3C WS-Arch working group is doing a nice job of identifying the various areas that need to be addressed to flesh out a complete Web services infrastructure. Examples of these areas include asynchronous messaging, message correlation, message routing, alternative message exchange patterns, session management, policy, and caching. As of this writing, there are no formal efforts to define standards for these advanced features. There are quite a few vendor-published specifications to consider, though.

WS-Arch is identifying other advanced middleware features

Chapter 5 Advanced Web Services Standards

Microsoft has published a number is specifications as part of GXA

Microsoft has published a number of specifications as part of its Global XML Web Services Architecture (**GXA**). Microsoft positions GXA as a set of technologies that aims to make Web services appropriate for cross-platform application integration. The GXA specifications include WS-Attachments, WS-Inspection, WS-Routing, WS-Referral, WS-Security, WS-Policy, WS-ReliableMessaging, WS-Addressing, WS-Coordination, and WS-Transaction. Microsoft says that these specifications or derivatives thereof may be submitted to a standards group at some point in the future.

Microsoft, IBM, and friends have published six security specifications

Since launching the GXA initiative, Microsoft has joined forces with BEA, IBM, RSA Security, SAP, and VeriSign to develop a number of advanced security specifications. In December 2002 these six companies released six security-based specifications that focus on trust and policy. The group intends to submit these specifications to a standards group in the future.

BEA has published a set of specifications for asynchronous conversations

In March 2003 BEA published a set of SOAP extension specifications to support asynchronous and conversational SOAP interactions. These specifications—WS-Acknowledgement, WS-Callback, and WS-MessageData—are designed to work with and augment the WS-Addressing and WS-ReliableMessaging specifications. BEA has published these specifications on a royalty-free basis.

The vendors are committed to developing interoperable Web services technologies

One thing is clear. The vendors are committed to Web services. They are investing time and effort in the development of advanced Web services technologies. And they are committed to making sure that their systems are interoperable. We've made excellent progress in security. Management and portals are coming along nicely. There are competing efforts regarding transactions, choreography, and reliability, but progress is definitely being made. For the most part, the degree of cooperation is unprecedented.

6

The Promise of Web Services

If you listen to the hype about Web services, you might get the impression that they can help us end war and solve world hunger. As with any breakthrough technology, its advocates get carried away and start painting glorious pictures of the way things could be.

There's been a lot of hype about Web services

Hype is a useful marketing tool. Suppose you come up with a new idea that has real potential. You go out and raise awareness. You evangelize this new technology as the next revolution in technology or business. If you market it well, you create a buzz. The next thing you know, you've got lots of people talking about it. New businesses start popping up. Money starts to flow. Suddenly you're on your way to endless riches.

Hype helps establish a new technology

But hype can be a double-edged sword. If you're not careful, expectations can get out of hand. What starts as a good idea can get whipped up into something completely different. Something exaggerated. Something totally unattainable. Then, when you don't deliver these unattainable solutions in an unrealistically short time, the public begins to doubt the viability of the technology. If you aren't careful, the bubble will burst, and the money will wash away.

Hype can also kill a new technology

Web Services Hype

Web services have been a victim of the hype hurricane. We've heard the far-fetched stories: Web services will revolutionize computing; Web services will enable dynamic assembly of software components; Web services will enable dynamic business relationships. Although technically most of these stories are plausible, realistically many of them are science fiction.

Some of the hype about Web services is science fiction

Chapter 6   The Promise of Web Services

There is a germ of truth in all these stories

I believe that Web services have the potential to revolutionize computing. I know that Web services can enable much more dynamic interaction than we've ever been able to achieve before. I'm just worried that the hype about Web services goes too far. The biggest issue that I have with these stories is that they seem to ignore typical personal and business practices. Even so, there's a germ of truth in all these stories. Let's spend a moment looking at a few scenarios to see what's real and what's not.

Super-powered PDA

Scenario 1: Your PDA can reschedule your travel arrangements

To make the technology more comprehensible, most sample scenarios focus on an individual making use of Web services. Here's a classic scenario.

> Your meeting with a prospective customer is going so well that you decide you need to stay longer than expected to close the deal. You flip out your wireless PDA to reschedule your return trip. You drag your calendar entry for your return flight to a slot that falls three hours later. Then you set your PDA aside and go back to your meeting. While you're busy negotiating, your PDA gets to work. It reschedules your flight and your limousine pickup; it sends an e-mail to your spouse saying that you'll be home late; and it places an order to have flowers delivered to the house.

You would spend forever setting up the application

I certainly wish that my PDA could work this type of magic. I like this scenario. It's a bit far-fetched, but it is technically plausible. It's relatively easy to create a trigger that sends an e-mail and converses with three different Web services (the airline's booking service, the limousine's booking service, and the florist's ordering service) when you move a calendar entry. The bigger challenge is in the setup. How does the PDA know that this calendar entry represents a travel itinerary? How does it know which airline to contact? How does it know which flight you're currently booked on? How do you make sure that the PDA application thoroughly understands your preferences and can make the appropriate judgment calls about things such as carrier, fare, connections, and schedule? So even though this scenario is theoretically possible, you would need an incredibly sophisticated PDA application, and, more to the point, you would have to devote an impractical amount of time to set it up.

I suspect that the more advanced PDA systems will eventually provide this kind of sophisticated application. You will have the ability to create a calendar entry that represents a travel itinerary. In doing so, you would give the PDA application the critical pieces of information it needs to make changes to the itinerary, such as your airline and flight number. I suspect that these future PDA applications probably won't reschedule your flight completely by themselves. More likely the PDA application will require a bit more human interactivity. When you drag the travel itinerary calendar entry, the trigger will ask you whether you want to reschedule your flight. When you respond "yes," it will query the airline's booking service and present you with a set of options. You select the one you want, and it will rebook your flight. I estimate that we should see something like this type of scenario as early as 2004.

We should see something like this scenario by 2004

Software-as-a-Service

Another popular scenario features software-as-a-service.

> Your company no longer has its own IT organization. Rather than waste your resources and capital to build, manage, and maintain internal application systems, you manage your business operations using Web services supplied by a variety of Internet-based service providers. You can now focus your resources and capital on your core competencies.

Scenario 2: Do away with your IT organization and use Internet-based Web services to run your business

Chapter 6 The Promise of Web Services

Or you can monetize your existing systems by selling them as a software service

There's another side to this scenario, too:

> Your company has invested millions (maybe billions) of dollars in your IT organization. Now you want to monetize these investments by selling your application systems as a service to other companies.

It's hard to design a successful software-as-a-service business model

I think this software-as-a-service scenario is dangerously exaggerated. First, I suspect that very few companies will be successful selling software-as-a-service. The application service provider (ASP) market was all the rage in the late 1990s. By the turn of the century, though, "ASP" had become a bad word. Now even companies that are successfully selling software services didn't like the label. For the most part, it's difficult to design a product and create a business model that can support an ASP business. To be successful, you must offer a clear differentiating advantage. There are some exceptions (ADP and Salesforce.com come to mind), but I'd be very reluctant to invest in an ASP business these days.

This scenario ignores the fact that IT systems can provide strategic value

Second, I find it extremely doubtful that you view your IT systems as a waste of resources and capital. Instead your IT systems can be a source of strategic advantage. Just ask companies such as Wal-Mart and FedEx. Wal-Mart achieves its remarkably low cost of operations from its effective use of information technology. And as FedEx Chairman Fred Smith says, "The information about a package is as important as the delivery of the package itself." You lose a competitive advantage by relinquishing control of your business applications.

It makes sense to outsource nonstrategic business functions

Certainly there are many situations when it makes sense to outsource certain pieces of your application infrastructure. Very likely, you already do. Lots of companies outsource functions such as payroll, fulfillment, and logistics. It's reasonable to consider outsourcing any function that doesn't provide a strategic or tactical advantage to your business. But I view it as very unlikely that many organizations want to outsource everything.

The point I want to reiterate here is that Web services don't constitute a business model. A Web service is a programming interface to a business function. If you choose to outsource certain IT functions, you aren't buying a Web service; you're buying a business service. The service provider probably supplies a number of interfaces into that business service. Some of those interfaces are designed for human interaction; others are designed for program interaction. The human-oriented interface isn't a Web service. In the case of Salesforce.com, for example, it's a browser application. Only the programming interfaces would be Web services. (You definitely want to push your service provider to supply Web service interfaces. They will make it much easier for you to integrate your other systems with the outsourced business functions.)

You buy a business service, not a Web service

I always get uneasy when I hear people equate Web services with software-as-a-service. IDC published a sobering report in October 2002. In this report, IDC research director Rikki Kirzner implied that software-as-a-service is the perceived ultimate vision for Web services. She went on to say, "But most of the Web services vision is just pure speculation, with no real consideration of what is achievable and what it will cost to actually build out the vision for full use on the open Internet." She predicted that it would take 10 years or more for the software-as-service vision to become a reality. I view this prediction as optimistic. Even with Web service interfaces, it still takes time and effort to connect systems. I think it will take quite a while before we'll be able to run a business using dynamically assembled Internet-based services.

Don't view software-as-a-service as the ultimate vision for Web services

I prefer not to get distracted by the software-as-a-service vision. Web services are about integration and the advantages afforded by that integration. They are about increasing developer productivity.

Web services are about integration

Chapter 6   The Promise of Web Services

They are about reducing time to market. They are about reducing costs and improving your business process. They are about making it easier for your customers and partners to do business with you. They aren't about software-as-a-service.

Dynamic Discovery of Business Partners

Scenario 3: UDDI can perform comparison shopping

A third popular hype scenario is the one about comparison shopping.

You're a buyer for a hospital, and you need to order some surgical gloves. You log on to your corporate portal and call up your shopping agent software. You tell the agent that you need 1,000 boxes of surgical gloves to be delivered no later than tomorrow morning at 10:00 A.M. The agent uses the public UDDI Business Registry (UBR) to dynamically discover all vendors that sell surgical gloves and to identify which vendor offers the best price with the best delivery options. When it has identified the best deal, it places the order.

This scenario ignores standard business practices

Based on standard business practices, this scenario is straight out of science fiction. Although it's technically feasible to build a comparison shopping agent that obtains pricing and delivery information from multiple suppliers and then places an order, this scenario doesn't take into account standard business practices.

Hospitals won't buy surgical supplies from just anyone

This scenario might be practical when we're talking about paper clips, but not surgical gloves. I would hope that a hospital wouldn't buy surgical gloves from just anyone. A hospital requires a certain level of quality in its surgical gloves. If the gloves fail during an operation, the hospital would be liable for any infection that the patient or doctor might develop. A hospital generally buys surgical supplies only from a reputable supplier with which they have an established purchasing agreement.

This scenario makes a number of unrealistic assumptions about the suppliers. First, it assumes that all the suppliers provide a set of Web services that allow you to get a price quote, get a delivery quote, and place an order. Second, it assumes that all the suppliers have registered these Web services in the public UBR. But many suppliers might be cautious about exposing their internal application systems to the general public. (Only discount suppliers that compete on price would have the incentive to do so.) Third, it assumes that your comparison shopping agent can programmatically figure out the semantics of each supplier's Web services. This assumption is feasible only if you make a fourth assumption: that an industry group has defined a set of standards for these Web services and that all the surgical suppliers implement these standards.

This scenario assumes that all suppliers support public Web APIs based on industry standards

This scenario also disregards the relationship you have with your suppliers. If your only selection criterion is the price on this one purchase, then you might want to use a price comparison service such as Pricewatch, Pricegrabber, or MySimon. There are a few discount suppliers in every business that compete on price, but usually at the sacrifice of service. Many suppliers compete on some other type of service differentiation. They offer discounts based on volume or combined orders. They offer flexible payment terms. They offer guaranteed delivery of scarce supplies when you need them. In short, there's more to your procurement relationship than price. It's hard for a price comparison agent to accommodate these other factors.

There's more to your procurement relationship than price

So let's modify this purchasing scenario to make it a bit more realistic. If we remove the concept of dynamic discovery of suppliers, the scenario works just fine. Let's assume that you are a buyer for a hospital, and the hospital has business agreements with a set number of suppliers. Your suppliers provide you with Web APIs that enable you to get price quotes and delivery estimates and to

This scenario works if we remove dynamic discovery

place orders online. These Web APIs are registered in the hospital's private UDDI registry for partner relationships. You have a comparison shopping agent that knows how to get and interpret price quotes from each of these suppliers.

UDDI should be used at development time rather than at runtime

You instruct the agent to hunt for the best deal for 1,000 boxes of surgical gloves. It sends a query to each known supplier, which returns a price quote. Because there's no Web services standard for price quotes, every supplier probably uses a slightly different format, but the agent understands each format. The agent compiles the quotes and displays your options in your portal view. It also pops up notices of special deals or arrangements you have with each supplier. You then select what you deem the best deal and place the order. Because your agent knows all the suppliers and all the interfaces to their systems ahead of time, it doesn't need to use UDDI at runtime. But the developer would almost certainly have used UDDI when developing the agent. This scenario is realistic and can be implemented today. The fully dynamic comparison shopping agent doesn't really make sense because it doesn't accommodate the other aspects of your business relationships.

Enabling Dynamic Discovery

Applications can't understand interface semantics the way a human can

Enabling an application to dynamically discover and interact with a Web service works only if the application has the means to understand the semantics of the application interface. What does the operation "placeOrder" mean? Is it the same as "submitOrder"? A human can look at these names and immediately recognize the similarity between the two operation names, but it's much harder for an application program to do it. A human can look at a previously unknown form and easily figure out that the shipping address should go into the "Ship to" field, but an application program probably can't make that leap. An application can't dynamically discover and use a Web API unless it already knows the API's semantics.

The only exception to this rule occurs when a human has the opportunity to interpret the semantics of the API at runtime through some type of interactive interface. For example, dynamic discovery has tremendous potential for portal applications. The OASIS WSRP specification is defining a remote portlet standard that will enable dynamic discovery and use of interactive Web services within portals.[1] An interactive Web service provides its own interactive interface that can be displayed in a portal on a desktop, PDA, wireless handset, or other device a human can interact with. These Web services rely on humans to interpret the semantics of the API.

Dynamic discovery and use of a Web service are plausible only if it is an interactive Web service

One caveat about WSRP: Keep in mind that it doesn't let you add your own look and feel to dynamically discovered content in your portal. If you have strict branding requirements for your portal applications, you may not be able to take advantage of some of the dynamic features of WSRP.

WSRP doesn't let you add your own look and feel

At some point in the future, applications may be able to dynamically interpret the semantics of an application interface. The W3C Semantic Web project is working in collaboration with a number of research organizations and industries to create the next-generation Web, in which Web resources can supply a machine-readable description of their semantics using common and well-known ontologies. But until the Semantic Web gets beyond the research stage, we need to use other means to provide applications with semantic understanding.

The Semantic Web project may enable dynamic discovery in the future

Domain-specific Industry Standards

For now, to make the most of programmatic Web services, we need to rely on predefined semantics. If we want to enable dynamic connections, applications must agree ahead of time on these semantics.

Domain-specific industry standards define common semantics

---

[1] See Chapter 5 for more information about WSRP.

Chapter 6 The Promise of Web Services

One of the simplest and most effective ways to define common semantics is to define and adopt domain-specific industry standards. Many vertical industry groups have established a set of standard forms and message formats that simplify business interactions within that particular industry.

ACORD develops electronic standards for the insurance industry

For example, ACORD is a nonprofit insurance association that develops electronic standards for the insurance and related financial services industries. According to its mission statement, ACORD is committed to providing standards and services that improve efficiency and expand market reach by reducing costs, lessening duplication of work, reducing ambiguous communication exchanges, improving accuracy, facilitating e-business, and supporting multiple distribution models. ACORD estimates that the insurance industry could save $250 million annually in integration costs if the ACORD standards were adopted universally. As of October 2002, ACORD had 440 members, including 7 of the top 10 life and annuity carriers, more than 75 percent of the top 50 property and casualty carriers, 7 of the top 10 reinsurers, and the top 5 reinsurance brokers. The next time you fill out an insurance form, you're likely to find the ACORD logo on it.

ACORD XML defines business operations and message formats

ACORD defines standards for the life and annuity, property and casualty, and reinsurance industries. Initially ACORD developed a set of common data models to represent insurance information and EDI standards to enable e-business. More recently ACORD has translated these standards into XML. ACORD XML defines a set of business operations and message structures, which map easily to Web services.

Similar efforts are under way in many industries

Similar XML standardization efforts are under way in many industries. Here are some examples:

- Standards for Technology in Automotive Retail (STAR) is a nonprofit consortium that develops electronic standards for the North American retail automotive industry. STAR members include 19 North American automotive manufacturers, 10 software application vendors, and the National Automotive Dealers Association (NADA), which represents more than 19,000 car and truck dealers. STAR has been working with the Open Applications Group, Inc. (OAGI), another nonprofit standards group that focuses on developing XML messaging standards for e-business. Together these organizations have developed a set of XML specifications that define standards for automotive dealer-to-manufacturer business transactions.
- OpenTravel Alliance (OTA) is a nonprofit consortium that develops XML standards for the travel industry. OTA is composed of more than 150 member companies representing the airlines, car rental firms, hotels, leisure suppliers, service providers, tour operators, travel agencies, and trade associations. OTA XML specifications provide a standard format for exchanging data among travelers and travel-related businesses.
- The International Swaps and Derivatives Association (ISDA) is a global trade association representing more than 600 companies in the privately negotiated derivatives industry. The ISDA Financial Products Markup Language (FpML) is the XML standard supporting over-the-counter trading of financial derivatives.
- The ComCARE (Communications for Coordinated Assistance and Response to Emergencies) Alliance is a nonprofit coalition of more than 80 organizations in the medical, emergency response, telecommunications, transportation, and technology sectors dedicated to improving response in emergency situations. The ComCARE Automotive Crash Notification (ACN) initiative has defined an emergency alert system that uses wireless technology to send an immediate alert to a private

emergency call center when a passenger presses the car's mayday button or the car's air bag deploys. The ACN initiative is now working on the next generation of ACN systems, which can collect sophisticated crash information using on-board telematic systems. In the event of a collision, the ACN system will transfer this crash information directly from the car to multiple public safety agencies, hospitals, transportation agencies, and paramedics. This information, formatted in XML, will permit the emergency agencies to predict injury severity and dispatch the appropriate care and will allow hospital emergency rooms to prepare for arrival.

Cross-industry organizations are developing general business XML standards

A number of cross-industry organizations and consortia also develop general business XML standards. Here are examples:

- XBRL International is a nonprofit consortium that develops financial reporting and accounting standards. This group is made up of more than 170 companies, including the world's leading accounting, technology, government, and financial services bodies. The Extensible Business Reporting Language (XBRL) is an XML standard for simplifying the flow of financial statements, performance reports, accounting records, and other financial information among software programs.
- The HR-XML Consortium is a nonprofit organization dedicated to the development and promotion of a standard suite of XML specifications to enable e-business and the automation of human resources-related data exchanges. As of December 2002, HR-XML had developed 25 XML specifications related to staffing, stock plans, benefit enrollments, time and expense reporting, background checks, resumes, and other HR topics.
- The Uniform Code Council (UCC) is a nonprofit standards organization that administers the Universal Product Code (UPC). The mission of the UCC is to enhance supply chain management by establishing and promoting multi-industry

Dynamic Binding

standards for product identification and related electronic communication. In addition to administering the UPC, the UCC has worked with EAN International and the Voluntary Interindustry Commerce Standards (VICS) Association to develop a number of XML standards and schemata for supply chain management. Among these standards is an XML translation of the VICS Collaborative Planning, Forecasting and Replenishment (CPFR) standard.

As you can see, many industry groups are defining standard operations and message formats in XML. These XML specifications define a set of shared semantics that give applications a common frame of reference. Web services give you an infrastructure that allows you to take advantage of these shared semantics to enable dynamic interaction.

Shared semantics enable dynamic interaction

Dynamic Binding

As described in Chapter 3, Web services support dynamic binding, a powerful capability that no other middleware technology provides. Using dynamic binding, an application can talk to multiple Web services through a single common interface. Figure 6-1 is almost identical to Figure 3-4, but I want to repeat this point because it is fundamental to the power of Web services. This time I flesh it out with examples using industry standards.

Dynamic binding is powerful

Figure 6-1 assumes that many suppliers have chosen to adopt a domain-specific standard for order processing, such as the Core Order business message defined by the UCC. The UCC Core Order business message allows a buyer to place an order for specified quantities of goods and services from a seller for a single shipment to a single location.

UCC defines a standard for order processing

In Web services, this UCC Core Order business message corresponds to an abstract interface defined by a WSDL *what* part. Suppliers that

The business message standard corresponds to a WSDL what part

Chapter 6 The Promise of Web Services

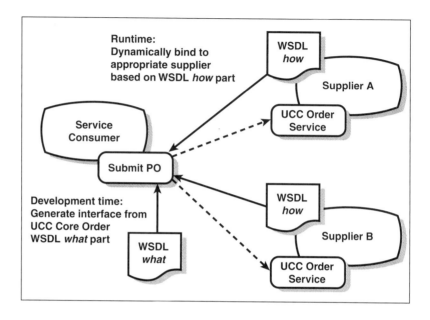

Figure 6-1:
Dynamic binding is fundamental to the power of Web services. A client can dynamically connect to any service that implements the abstract interface defined by a WSDL *what* part.

support the standard will offer a Web service that implements this WSDL *what* part.

A client can dynamically connect to any service that implements the standard

Here's where industry standards really facilitate dynamic interaction. A developer can write a client application that can connect to any service that implements the standard. The developer generates a client interface from the WSDL *what* part for the UCC Core Order service. At runtime the application uses dynamic binding and the WSDL *how* part to connect to a specific UCC Core Order-compliant service.

The separation of what *from* how *has technical and business benefits*

The specifics of how to talk to an individual Web service implementation are stipulated in the WSDL *how* part. It specifies which protocols to use, such as SOAP over HTTP; it specifies how to format and represent the information in the SOAP message; and it specifies which SOAP headers must be included in the message to support functions such as security, reliability, or message correlation. This binding information is not specified in the core industry standard. Instead each

148

service provider must specify its unique binding information. At runtime the client application obtains the WSDL *how* part for the specific Web service implementation that it wants to use and then uses the specified binding information to dynamically connect to that service implementation. The separation of *what* from *how* enables a style of interaction that is much more flexible from both the technical viewpoint and the business perspective.

This dynamic binding capability is also what separates Web services from simple XML messaging. Most of the domain-specific industry standards define XML message formats. To implement your e-business operations based on these standards, you send these XML message formats over HTTP using basic XML processing technologies. You don't have to use SOAP and WSDL. But if you don't use SOAP and WSDL, then you must write a much more sophisticated application that constructs and packages the XML messages, establishes a connection to each individual business partner, and manually negotiates the expected formats, protocols, and security. Chances are high that you will wind up duplicating your efforts by developing a different application connection for each of your business partners. By using SOAP and WSDL, you can let Web services, rather than your application logic, do the tedious application connection work. And you can use a single application to talk to any number of business partners.

Dynamic binding makes Web services more powerful than simple XML messaging

Now consider the advantages of adding UDDI to the mix. UDDI takes dynamic binding one step closer to true dynamic discovery. Standard business practices will still prevent you from arbitrarily picking some unknown parts supplier to serve your manufacturing requirements, so the public UBR still has its limitations. But imagine that you have set up a private UDDI registry for your supply chain operations. You probably use a number of industry standards in your supply chain, and perhaps you also use some customized message formats to suit your specific needs. You register all these

UDDI takes dynamic binding one step closer to true dynamic discovery

Chapter 6 The Promise of Web Services

industry and corporate standards in your private UDDI. Then your business partners register their Web services in your private UDDI, associating each Web service with the standards it supports and specifying the unique binding information required to connect to the service. You can now develop an application that dynamically queries your private UDDI registry at runtime to obtain the specific binding information needed to connect to a particular supplier. This capability is particularly helpful if the supplier needs to make a change to its Web service that might require a change to the binding information.

UDDI makes it easier for you to connect with a new business partner

Now imagine that your company has just signed an agreement with a new parts supplier. You want to quickly and easily enable your purchasing application systems to make use of this new supplier because it's offering steep introductory discounts. You point this supplier to your private UDDI registry so that it can easily find the specifications for your corporate standards. After the new supplier has implemented support for your Web APIs, it simply registers its services in your private UDDI. All your applications instantly gain access to this supplier's discounted products.

What Makes Web Services Special

Web services have weathered the hype hurricane

Perhaps UDDI won't let you form new business partnerships on-the-fly, but it does help you build extremely flexible and dynamic applications. In 2002, the science fiction hype was threatening to knock Web services off course. Even so, it appears as if Web services have weathered the hype hurricane. If we tone down the stories a bit and look at the technology in terms of what it can do rather than what it can't do, Web services will thrive.

Interest in Web services has not died off. In fact, Web services technology is poised to cross the chasm from early adopters to early majority in 2003.[2] The platform providers have added inherent support for Web services to operating systems, languages, and application servers. Application software vendors are starting to add support for Web services to their products. The innovators have deployed application systems. The early adopters have pilots in place and are planning broad-scale deployments. And the early majority users are actively exploring the technology.

Web services will cross the chasm from early adopters to early majority in 2003

Web Services Adoption

A survey conducted by the Software Information Industry Association (SIIA) and Systinet provides corroborating evidence of my claim. The survey report, titled "How Web Services Are Being Adopted Today," was published in October 2002. The survey was conducted during third quarter 2002. The two organizations queried 779 people representing a diverse set of companies. Most respondents were IT professionals, although 17 percent were business executives. In the group overall, 25 percent of respondents identified themselves as end-user companies, 25 percent as consultants and system integrators, 41 percent as software vendors, and 7 percent as "other." The respondents represented many different industries, including finance, insurance, manufacturing, retail, transportation, education, health care, government, construction, media, public utilities, and professional services. Half the companies had annual revenues less than $10 million, and 15 percent were more than $1 billion.

SIIA and Systinet conducted a survey on Web services adoption in Q3 2002

More than 30 percent of respondents said that they had already deployed Web services technology as of September 2002. More than 60 percent said that they were at least experimenting with Web services technology. In general the independent software

79% of respondents will deploy Web services in 2003

---

[2] Please see *Crossing the Chasm*, by Geoffrey A. Moore and Regis McKenna, ISBN 0060517123.

Chapter 6   The Promise of Web Services

vendors (ISVs) were more aggressive in their experimentation, but even among the end-user companies, 38 percent had developed a pilot application, and 28 percent had deployed Web services. Approximately 79 percent of respondents said that they will use Web services technology within the coming year, and more than 50 percent stated that Web services would be a significant part of their IT architecture by the end of Q3 2003 (see Figure 6-2).

Many market research firms agree

Many market research firms have published similar findings. Jupiter Research, for example, reported in October 2002 that 82 percent of the 403 IT executives it interviewed said they had deployed Web services. The report went on to say that although Web services technology will not reach full maturity until 2005 or later, nearly everyone was experimenting with the technology. A TechRepublic survey in November 2002 showed that 68 percent of the participants had already made the decision to rearchitect their IT infrastructure to use Web services.

Most analysts agree that Web services will take off in 2003

Most software analysts also agree with my prediction that Web services will cross the chasm in 2003. In August 2002, Daryl Plummer at Gartner said that Web services had already filtered into standard IT practice and that 2003 would be the year for even cautious

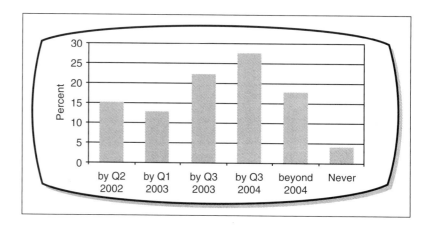

Figure 6-2: According to the SIIA survey, more than 50 percent of respondents think Web services will play a significant part in their IT infrastructure by Q3 2003.

What Makes Web Services Special

companies to begin Web services pilots. Ted Schadler at Forrester Research told me that as of December 2002 the market was still in the early adopter stage, but it would change to early majority in 2003. Sue Aldrich at Patricia Seybold Group said that as of December 2002, 85 percent of its customers were considering Web services, and 85 percent of those companies plan to deploy them by the end of 2003.

META Group predicts that Web services will rush right into the late majority stage. In a report published in December 2002, META predicted that 90 percent of large organizations would be using Web services to externalize their legacy applications by 2007.

Adoption will increase rapidly over the next four years

Clear Benefits

What is it about Web services technology that makes it so special? Why has this technology taken the industry by storm? First and foremost, I think that Web services are successful because they solve real problems at very low cost. Integration is at the heart of almost every application project, and Web services simplify the effort of making two systems talk to each other. Web services technology is simpler and easier to use than other middleware technologies. And Web services technology has a much lower price tag.

Web services solve real problems at low cost

The primary reason that Web services solve the integration crisis so well is that they have total industry buy-in. No other middleware technology has ever managed to unite all major systems vendors. IBM, Microsoft, and Sun have set aside their differences and are working together to define the Web services infrastructure. Almost everyone else you can think of is also involved, including Accenture, Akamai, AMD, AOL, Apple, ATG, AT&T, Borland, Cingular, Cisco, CommerceOne, Computer Associates, EDS, Entrust, Ericsson, France Telecom, Fujitsu, Hitachi, HP, Intel, IONA, Macromedia, Matsushita, Motorola, MITRE, NCR, NEC, Netegrity, Nokia, Nortel Networks, Novell, NTT, Panasonic, Peoplesoft, Progress, RIM, SAP,

Web services have total industry buy-in

Chapter 6   The Promise of Web Services

Sharp, Siemens, Software AG, Sony, Sybase, Tibco, Unisys, VeriSign, and Xerox, not to mention about a hundred startups and numerous end-user companies, such as Boeing, Canon, Chevron-Texaco, Citicorp, DaimlerChrysler, Fidelity, Kodak, Nationwide, Procter & Gamble, Sabre, United, and VISA. Some 140 companies are working together at WS-I to ensure that Web services support vendor-neutral interoperability.

Web services make it easy to connect applications

These vendors are committed because Web services make it easy to connect applications. Web services solve the Traditional Middleware Blues. Any application, written in any language, running on any platform, can communicate using Web services. What's more, Web services enable dynamic interaction.

Truth in Hype

Web services will let us do things we couldn't do before

There's a reason the Web services hype has gotten a bit out of hand. The dynamic features of Web services have sparked people's imaginations. Web services will let us do things that we've never been able to do before. That's why the system and application vendors have adopted the technology with gusto.

Web services make integration easier

Application integration lets us make our systems work better. It lets us reduce costs, increase efficiency, and improve quality. Web services help us do integration. They solve a number of technical issues so that it's easier to get one application to talk to another application. They solve the problems associated with the Traditional Middleware Blues.

Web services can exploit the power of the Web, XML, and domain-specific standards

But Web services have the potential to do much more. Web services allow us to exploit the power of the Web and XML as well as the efforts of the domain-based industry groups. These domain-specific industry standards are an important piece of the puzzle of what makes Web services promising. If domain-based standard Web APIs get defined for Web services and if Web service providers adopt these standard APIs, suddenly Web services technology becomes much more valuable than just point-to-point integration middleware.

The good news is that vendors are building support for Web services into their applications. Within a short time, packaged applications will include support for Web services and a variety of domain-based standards. You will be able to build in-house applications that can take advantage of these standards. When we bring all these features together, we can achieve dynamic interaction, as shown in Figure 6-3.

Web services enable dynamic interaction

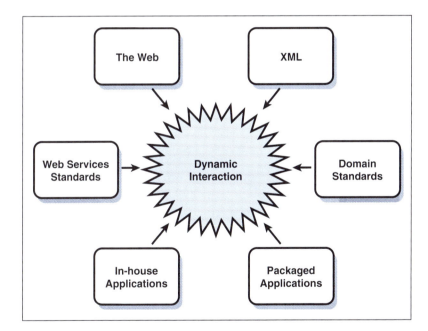

Figure 6-3: Web services can exploit the power of the Web, XML, and industry standards to enable dynamic interaction. These capabilities apply to both in-house and packaged applications.

7

When to Use Web Services

There are many compelling reasons to use Web services. It seems as if everyone is at least playing with Web services. Almost every software vendor is building support for Web services into its platforms, languages, and tools. Web services enable any-to-any integration, supporting any programming language, any runtime platform, and any network transport. Technologies such as SOAP and WSDL are simpler to use than traditional integration middleware technologies, and they offer much more flexibility. When combined with domain-specific industry standards, Web services enable unprecedented dynamic interaction. More to the point, they can make it easier for your partners and your customers to do business with you. Best of all, the low cost, pervasiveness, and simplicity of the technology lets your existing staff do more with less.

Web services let your existing staff do more with less

Web services can be used for many types of applications. Nearly every application requires some integration effort, so I'm sure you can find a way to use Web services in almost any project. After you get a little experience under your belt, you'll very likely adopt Web services as a standard integration technology. When you're just getting started, though, it's always best to limit your scope. Start small. Spend some time learning about the technology. Then you can apply your learning to larger projects. One nice feature of Web services is that you can use them incrementally. There's no need to tackle an enormous project all at once. I recommend that you use Web services in places where they are likely to have a big impact.

Web services apply to almost any application project

Chapter 7 When to Use Web Services

Bell Ringers

What are the key criteria that tell you to use Web services?

Which applications would benefit most from Web services? Where should you start? What are the key criteria that should ring a bell in your head and make you think, "This is a job for Web services"?

Heterogeneous Integration

Use Web services to integrate heterogeneous applications

The first and most obvious bell ringer is the need to connect applications from incompatible environments, such as Windows and UNIX, or .NET and J2EE. Web services support heterogeneous integration. They support any programming language on any platform. One thing that's particularly useful about Web services is that you can use any Web services client environment to talk to any Web services server environment.

JPMorgan uses Web services to connect Excel to UNIX-based data

For example, JPMorgan uses Web services to connect Excel spreadsheets to UNIX-based financial data. JPMorgan operates the global wholesale businesses for J.P. Morgan Chase. JPMorgan is a leader in investment banking, asset management, private equity, custody and transaction services, middle market financial services, and e-finance. The firm has financial analysts in more than 50 countries around the world. These analysts needed a way to upload and download financial, forecast, and other relevant data used in their spreadsheets to and from various legacy application systems.

Web services let you use the right tool for each side of the equation

Knowing that it's difficult to find a single-vendor solution that would allow it to connect Excel with various UNIX-based systems, JPMorgan decided to use Web services. Web services permit the firm to use the right tool for each side of the equation. JPMorgan created a set of Web services using Systinet's Web Applications and Services Platform (WASP) to enable easy access to the legacy applications. Now the financial analysts can access these services from Excel using Visual Basic for Applications (VBA) macros and the Microsoft SOAP Toolkit, as shown in Figure 7-1.

Bell Ringers

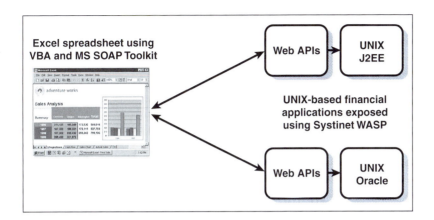

Figure 7-1: JPMorgan uses Web services to connect Excel spreadsheets to UNIX-based financial applications.

Unknown Client Environment

The next bell ringer is any situation in which you have little or no knowledge of or control over the client applications that will be used to access the service. Because Web services don't require a specific software environment, you don't need to worry about compatibility issues.

Use Web services if you have no control over the client application

For example, Con-Way Transportation Services uses Web services to support electronic exchange of shipping data with its customers and business partners. Con-Way is a $2 billion transportation company based in Ann Arbor, Michigan. More than two-thirds of its customers are small to medium-sized businesses. Con-Way wanted to provide these customers with a mechanism that would support tight integration with Con-Way's transportation systems. The challenge was that these customers use a variety of transportation applications on a variety of deployment platforms. Con-Way realized that it didn't have the option of asking these customers to install a proprietary API with limited deployment options to support integrated Con-Way business transactions. Instead Con-Way developed a set of Web APIs using IBM WebSphere. These APIs support invoicing, bill of lading, order pickup, and sales management services. Customers can interface with these services through

Con-Way Web APIs allow customers and partners to connect from any type of client

Chapter 7   When to Use Web Services

Figure 7-2: Con-Way's Web APIs support any type of client application, including packaged transportation applications from companies such as Prism and FreightDATA. Con-Way's clients can use any Web services package to make the connection.

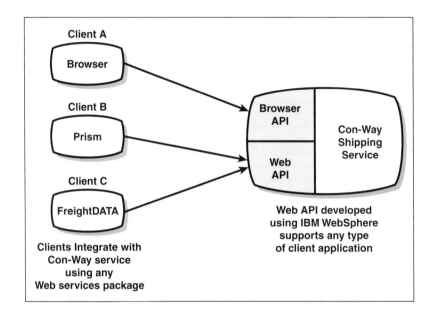

the Con-Way Web site or use the Web APIs to connect directly from their corporate application systems. The Web APIs support any type of client application—in-house applications as well as packaged applications—as shown in Figure 7-2.

Multichannel Client Formats

Use Web services if you need multichannel client support

A third bell ringer is the need to support many types of client formats, such as browser clients, rich desktop clients, spreadsheets, wireless devices, interactive voice response (IVR) systems, and other business applications. A Web service returns its results in XML, and XML can be transformed into any number of formats to support different client formats.

Wachovia uses Web services to support rich desktop clients and browser interfaces

For example, Wachovia uses Web services to support both browser-based clients and rich desktop clients for Einstein, its customer information system. Wachovia is a leading provider of financial services, with nine million U.S. customer households. Einstein is a GUI application that gives bank staff complete information about a customer, aggregating information from multiple backend systems. Some bank staff use a browser to access Einstein. Others require a richer desktop interface.

As shown in Figure 7-3, Einstein was developed as a multitier Web service application. The backend business functions and data sources are legacy applications implemented in CICS and DB2 on the mainframe. The middle tier, which accesses and aggregates the customer information, is implemented as a set of J2EE Web services using IBM WebSphere. The client environments are implemented using Microsoft .NET. The browser client is implemented using Microsoft .NET WebForms, and the desktop client is implemented using Microsoft .NET WinForms. Einstein's architecture also allows Wachovia to implement other types of client interfaces to support IVR systems, wireless handsets, two-way pagers, and other devices.

Einstein can support many types of client systems

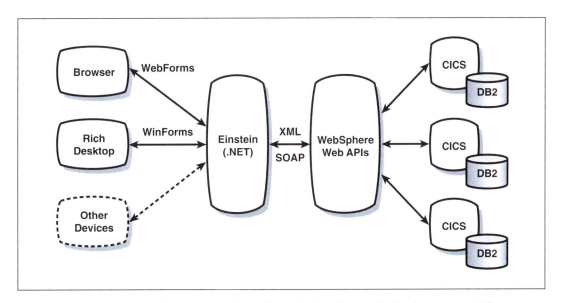

Figure 7-3: Einstein supports browser and rich desktop clients, allowing Wachovia to support other devices if needed. Written using .NET, Einstein aggregates information from numerous CICS-based backend systems via Web services implemented using WebSphere.

Chapter 7 When to Use Web Services

Other Web Services Applications

Web services can support many business goals

Web services can help you accomplish many types of business goals. You can use Web services to solve immediate tactical problems. You can use them to help you manage your software assets, leverage legacy applications, and reduce development costs. Web services can also help you optimize your business process and improve customer relationships.

Point-to-Point Integration

Cape Clear uses Web services to connect e-mail and CRM

The first and most basic way to use Web services is for simple point-to-point integration. For example, Cape Clear uses Web services to connect employees' e-mail clients with its CRM solution. Cape Clear is a Web services software startup. It uses Salesforce.com as its CRM solution. Salesforce.com provides a hosted CRM solution using an ASP-style model. Users typically interface with the CRM solution through a browser, recording customer contact information and correspondence.

Cape Clear wanted a way to automatically capture e-mail correspondence

Like most software startups, Cape Clear provides e-mail-based customer support. As a result, quite a bit of customer correspondence takes place via e-mail. But Salesforce.com didn't provide a simple, easy way for Cape Clear employees to log this correspondence in the Salesforce.com database. Users had to copy and paste the e-mail from Outlook into the Salesforce.com browser interface. Cape Clear found that lots of correspondence wasn't getting recorded.

Now a user simply clicks on a button to save an e-mail in Salesforce.com

Salesforce.com provides a programming API, so Cape Clear decided to eat its own dog food and address this problem using Web services. First Cape Clear used Cape Clear Studio to develop a Web service adapter for the Salesforce.com native programming API. This adapter accepts a SOAP request and translates it into the Salesforce.com native API. Next Cape Clear developed an Outlook

Other Web Services Applications

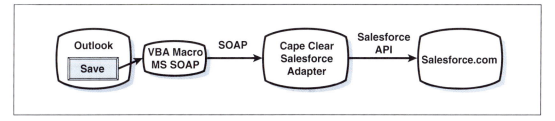

Figure 7-4: Cape Clear developed a VBA macro using Microsoft SOAP Toolkit that takes an Outlook e-mail and uses SOAP to pass it to the Salesforce Adapter Web service. The Adapter service then passes the message to Salesforce.com using the Salesforce API.

macro using VBA and the Microsoft SOAP Toolkit. This Outlook macro adds a button to the standard Outlook tool bar labeled "Save to Salesforce." As shown in Figure 7-4, when the user clicks on this button, the Outlook macro captures the e-mail message, packages it as a SOAP message, and sends it to the Salesforce.com adapter Web service. The Web service then forwards the e-mail using the native API to Salesforce.com, which logs it.

After seeing the advantages of using SOAP for integration, Salesforce.com has decided to develop its own set of Web APIs in addition to the native programming APIs. If you are a Salesforce.com customer, you won't need to build your own adapter Web services.

Salesforce.com now provides Web APIs

Consolidated View

One of the most popular internal integration projects is enabling a consolidated view of information to make your staff more effective. For example, you probably have many people in your organization who interact with customers. Each time your staffs interact with the customer, you want to let them have access to all aspects of the customer relationship. Unfortunately, the customer relationship information is probably maintained in variety of systems. The good news is that a consolidated customer view provides a single point of access to all these systems.

A consolidated customer view lets your staff see all aspects of a customer relationship

Chapter 7   When to Use Web Services

Coloplast uses Web services to get a 360 degree view of customers

You can use Web services to implement this type of consolidated view. For example, Coloplast is using Web services to improve its sales and customer support functions. Coloplast is a worldwide provider of specialized healthcare products and services. As part of an initiative to improve customer relationships, Coloplast wanted to set up a state-of-the-art call center system that would give customer representatives real-time access to complete customer histories and product information. The company selected Siebel Call Center as the base application, but it needed to connect this system to its backend AS/400-based ERP systems, which manage the sales, manufacturing, and distribution functions. It did so using Web services. Coloplast used Jacada Integrator to create Web services adapters for the legacy AS/400 application systems. As shown in Figure 7-5, Siebel Call Center uses these Web services to deliver a 360 degree view of customer relationships, including access to backend

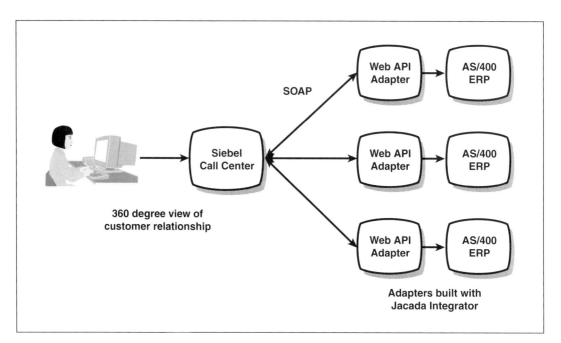

Figure 7-5: Coloplast uses Web services to connect the Siebel Call Center application to its backend AS/400 ERP systems. Coloplast used Jacada Integrator to create Web APIs to the backend systems.

Other Web Services Applications

processes such as open order status, inventory information, customer credit checking, and special pricing. This solution improves efficiency and enhances employee and customer satisfaction.

Managing Legacy Assets

Web services can make it easier to manage and maintain your legacy application assets. For example, AT&T estimates that Web services technology has reduced the time it takes to make modifications to some of its oldest application systems by 78 percent.

AT&T uses Web services to ease a legacy maintenance nightmare

TIRKS (Trunks Inventory Record Keeping System) is a critical application for AT&T. TIRKS was first developed in the 1960s, and it is connected to more than 100 other application systems. Because of the brittleness of these application connections, every time AT&T makes a modification to TIRKS, it must also make a corresponding modification to the other systems. Using Web services, AT&T has developed much more flexible application connections that don't break every time a change is made to the application. AT&T is using IONA XMLBus to replace the more than 100 brittle application connections with a much smaller set of flexible, reusable Web APIs to TIRKS. Now each modification to TIRKS no longer requires the associated changes in all the other application systems.

Web services connections are much more flexible than traditional application connections

Reducing Duplicative Applications

One of the more popular ways to use Web services is to reduce redundant applications. A service can support many types of application clients. If you need to perform the same type of function via multiple applications, it makes a lot of sense to develop a single service shared by all these applications rather than duplicate the functionality in each application.

A service can support many application clients

Reduction of redundant applications is a key objective of the U.S. government's E-Gov initiative. The U.S. government encompasses hundreds of federal agencies and bureaus, and there is

The U.S. government has numerous redundant systems

165

Chapter 7 When to Use Web Services

significant overlap and redundancy of systems across these agencies. A 2001 study by the E-Gov Task Force analyzed the agencies to identify the various business activities performed by the government. The study identified 30 general lines of business, such as economic development, public safety, environmental management, and tax collection. On average, each agency is involved in 17 lines of business, and each line of business is performed by 19 agencies. Some lines of business—such as payroll, travel, HR, procurement, logistics, administration, and finance—are performed by every agency.

The U.S. government expects to save billions of dollars annually by reducing redundancy

The U.S. government spent $48 billion on information technology in 2002 and will spend $52 billion in 2003. The Office of Management and Budget estimates that the government can save more than $1 billion annually in IT expenditures by aligning redundant IT investments across federal agencies. In addition, this alignment will save taxpayers several billion dollars annually by reducing operational inefficiencies, redundant spending, and excessive paperwork.

E-Travel will consolidate numerous stovepipe systems

In October 2001, the President's Management Council approved 24 high-payoff government-wide initiatives that integrate agency operations and IT investments. One of those initiatives is E-Travel, which is being run by the U.S. General Services Administration (GSA). E-Travel delivers an integrated, government-wide, Web-based travel management service. Federal government employees make approximately four million air and rail trips each year, and until recently each agency and bureau managed its own travel department. Cumulatively, these various departments used four travel charge card providers, six online self-service reservation systems, 25 authorization and voucher processing systems, 40 travel agencies, and a unique payment reimbursement system for almost every bureau.

Other Web Services Applications

By consolidating these travel systems into a single, centralized travel management system, the U.S. government expects to save $300 million annually, achieving a 649 percent return on investment. In addition, the consolidated system will deliver a 70 percent reduction in the time it takes to process vouchers and reimbursements.

E-Travel should save U.S. taxpayers $300 million annually

GSA delivered the first phase of E-Travel in December 2002—an online self-service reservation system. The total end-to-end travel management system is scheduled to be complete by December 2003. The system will use a service-oriented architecture, based on XML and Web services, to ensure easy integration with existing agency systems and future adaptability. The E-Travel team refers to this architecture as "Velcro integration," indicating that modules can be easily replaced when necessary.

Web services support "Velcro integration"

Managing Portal Initiatives

Web services can also be very useful as a means to manage and coordinate your portal initiatives. A portal is an integrated, Web-based view into a host of application systems. A portal contains a piece of application code (a portlet) for each backend application. A portlet contains the code that talks to the backend application as well as the code that displays the application in the portal.

Web services help you manage your portal initiatives

Web services technology enhances portals in two ways. First, Web services deliver content to the portal as XML. It's then easy for a portal engine to take this XML content and display the information in a portal frame. It's also easy for the portal engine to reformat the XML content to support other client devices, such as wireless handsets or PDAs. Second, Web services technology defines a simple, consistent mechanism that portlets can use to access backend applications. This consistency allows you to create a framework to make it quicker and easier to add new content to your portal. Furthermore, as mentioned in Chapter 5, the new

Web services make it quicker and easier to add new content to your portal

Chapter 7   When to Use Web Services

OASIS WSRP specification will allow you to add new content to the portal dynamically. Figure 7-6 shows an overview of WSRP.

The U.S. government has more than 22,000 Web sites

Another goal of the U.S. government's E-Gov program is to get a handle on government portals. As of February 2003, the U.S. government was managing more than 22,000 Web sites with more then 35 million Web pages. These Web sites have been developed, organized, and managed using the same stovepipe mentality as used in the backend agency applications. Such decentralization and duplication make it difficult for citizens and communities to do business with the government. For example, a community that is attempting to obtain economic development grants must do a tremendous amount of research to learn about federal grants. There's no single source of information. More than 250 agencies administer grants, and you would have to file more than 1,000 forms (most with duplicate information) to apply for all of them. Some of these forms are available online; others aren't. Currently all forms must be filed by postal mail.

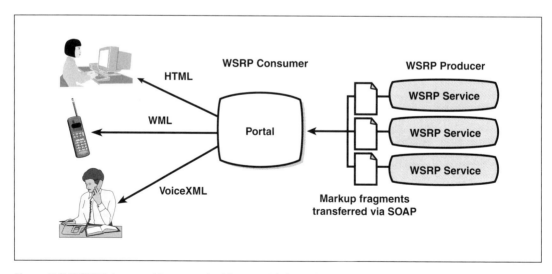

Figure 7-6: WSRP lets you add new content to a portal dynamically. A content provider makes content available as a WSRP service, and the portal accesses the content using SOAP and delivers the result in the appropriate markup format.

Other Web Services Applications

The government is working to consolidate this myriad of Web sites into a much more manageable number of portals, each providing a single point of entry to a particular line of business. Each portal will use Web services to access the backend applications that implement the business process. In many cases the government will consolidate backend applications to reduce redundant systems and to ensure a simpler experience for the portal users. For example, the forthcoming E-Grants portal will provide a single point of entry for anyone looking to obtain or administer federal grants. This site will help citizens learn about all available grants and allow them to apply for these grants online. The government expects to save $1 billion by simplifying grant administration as well as saving $20 million in postage.

Government portals will use Web services to access backend applications

All government portals will be coordinated through the FirstGov portal at http://www.firstgov.gov. From this one portal, citizens, businesses, and government agencies will have a single point of entry to all other government portals.

The FirstGov portal provides access to all other government portals

Collaboration and Information Sharing

Web services can make it easier for your employees to share information and collaborate. For example, the University of Texas M.D. Anderson Cancer Center used Web services to implement a shared information retrieval system called ClinicStation. The center uses a unique collaborative approach to cancer treatment that makes it one of the most respected cancer centers in the United States. Rather than rely on a single physician to manage a patient's case, M.D. Anderson brings together a team of multidisciplinary specialists to collaborate on the best treatment for each individual.

Web services can enable collaboration and information sharing

Such collaboration requires a means to dynamically share patient information, such as the patient's chart, test results, x-rays, and other diagnostic images. Because the clinic spans multiple buildings, it's inefficient to try to assemble everyone in the same room to view physical images and discuss a course of treatment. Instead the

ClinicStation integrates 10 backend systems

Chapter 7   When to Use Web Services

clinical data is digitized so that it can be viewed electronically. One challenge, though, is that this clinical information is stored in 10 systems on a wide range of platforms. To bring all these systems together, ClinicStation uses Web services built with Microsoft .NET to provide access to all patient information from any browser throughout the center. Physicians can now collaborate over the phone while looking at patient records online.

ClinicStation should deliver a 3000% ROI in 3 years

M.D. Anderson developed this application in nine months using three in-house developers. The total hardware and software costs were less than $200,000. The center expects to save $6 million over the next three years, largely through increased clinical efficiency.

B2B Electronic Procurement

Web services are much less expensive than EDI

One of the most popular B2B applications is electronic procurement. Companies have been using Electronic Data Interchange (EDI) to automate purchasing applications for years. But EDI is expensive and often requires extensive customization. Web services technology can reduce the cost and time required to create these B2B connections.

Premier Farnell uses Web services to support B2B procurement

Premier Farnell uses Web services technology to implement a B2B procurement system for its customers. Based in London, Premier Farnell is a small-order distributor of electronic components and industrial products to the design, maintenance, and engineering industries throughout Europe, North America, and Asia Pacific.

Premier Farnell supports purchase orders from any procurement system

The Premier Farnell B2B trading solution, implemented using IONA Orbix E2A Web Services Integration Platform, supports customers using any electronic procurement system, including SAP, Oracle, Ariba, Commerce One, and custom systems. As shown in Figure 7-7, even if each of these systems sends a slightly different purchase order format, the Web service can handle the situation. It

Other Web Services Applications

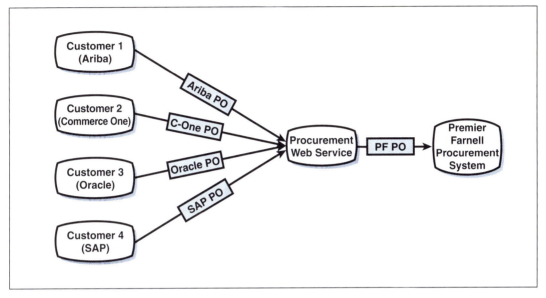

Figure 7-7: Premier Farnell's procurement Web service can accept purchase orders from a variety of procurement systems. It transforms the PO into the format required by the Premier Farnell procurement system.

automatically converts all incoming purchase orders into the format required by the Premier Farnell systems.

Trading Partner Network

Web services provide an excellent foundation for building a trading partner network. The Integrated Shipbuilding Environment Consortium (ISEC) is building a trading partner network for U.S. shipbuilders. ISEC is a project of the National Industrial Information Infrastructure Protocols Consortium (NIIIP), a group of information technology suppliers, industrial manufacturers, academic institutions, and standards organizations. NIIIP is defining an infrastructure based on Web services that can support the creation of a dynamic virtual enterprise: an ad hoc or long-term alliance of companies that work together on a project or opportunity. Although each member of the virtual enterprise operates its own internal business systems,

ISEC is building a trading partner network for U.S. shipbuilders

Chapter 7   When to Use Web Services

the integration features of the virtual enterprise infrastructure make it seem as if all members belong to the same organization.

ISEC is developing standards for a shared parts catalog

NIIIP's first project is focused on the U.S. shipbuilding industry. ISEC will use the NIIIP infrastructure to enable an integrated supply chain that will reduce costs and cycle time for commercial and Navy shipbuilders. Part of the ISEC project is the development of an open, shared parts catalog and a set of standard Web APIs for accessing it.

NIIIP will host a public UDDI registry for the ISEC community

NIIIP will host a public UDDI registry for the ISEC community. The ISEC catalog service descriptions and Web APIs will be registered in this public registry. The U.S. shipbuilding suppliers will then be invited to implement catalogs that conform to the ISEC standards and to register their catalogs in the public registry. The shipyards will be able to query the public registry to obtain information about the various suppliers and obtain the binding information necessary to access the individual catalogs. Shipyards are also invited to replicate a subset of the public information in their own private UDDI registries and to customize the information for their specific needs. For example, a private shipyard UDDI registry might contain information about the specific subset of approved suppliers for that shipyard. A shipyard might also want to define a set of custom taxonomies to indicate contract history, negotiated discounts, or other information about supplier relationships. Figure 7-8 shows the relationship between the consortium-hosted public registry and a shipyard's private registry.

Software-as-a-Service

A successful ASP must provide a service that customers can't easily do for themselves

You can also use Web services to provide a programmatic interface to a business service that you license using the software-as-a-service business model. For the most part, I'm leery of promoting the association of Web services and software-as-a-service. Web services are Web APIs. You don't sell APIs. Instead you sell the business function that customers access through the APIs. As I mentioned in

Other Web Services Applications

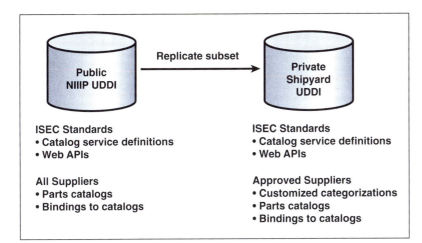

Figure 7-8: The ISEC standards and all shipbuilding suppliers will be registered in the Public NIIIT UDDI registry. Subsets of this information can be replicated and categorized in a private UDDI registry operated by an individual shipyard.

Chapter 6, it's hard to be successful using an ASP-style business model. Looking at history, we can see the secrets to a successful ASP model:

❏ The service must be based on strategic intellectual property, something that your customers can't easily do themselves.
❏ The service must provide a disruptive value proposition—a new and unique advantage that's dependent on the service provider model, such as aggregate information gained through collaboration.[1]
❏ The service provider must establish and maintain a reputation for neutrality and trustworthiness.
❏ The service provider must devise a reasonable revenue model that is comfortable for the customer.

My general take on software-as-a-service is that the business model must be viable on its own without Web services. A Web API is simply a better way to provide programmatic access to the service. If you think you have a new, viable idea for an ASP-style

A Web API provides programmatic access to a software service

---

[1] Please see *The Innovator's Dilemma*, by Clayton M. Christenson, ISBN 0875845851, for an explanation of disruptive versus sustaining innovations and value propositions.

Chapter 7   When to Use Web Services

service, then you should provide Web APIs for that service. As I mentioned earlier in this chapter, Salesforce.com has added Web APIs to its already successful ASP model, making it easier for clients to integrate their in-house systems with the hosted CRM solution. Now let's look at another example.

Yahoo licenses aggregated content as a service

Yahoo is an excellent example of a company that has been successful using the ASP model. Yahoo is the world's leading aggregator of content. The vast majority of Yahoo's clients access this content for free through the Yahoo public portal. As with most public portals, Yahoo generates revenue through advertising. But Yahoo also licenses this content to other businesses as a service. If you are a Yahoo enterprise service customer, you can display Yahoo content in your corporate portal, and users can personalize their corporate portal just as public users can personalize their my.yahoo.com portal.

Yahoo Web APIs will support content integration with CRM and other applications

Yahoo is extending its enterprise software service offering by adding a set of Web APIs. These Web APIs will let you integrate Yahoo content with your business applications. For example, you could integrate Yahoo content with your CRM application. When a salesperson looks up a customer contact in the contact management system, the application can send a query to Yahoo to retrieve and display the latest headlines about the customer. Although it's true that this information is available for free through the Yahoo portal, there's an obvious value to being able to integrate news with a CRM solution. Yahoo plans to license the Web APIs as part of the Yahoo enterprise service offering. Yahoo may also license these APIs to CRM application providers to enable a prepackaged Yahoo-ready solution.

When Not to Use Web Services

Web services aren't appropriate for some applications

As much as I like Web services, I want to caution you that they aren't always the appropriate solution. XML is tremendously versatile, but it isn't the most compact or efficient mechanism for

When Not to Use Web Services

transferring data. A SOAP message is much bigger than a comparable native binary message used with RPC, RMI, CORBA, or DCOM. It also takes a lot more time to process an XML message than a binary message. Even with the best-performing implementations, SOAP messaging can take 10 to 20 times longer than RMI or DCOM.[2] The performance differential gets worse as the message grows in size and complexity. You want to be cautious when trying to use Web services in situations with stringent requirements for real-time performance. I don't recommend using Web services to transfer very large files (> 10MB).

You shouldn't view SOAP as a total replacement for traditional middleware technologies, such as RPC, RMI, CORBA, and DCOM. These technologies still have an important place in application development. They were designed to provide a seamless, high-performance mechanism to communicate among various components within a homogeneous application system or service.

SOAP doesn't completely replace traditional middleware

It's quite appropriate to use these technologies to build individual applications. For example, if you were developing in Java, you would probably want to build the application using J2EE component technologies, such as servlets and Enterprise JavaBeans. These components communicate with each other using RMI.

Use traditional technologies to build individual applications.

After you have developed your application, you probably want to expose it to the rest of the world using SOAP and WSDL. The traditional technologies weren't designed to integrate heterogeneous application systems, and they certainly weren't designed to communicate across the Internet. The point is that you want to use the

Use Web services to connect disparate systems

---

[2] Each new generation of Web services technology makes tremendous improvements in performance and scalability. It's quite possible that these performance issues may go away in subsequent generations.

Chapter 7 When to Use Web Services

right tool for the job. Web services were designed to support heterogeneous integration and Internet communication.

SOAP doesn't provide the same level of reliability as message queuing software

You might consider using SOAP in place of some proprietary messaging infrastructures, particularly if you are using these technologies to perform simple point-to-point integration. Keep in mind, though, that as of this writing, basic SOAP doesn't provide the same level of reliability as message queuing software, nor does it give you inherent notification facilities to support publish and subscribe functionality.[3]

Web services don't replace EAI

A number of folks position Web services as the death knell for EAI software. My view is that if Web services can replace your EAI software, then EAI software is overkill for your project. EAI software does many things that SOAP, WSDL, and UDDI simply can't do by themselves. The software category known as EAI consists of a collection of various types of software that work together to deliver a comprehensive integration solution. EAI software includes messaging infrastructure, application adapters, data extraction and transformation tools, message brokers, and rules engines. Web services technology could replace the messaging infrastructure, but it can't replace the rest of the pieces. These other pieces, particularly the application adapters, are complementary to Web services technology. Most EAI vendors are adding support for Web services to their products. Over time I suspect that we'll see most of the EAI vendors adopt Web services technology in place of their current proprietary messaging infrastructure.

---

[3] By "basic SOAP" I mean SOAP over HTTP. You can achieve the same level of reliability as MOM by transporting your SOAP messages using a reliable transport. The standards community is also developing SOAP extensions to support reliable messaging. I expect most SOAP implementations to support reliable messaging by early 2003.

Executive Summary

Because nearly every application project involves integration, you can use Web services almost anywhere. But when you have a hammer, everything looks like a nail. As with any situation, it's always a good idea to use the right tool for the job.

Use the right tool for the job

Web services are useful and versatile, but they have their limits. Let's review what they're good at:

Let's review where Web services excel

- ❏ Web services excel in connecting disparate systems. For example, you can use Web services to connect multiple platforms, such as Windows, Macintosh, Linux, UNIX, AS/400, and mainframe systems. You can also use Web services to connect various programming languages, such as Visual Basic, Excel, Java, C++, RPG, COBOL, and Perl.
- ❏ Web services excel in dealing with uncontrolled conditions. For example, if you want to expose some business functionality to many different users, and particularly if you don't have any control over those users' systems, Web services give you the most flexible and versatile solution.
- ❏ Web services excel in supporting multichannel clients. For example, you can use Web services to deliver the same application to rich desktop clients, browser users, mobile devices, and IVR systems.
- ❏ Web services excel in dealing with dynamic conditions. If you anticipate that your system will need to adapt to changing conditions, Web services are a great choice. If you anticipate churn in your user base or if you anticipate the need to add or modify parts of your system, Web services can deal with these changes gracefully.
- ❏ Web services excel in aggregating information. You can use Web services to pull together information from many sources

Chapter 7 When to Use Web Services

for portal applications, customer care applications, and collaborative applications.

❏ Web services excel in reducing redundancy. If you have many applications that perform essentially the same work, you can use Web services to centralize that functionality into a single set of shared services.

Other middleware systems still have their place

Although Web services are versatile, they aren't a complete replacement for all other types of middleware. Web services don't do all the things that other middleware systems do. Other middleware systems still have their place:

❏ Web services don't provide a development component model, and therefore you don't build applications using Web services. You generally build applications using component technology based on your programming language, such as Java or Visual Basic. You want to use the native communication technology supplied by the language (for example, RMI or DCOM) to connect the various components within the application. You can then use Web services to expose the application functionality to other environments.

❏ Web services don't perform as well as traditional middleware systems. If you have stringent performance and scalability requirements, Web services may not be appropriate for your project.

❏ Web services don't do all the things that an EAI middleware solution does. If you need to extract, aggregate, transform, and route information for business process automation purposes, you'll need more capability than Web services offer. EAI middleware often complements Web services.

8

Web Services Infrastructure

Thus far we've talked a lot about why and where you might use Web services. Although we've looked at the basic technology that supports Web services, we have yet to talk about what you need if you want to build Web services. You don't build applications with technology; you build applications with software products. In this chapter we'll discuss the kind of software products that you can use to build, deploy, manage, and use Web services. These products implement XML, SOAP, WSDL, UDDI, and other Web services technologies. I call these products Web services infrastructure products.

Web services infrastructure refers to the products you use to implement Web services

As mentioned in Chapter 2, the realm of Web services suffers from scope creep. Depending on how broadly you're willing to define the term "Web services," nearly any software product can somehow fit into the picture. Increasing numbers of software vendors are justifiably claiming that they "support" Web services. But what exactly does that mean?

Nearly any software product can "support" Web services

I like to organize Web services products into two major categories, which in turn are divided into subcategories. The two major categories are *core* products and *associated* products. You use the core products to build, deploy, and manage Web services. The associated products use or rely on the core products. Figure 8-1 provides a roadmap to this discussion.

Some products supply Web services infrastructure, and others use it

Chapter 8   Web Services Infrastructure

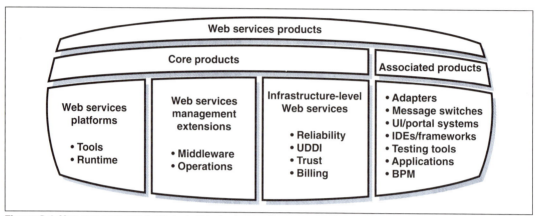

Figure 8-1: You use core products to build, deploy, and manage Web services. Associated products use or rely on the core products.

Core Products

Web services infrastructure products implement the Web services technologies

The core products provide the basic infrastructure that supports Web services. These products, which implement the Web services technologies, can be divided into three subcategories: **Web services platforms**, **Web services management extensions**, and **infrastructure-level Web services**. Figure 8-2 shows an overview of these types of products.

Figure 8-2: The core products are divided into Web services platforms (tools and runtime), Web services management extensions, and infrastructure-level Web services.

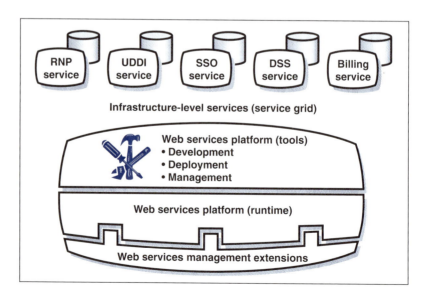

Core Products

A Web services platform consists of a SOAP runtime environment and the tools you need to develop, deploy, and manage Web services. The Web services management extensions add advanced features to the Web services platform, such as security, version control, and monitoring. The infrastructure-level services are Web services that implement parts of the infrastructure. Sample services include a reliable network provider (**RNP**) service, a UDDI service, and a single sign-on (SSO) service. Together these infrastructure services form a service grid to support advanced Web services operations.

You use all three types of products to create your Web services infrastructure

Web Services Platforms

A Web services platform provides the basic environment that you use to build and deploy Web services. A Web services platform also provides the framework that your applications use to communicate using SOAP. Many people refer to this type of product as a **SOAP stack**, a **SOAP engine**, a **SOAP server**, or a **SOAP implementation**. A Web services platform supplies a SOAP runtime environment and a set of development and deployment tools. Examples of this type of product include Microsoft's .NET Framework and IBM's Web Services Developer Kit (WSDK[1]). (Please don't construe the naming of a product in this chapter as a special endorsement of the product. I am naming products to give you some context for the discussion. Please see Appendix A for a much more comprehensive list of products.)

A Web services platform supplies a SOAP runtime and tools

Many industry analysts break this product sector into two categories: SOAP tools and SOAP servers. But a set of SOAP tools is closely associated with a specific SOAP runtime environment. When you use a tool, it generates code for your application, and that code relies on a specific SOAP implementation. If you build a Web service using Microsoft .NET tools, you must deploy the service using Microsoft's .NET Framework. Similarly, if you build a Web service client using

A SOAP tool generates code for a specific SOAP implementation

---

[1] WSDK is the Web services platform within WebSphere.

Chapter 8   Web Services Infrastructure

IBM WSDK, the client must use IBM's SOAP implementation at runtime. You can mix and match client and server environments. (In fact, that's the whole point.) For example, you can use your IBM WSDK client to talk to your .NET service.

.NET Versus Java

Both .NET and Java are excellent platforms

A lot of people ask me which is better for Web services: .NET or Java. My usual answer is yes. Both .NET and Java are excellent platforms for developing Web services. .NET is easier to use, and Java offers more options and versatility. As with any situation, you need to select your platform based on the requirements of your project. Chapter 9 provides guidelines to help you choose a platform.

Choose your platform based on programming language and deployment platform

Your most basic decision factors are your programming language and your deployment platform. If your application is written in Visual Basic and runs on Windows 95, you need to use a Web services platform that supports Visual Basic on Windows 95. If your application is written in Java and runs in WebLogic Server on Solaris, you need to use a Web services platform that supports Java running in WebLogic Server on Solaris. If your application is written in Python and runs on Linux, you need to use a Web services platform that supports Python on Linux.

Most organizations use multiple Web services platforms

Most organizations use a variety of programming languages on a variety of platforms, and therefore most organizations will use multiple Web services platforms. This is one of the beautiful things about Web services. You don't need to rely on a single product or a single vendor.

The .NET Framework

.NET supplies the foundation for Microsoft's new operating systems

The .NET Framework provides the foundation for Microsoft's latest generation of operating systems. .NET essentially replaces the COM-based infrastructure introduced in Windows 95 and Windows NT. Figure 8-3 shows an overview of the .NET Framework.

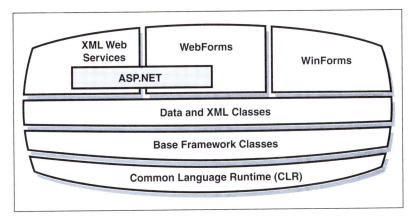

Figure 8-3: The .NET Framework includes a runtime environment, an extensive set of class libraries, and three interface modules that support programmatic access (Web services), browser clients (WebForms), and rich desktops (WinForms).

At its core, the .NET Framework is based on the runtime environment for the C# programming language. This runtime environment is called the Common Language Runtime (**CLR**). .NET supports any number of programming languages, but at compile time, all these languages get compiled into the Common Intermediate Language (**CIL**).[2]

.NET is based on C#

The .NET Framework includes a number of useful features to support rapid application development. It includes a core set of C# classes as well as classes for manipulating data and XML. It also provides three complementary interface modules, which support programmatic access (Web services), browser clients (WebForms), and rich desktop clients (WinForms). The Web services and WebForms modules rely on ASP.NET to support Web access. ASP.NET is Microsoft's Web application server environment that runs in Internet Information Services (IIS). WinForms applications can be deployed on any Windows desktop.

.NET supports rapid application development

[2] The CIL is also known as the Microsoft Intermediate Language (MSIL).

Comparing .NET and Java

There are many similarities between .NET and Java

From an architectural perspective, the .NET Framework is very similar to the Java platform. You write applications and compile them into intermediary code, and then you deploy and execute the intermediary code in a virtual machine. In Java terminology, the intermediary code is called Java **bytecode**, and the virtual machine is called a Java Virtual Machine (**JVM**), which is part of a Java Runtime Environment (**JRE**). In .NET terminology, the intermediary code is called CIL, and the virtual machine is called the Virtual Execution System (**VES**), which is part of the CLR.

But there are differences

Although the platforms are very similar, there are important differences between them. Table 8-1 summarizes the most pertinent differences.

Language Support

.NET lets you use your language of choice

One of the most basic differences between .NET and Java lies in the programming languages you can use. .NET permits you to use almost any language except Java.[3] For practical purposes, the only

Table 8-1: Key Differences between .NET and Java

Differentiator	.NET	Java
Language support	Many languages	Java
Vendor options	Microsoft	Many vendors
Platform options	Windows	Any platform
XML/SOAP support	Integrated	Added via extensions
Standardization	C# is an ISO standard; .NET is more than C#	JCP is open to anyone
Licensing	Nonrestrictive for C#	Restrictive

[3] Java and C# are mutually exclusive because they compile into different intermediate languages. Microsoft provides a language very similar to Java, though, called J#.

Core Products

programming language that you can use with Java is Java. Interestingly, this distinction is based on a marketing decision rather than a technical limitation.

Although .NET is fundamentally based on C#, Microsoft has chosen from the outset to promote the .NET Framework as a multilanguage environment. Nearly any language syntax can be compiled into CIL. Microsoft provides a number of CIL language compilers in Visual Studio .NET, allowing you to develop .NET applications using various languages, such as Visual Basic, Visual C++, Visual J#, and Visual FoxPro. When you use the Visual Studio .NET development environment, all these languages compile into CIL and can run in the CLR. Other language vendors also provide CIL language compilers. For example, Borland makes CIL compilers for Delphi and C++ Builder, and Fujitsu makes a CIL compiler for COBOL. Any component or application compiled to CIL can be easily integrated into other CIL-based applications.

.NET is based on C#, but Microsoft promotes it as a multilanguage platform

The Java platform has the same ability to support multiple language syntaxes, but Sun has never promoted this idea. Just as with CIL, almost any language syntax can be compiled into Java bytecode. Although most people view Java as a single-language environment, you can find bytecode compilers for other language syntaxes, such as Ada, Basic, C, C++, COBOL, Fortran, Lisp, Perl, PL/SQL, Python, Rexx, and Smalltalk. Very few people use these alternative syntaxes for production applications, though, so for most practical purposes, the only language that you can use with the Java platform is Java.

Java has the same ability to support multiple languages, but Sun has never promoted this feature

Vendor and Platform Options

Another basic differentiator is in terms of vendor and platform options. As of this writing, .NET is available only from Microsoft, and it runs only on Windows. Java is available from many vendors, and it runs on any platform.

.NET runs only on Windows, and Java runs anywhere

Chapter 8   Web Services Infrastructure

.NET doesn't run on Windows 3.1 or Windows 95

The .NET Framework is available for Windows CE, Windows XP Embedded, Windows 98, Windows ME, Windows NT 4.0, Windows 2000, Windows XP, and Windows Server 2003. It is not available for Windows 3.1 or Windows 95.

Mono and DotGNU are building support for C# on UNIX and Linux

At some point in the future you may be able to deploy .NET applications on UNIX and Linux. Two open source efforts are under way to develop portable implementations of the core .NET environment for UNIX and Linux systems. The **Mono** project is sponsored by Ximian, and the **DotGNU** project is sponsored by the Free Software Foundation and the GNU Project. As of this writing, these projects are still a work in progress.

.NET Web services require ASP.NET

These groups are building their platforms based on the **ECMA** Common Language Infrastructure (**CLI**) specification, the standard specification for Microsoft's CLR. These systems will be able to execute C# applications (and any application compiled into CIL). Keep in mind, though, that .NET is more than just the CLR. The CLI specification doesn't include the higher-level class libraries used to build Web services, browser applications, and rich desktops. .NET Web services on UNIX will also require the equivalent of ASP.NET, which isn't part of the CLI standard.

Java runs everywhere

Many vendors supply implementations of the Java platform, and you can run Java applications on almost every computing platform. Web services platforms for Java are available from more than a dozen organizations, including Apache, BEA, Borland, Cape Clear, Enhydra, IBM, IONA, Killdara, Macromedia, Novell, Oracle, SAP, Sun, Systinet, Sybase, The Mind Electric, and Wingfoot.

The number of available vendors has one crucial ramification. With .NET you have only one vendor. As a result, you have one very tidy, very coordinated, very integrated environment. With Java you have many vendors, and each implementation is slightly different from the others. You have different tools, different services, different feature sets, and different runtime configurations. As a result, the Java environment looks much less integrated and standardized. But the truth is that there are more standards in the Java environment than there are in the .NET environment. The Java community has defined standard Java APIs and standard data mappings between Java types and XML types. You don't need the equivalent standards in .NET because you have only one vendor.

The .NET platform seems more standardized than the Java platform because you have only one vendor

Support for XML and Web Services

Another distinction between .NET and Java is in the way each supports XML and Web services. .NET provides native support for XML and Web services. Java adds support for these technologies through a set of standard Java extensions.

Java views XML and Web services as an extension

As mentioned earlier, the .NET Framework provides class libraries for manipulating data and XML. From a developer's perspective, XML is a first-class data format that's as integrated into the environment as relational data. This integration makes it easy for developers to work with XML. .NET also includes the Web services interface module, which has full support for SOAP, WSDL, and UDDI.

.NET treats XML as a native data format

As explained in Chapter 4, Java supports XML manipulation and Web services through a new set of APIs, often referred to as the JAX APIs. Although these APIs provide complete support for XML and Web services, they aren't as tightly integrated into the platform as their counterparts are in .NET.

XML and Web services aren't as integrated in Java as they are in .NET

Technology Ownership and Management

The final key differentiator focuses on technology ownership and management. This issue is political rather than technical, and it may not be of interest to you unless you are a software vendor or you would like to participate in the management of the technology. This issue has two aspects. The first is whether you (or anyone else)

C# is managed by ECMA; Java is managed by JCP

Chapter 8 Web Services Infrastructure

can exert any influence over the future of the technology. The second is whether the licensing requirements for the technology might restrict its use.

The politics are complicated

Both Microsoft and Sun claim that their platforms are managed through a formal standards process. Thus you should have the ability to participate in the development of the technology. Although these claims are true, it's a bit complicated. Both vendors support an open standardization process, but they both retain tight control of their technologies.

Java is managed by the JCP

Sun developed the original specifications for the Java programming language, the Java APIs, and the JRE. Since 1995 the Java platform has been developed and maintained by the Java Community Process (JCP), a quasi-standards organization sponsored and managed by Sun.

After two years of fruitless negotiation, Sun decided not to contribute Java to a standards group

In 1997 Sun initiated an effort to contribute Java to a formal standards body. At first the company tried to work out a deal with the International Standards Organization (**ISO**), and, when that didn't work out, it turned to ECMA. Sun wanted to get the endorsement of a standards organization, but it really wasn't willing to relinquish control of the technology. After two years of failed negotiation, Sun decided to make do with the JCP. Many Java licensees weren't particularly happy with the decision, and eventually Sun revamped the JCP to make it more open.

Anyone can participate in Java development

Anyone can participate in Java development. More than 500 corporate, academic, and individual member organizations participate in the JCP. Companies that have participated in the development of the Web services APIs for Java include Apache, ATG, BEA, Cisco, Commerce One, EDS, Encoda, Extol, Fujitsu, HP, IBM, IONA, Macromedia, Novell, NTT, Oracle, Progress, SAP AG, Software AG,

Sonic Software, Sterling Commerce, Sun, Sybase, Systinet, Vitria, and webMethods.

But the other side of the coin is licensing. Sun maintains tight control of the licensing rights to the Java specifications and to the Java brand. Although the development process is quite open, you must pay Sun for the right to implement a product based on a Java specification. Even if you participate in the development of a new Java API, you may still need to obtain a license.

You must pay Sun for the right to implement a Java specification

Microsoft also wanted the endorsement of a standards body for .NET, but Microsoft took a slightly different tack. Rather than try to contribute all of .NET, Microsoft elected to standardize only the lowest level of the platform. Microsoft won big points when it submitted C# to ECMA in 2000. The ECMA committee—consisting of representatives from Fujitsu, HP, Intel, IBM, ISE, Microsoft, Monash University, Netscape, OpenWave, Plum Hall, and Sun Microsystems—polished the specifications and submitted them to ISO. The C# specifications are formal international standards. Anyone can implement an international standard. No Microsoft license is required.

ECMA manages C#

Keep in mind, though, that the ISO standards cover only the C# language and the CLI. The higher-level class libraries and services that make up the remainder of the .NET platform—including the interface modules, the Web services class libraries, the development tools, and ASP.NET—are not part of the standard. These technologies are owned and managed by Microsoft. So although C# is managed by a standards organization, you really don't have much influence on the future of the .NET platform.

Microsoft owns and maintains the .NET Framework and the Web services class libraries

Chapter 8 Web Services Infrastructure

Integrated Versus Portable, Best-of-Breed Solutions

.NET offers an integrated solution with limited portability, and Java offers a best-of-breed solution across many platforms

As with any debate between Microsoft platforms and the Java platform, you must decide between an integrated solution with limited portability versus a best-of-breed solution with wide portability. If you use Java, you have more homework to do. There are about a dozen product-quality SOAP implementations for Java to choose from. Each has its own best-of-breed specialty features, such as developer productivity, performance, security, or legacy integration. When choosing a platform, you should evaluate multiple products to determine which works best for your specific requirements. Chapter 9 provides guidelines to help you with your evaluation.

Web Services Platform Features

Features vary by vendor

Table 8-2 shows an overview of the features that come with a Web services platform. These features and services vary widely from vendor to vendor, so this table is a generalization.

At a minimum, a Web services platform provides a SOAP runtime system

At a minimum, a Web services platform provides a set of runtime libraries that implements support for the SOAP specification. Each client and server application that communicates using SOAP needs access to a SOAP runtime system. A Web services platform also supplies a programming API that developers use to access the SOAP runtime libraries. This programming API supports a specific programming language, so you must have a different platform for each language you use. That's no problem, and in fact it's expected that you use multiple runtime libraries from multiple vendors on your various systems. Remember, heterogeneous interoperability is one of the major features of Web services.

Most Web services platforms support WSDL

Almost all Web services platforms include support for WSDL. Most SOAP tools can generate WSDL descriptions for your services, and they can use WSDL descriptions to generate client code. Many SOAP implementations use WSDL descriptions at runtime to help

Table 8-2: Web Services Platform Features

Platform Component	Features
Runtime environment	Client and/or server runtime libraries
	Support for extensions (interceptors)
	Advanced extensions (security etc.)
	Management and administration tools
Development tools	Language-specific programming APIs
	WSDL generators
	Code generators
	UDDI browsers
	Serialization/type mapping tools
	Command line tools
	Graphical tools
	IDE plug-ins
Deployment tools	Packaging tools
	Configuration tools
	UDDI registration tools

interpret and process the SOAP messages and to enable dynamic interaction. But not all platforms support WSDL, particularly some of the antique platforms, such as Apache SOAP and Sun's JAXM reference implementation.

I caution you against using a platform that doesn't support WSDL. You need WSDL to get the most from Web services. Without WSDL you lose most of your dynamic capabilities. More important, clients need WSDL descriptions to figure out how to access a service.

You need WSDL to get the most from Web services

Chapter 8 Web Services Infrastructure

I recommend that you stick with the more modern platforms that provide integrated support for WSDL. If you use a platform that doesn't support WSDL, you probably want to find a third-party WSDL editing tool, such as Altova xmlspy or Kamiak's OmniOpera, to help you create your WSDL files.

Support for UDDI may be built in or available separately

Support for UDDI varies widely. Some Web services platforms include a UDDI registry as part of the platform. Others include a comprehensive set of UDDI wizards and utilities, but the UDDI registry server is sold separately. Still others do not provide any direct support for UDDI, although they work easily enough with third-party UDDI registries and tools.

A UDDI registry is a separate product

From my perspective, a private UDDI registry service should be viewed as a separate product; in fact, I classify it as an infrastructure-level Web service rather than as a piece of the basic platform. A business is likely to need many licenses for many Web service platforms, but only one or two UDDI registries. A Web service platform should provide or make available the tools needed to access a UDDI registry, but it makes sense to obtain the registry separately.

A few platforms include advanced middleware functionality

A few Web services platforms provide advanced middleware functionality, such as security and management frameworks, reliable messaging, asynchronous communications, and cluster support. If you are using a platform that does not include these capabilities, you can augment your environment using a Web services management extension, described later in this chapter.

Most platforms provide administrative tools

Most platforms supply management and administration tools designed for your operations staff. These tools are distinct from the development and deployment tools that are designed for your developers. You probably don't want your developers to be responsible for the runtime operations of your production systems.

Web Services Development and Deployment Tools

In addition to the runtime libraries, a Web services platform must give you development and deployment tools. You use the development tools to generate SOAP code for your clients and services. You use the deployment tools to package and configure the runtime settings for your applications.

A platform provides development and deployment tools

Most Web services platforms provide **command line tools**, which will appeal to your advanced developers. Command line tools are extremely powerful but cryptic. Some platforms have associated but separate visual tools. These tools give you a graphical design environment, numerous wizards, and drag-and-drop editors. Your novice developers will no doubt find these tools beneficial. Some platforms make their tools available as modules that plug in to popular IDEs. These plug-in modules transparently add Web services development capabilities to popular code development environments, such as Borland JBuilder, Eclipse, IBM WebSphere Studio Application Developer (WSAD), Microsoft Visual Studio .NET, NetBeans, and Sun ONE Studio.

Tools are available as command line tools, visual tools, or IDE plug-ins

Most Web services platforms include development tools based on WSDL. A WSDL file is a machine-readable description of a Web service, and it can be compiled into application code.[4] As shown in Figure 8-4, a developer can use these tools to generate WSDL descriptions from application code or to generate application code from WSDL descriptions.

Most platforms provide WSDL development tools

The development of clients is typically separated from the development of services. The tools and platforms you use to build your clients can be different from those you use to build your services. The WSDL description is the point of integration.

You can use different tools to build your clients and services

---

[4] See Chapter 3 for a thorough discussion of WSDL.

Figure 8-4: A developer uses WSDL tools to generate SOAP code. Your tool should support the language you're using.

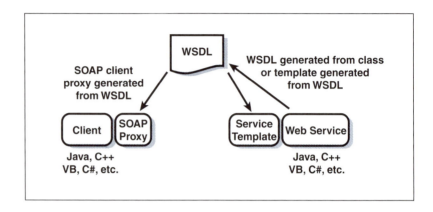

Service Development

A service can be new or wrap an existing application

There are generally two approaches to building Web services. In the first case, the developer builds a new service from scratch. In the second case, the developer creates a Web service interface for an existing application.

Building a New Service

A UDDI browser helps the developer find service type definitions

If you want to build a new Web service, you may want to build the service based on an existing service type. In this case, you must find the WSDL description that describes the service type. Some platforms provide UDDI browser utilities that can help you find an appropriate WSDL description.

A WSDL compiler can generate an application template from a WSDL description

After you have found the WSDL description, you can use a WSDL compiler to generate an application template for the service. This template consists of a set of functions that map to the operations defined in the WSDL description. You then fill in the template by writing the code that implements the functions. In some cases the service-side code generator produces generic code that can work with any SOAP runtime that supports the same language, but I wouldn't count on this type of tool to be portable across vendor implementations. Most generated templates contain code that is unique to a specific SOAP implementation.

Core Products

You implement the service's business functions using normal language components and constructs. For example, a Java developer would build a service using Java classes, JavaBeans components, and Enterprise JavaBeans (EJB) components. You should always follow the traditional best practices for SOA application development.

Always follow SOA best practices

Wrapping Existing Applications

If you have an existing application, you can use a tool to generate a WSDL description from your existing code. In a Java environment, this type of tool is usually called something like `java2wsdl`. A WSDL generator tool is fairly generic, so if you are using a platform that doesn't provide a WSDL generator, you should be able to use a tool from a different platform to generate your WSDL file. You may need to tweak the generated description, though.

A developer can generate a WSDL description from existing code

After you've generated the WSDL file, many SOAP implementations will let you take your existing application and simply deploy it into the Web services runtime container. Presto! Your application now has a Web API. In many cases you don't have to write a single line of new code.

Simply deploy the application to the server

One word of caution about this approach: If the existing application has a highly granular, low-level API, you probably don't want to expose this interface directly. Instead you probably want to build a wrapper that presents a higher-level business interface to the application's functionality. You would use this wrapper to generate your Web API.

Make sure the application has a business-level API

For example, let's say that you have an interactive order-entry application that displays an interface that lets users add items to the order one product at a time. This type of interface is quite reasonable for an interactive application, but it isn't particularly appropriate for a Web services application. It would require an excessive

Design Web APIs to reduce message exchanges

195

Chapter 8   Web Services Infrastructure

Figure 8-5: If your Web service has a highly granular, low-level interface (top), you should build a new, higher-level interface to the application functionality (bottom).

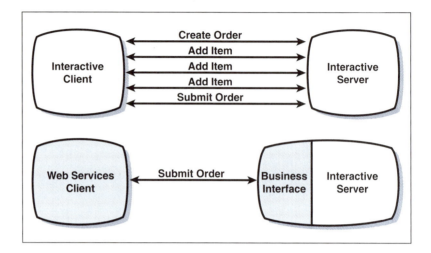

number of message exchanges, causing poor performance. When building Web service interfaces, you want to design the interface to reduce the number of message exchanges, as shown in Figure 8-5.

An adapter maps SOAP requests to a proprietary API

In some cases you may need to build a Web services adapter for a legacy application. As described in Chapter 1, an adapter acts as a mediator between an open API and a proprietary API. A Web services adapter maps SOAP requests to the proprietary API supported by the legacy application. As with the business interface scenario, you would use the adapter code to generate your Web API. Many EAI vendors provide adapter frameworks that support Web APIs.

Completing the Project

You may need to provide serialization routines to transform objects into XML structures

In addition to the Web API and the business logic, you may need to develop a few other routines. When you send and receive SOAP messages, the SOAP runtime system translates the messages between XML and your application's native data format. In some cases the developer may need to provide serialization routines that tell the runtime system how to map between the two formats. Some platforms perform this data mapping automatically. Other platforms can perform automatic mappings as long as the application objects are relatively simple and are constructed according to certain conventions. Some platforms provide visual tools to help you design the data mappings and then generate the serialization routines. Other platforms require that you write custom serialization routines. All serialization tools are tied to a particular runtime.

You may need to write specialized routines to handle middleware functions, such as security, reliability, version control, message transformation, and transactions. These routines are known as interceptors or header processors. The middleware information is usually passed using SOAP headers, and you may need to supply the code to process the SOAP header information. Some platforms provide built-in support for many of these middleware functions, so you don't necessarily need to write your own header processors. The mechanisms you use to implement header processors are unique to each specific runtime.

You may need to provide interceptors or header processing routines

After you have developed the serialization routines and header processors, you are ready to configure the Web service and create a deployment package. Figure 8-6 shows an overview of the deployment steps. Most SOAP implementations use some type of **deployment descriptor** to define the runtime configuration of the service. This deployment descriptor maps a particular WSDL operation to a particular application program, and it specifies any additional information that the runtime system needs to know. For example, it specifies the name of any serialization routines and header processors associated with the service. As of this writing, there are no standards for deployment descriptors, so each SOAP implementation uses a unique format, and the mechanism you use to create the deployment descriptor and deploy your service is unique to each particular runtime server. This issue should be resolved for Java applications at some point in the future as the JCP develops container standards for Web services.

The configuration and deployment tools are unique to each runtime

Chapter 8   Web Services Infrastructure

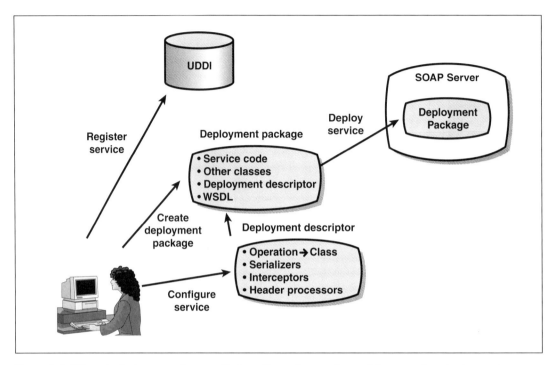

Figure 8-6: When deploying a service, you first configure the service and then create a deployment package to deploy it. You may also want to register the service in a UDDI registry.

Some platforms supply UDDI registration wizards

After you have deployed your service, you probably want to advertise it to your potential consumers. For example, you may want to advertise it in a private or public UDDI registry. Some platforms provide UDDI registration wizards that automatically register a new service in a public or private UDDI registry.

Client Development

A WSDL compiler generates a client proxy

When building a client, a developer obtains the WSDL description for the service and uses a WSDL compiler to generate a client proxy. The client uses the proxy to talk to the service. The proxy contains code that interfaces with the SOAP runtime. The proxy does quite a bit of work for the client application:

Core Products

- ❏ It constructs the SOAP message.
- ❏ It establishes a connection to the remote service.
- ❏ It sends the request message.
- ❏ It interprets the response message.

The client proxy always contains code that is unique to a specific SOAP implementation, so the tool you use to generate the proxy determines which SOAP runtime your client will use. As mentioned before, you can use different SOAP runtimes for your clients and services.

The client proxy works with a specific SOAP runtime

In addition to the client proxy, you must provide serialization routines and header processors for your client. If you are using the same SOAP runtime on both client and server, you can use the same serialization routines and header processors. If you are using different SOAP runtimes, you must supply different routines.

The client also needs serialization and header processing routines

Web Services Runtime Architecture

Web services can run on almost any size computer—anything from a massive mainframe or multiprocessor server, to a desktop machine, to a PDA, to an embedded processor in a light switch. A few platforms, such as EXOR eSOAP, kSOAP, and Wingfoot, are designed to support tiny-footprint devices. For the most part, though, you'll find that most Web services are deployed on servers, and most Web services platforms are designed to support that configuration.

Although they can run anywhere, most Web services run on servers

Figure 8-7 shows a typical runtime environment for Web services. Here you see a client application talking to a Web service. The client application can be any type of application, including a corporate application (such as your inventory control system), a desktop application (such as a spreadsheet tool), a wireless device (such as a RIM Blackberry pager), or a Web portal (such as your

A Web service client can be any type of application

Chapter 8   Web Services Infrastructure

Figure 8-7: A client application communicates with a Web service using a proxy generated from the Web service's WSDL description. The Web service runs in a SOAP runtime server, which usually executes in a Web server or application server.

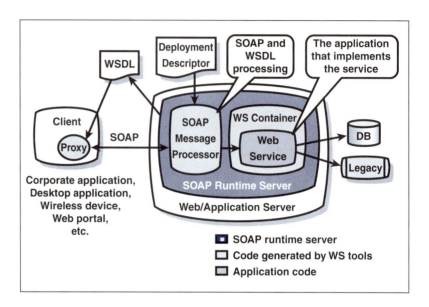

employee HR portal). The client uses a proxy to communicate with the service. The proxy is generated from the service's WSDL description. The proxy uses its associated SOAP runtime libraries to construct, send, and interpret SOAP messages.

A Web service has a WSDL file and deployment descriptor

A Web service is deployed in a SOAP runtime server. You'll notice in Figure 8-7 that the Web service has a WSDL description and a deployment descriptor associated with it. The WSDL description provides the information that a client needs to communicate with the service. The deployment descriptor provides the information that the SOAP runtime server needs to process the request.

A SOAP server consists of a SOAP message processor and a runtime container

When the client issues a SOAP request, the proxy converts the request into a SOAP message, establishes a connection to the SOAP runtime server, and sends the message. A SOAP runtime server consists of a **SOAP message processor** and a **runtime container**.

A SOAP message processor is responsible for interpreting the request and directing it to the appropriate application. The SOAP

200

message processor listens for requests, and, for each request received, it processes the SOAP message. It uses the deployment descriptor to figure out how to process the message. The deployment descriptor indicates how to process any SOAP headers that may be present, and it specifies how to translate the XML into program language objects. It also specifies which application program should be called to process the request. When the program completes its work, it returns a response to the SOAP message processor, which converts the response into a SOAP message and sends it back to the client.

A SOAP message processor processes requests as defined by the deployment descriptor

The application program normally executes within the runtime container in the SOAP runtime server. A runtime container manages the **lifecycle** of an application. The container is responsible for loading the program into memory, allocating the system resources that the program needs, and removing the program when it's complete. A runtime container may provide a number of optimization services, such as multithreading support and resource pooling, that can increase the performance and scalability of the environment.

A runtime container hosts the application code

The Web service application running in the container may contain the business logic that implements the service, or it may instead contain a wrapper service. A wrapper service is an application adapter that calls an external application to perform the actual business logic. The external application could be any type of application, such as an SAP R/3 function or a CICS transaction. The wrapper service communicates with the legacy application using the legacy application's native API.

A wrapper service serves as an adapter to a legacy application

A SOAP runtime server usually runs in a Web server or application server. A Web server, such as Microsoft IIS and Apache HTTP Server, provides support for HTTP, the most common protocol used to transfer SOAP messages. An application server, such as Apache Tomcat or BEA WebLogic Server, is a Web server that has been

A SOAP runtime server usually runs in a Web server or application server

Chapter 8   Web Services Infrastructure

extended to support Web applications. An application server usually supplies one or more runtime containers that provide lifecycle management for various types of Web applications.

Web Services and Java Application Servers

Java Web services don't require a full J2EE application server

I'm sure you've noticed that most J2EE application server vendors—including BEA, Borland, IBM, IONA, Macromedia, Novell, Oracle, and Sun—have added Web services to their products. You may also be aware that a number of other SOAP providers and vendors—such as Apache, Cape Clear, Killdara, Systinet, The Mind Electric, and Wingfoot—provide Web services platforms for Java that don't require a full J2EE application server. IONA, Novell, and Sun provide stand-alone platforms as well as J2EE-based platforms. So let's spend a moment talking about Java application servers.

J2EE defines two types of containers

As shown in Figure 8-8, J2EE defines two types of containers to support Web applications: a **servlet engine** and an Enterprise JavaBeans (**EJB**) container. A servlet engine hosts **servlets** and

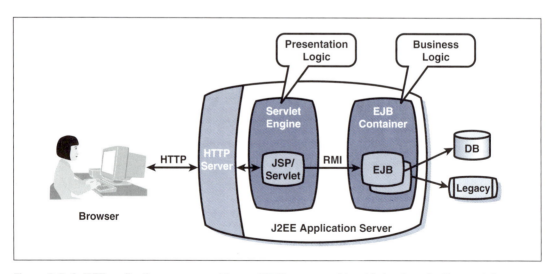

Figure 8-8: A J2EE application server provides an HTTP server and two kinds of application containers to support dynamic Web applications. A servlet engine hosts servlets and JSPs, which perform presentation logic. An EJB container hosts EJB components, which perform business logic.

JavaServer Pages (**JSPs**). An **EJB container** hosts EJB components. According to Sun's best practices blueprints, you should use servlets and JSPs to implement presentation logic and use EJBs to implement complex business logic.

Servlets and JSPs are lightweight Java components that communicate using HTTP. For the most part these components are designed to perform Web-based presentation logic. You normally invoke a servlet from a Web page by clicking on a link within your browser. The link tells the HTTP server to invoke the servlet, which is a Java application that dynamically creates an HTML page. I refer to servlets as lightweight, but they can do pretty much anything you want them to do. They can execute business logic, access databases, call legacy applications, and perform transactions. A servlet engine gives you a number of optimization features that support high performance and scalability. However, a servlet engine generally doesn't provide support for distributed transactions.

Servlets and JSPs perform Web-based presentation logic

EJB components are industrial-strength, secure, transactional business components. EJB components are designed to support complex business logic, distributed transactions, and extensive data manipulation. The EJB container is a runtime framework that automatically manages distributed transactions and access control facilities. An EJB container optimizes resources a little differently than a servlet engine does. These EJB optimizations impose more overhead but result in better overall performance and scalability when you're dealing with complex transactions. For relatively simple applications, though, a servlet engine is often adequate and offers better performance.

EJBs perform complex business logic

Unlike servlets, EJB components cannot communicate using HTTP. They can communicate only via RMI. You cannot invoke an EJB component from a Web page through an HTTP connection, so for Web applications, you must invoke an EJB component

EJB components communicate only via RMI

Chapter 8   Web Services Infrastructure

through an HTTP-enabled component, such as a servlet or a Web service.

Servlets are designed to speak with humans, and Web services are designed to speak to other applications

A Web service is a third kind of component that executes in yet another type of container. Figure 8-9 shows a J2EE environment with an added Web services container. Web services provide an alternative type of interface to your backend business applications. They are similar to servlets in that you communicate with them using HTTP, but they are different in that they are designed to serve application clients rather than human clients. Servlets return HTML, and Web services return XML.

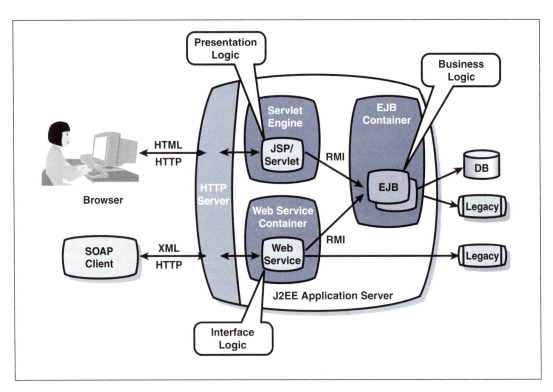

Figure 8-9: A Web service offers an alternative programmable interface to your business applications. A Web service container offers performance characteristics comparable to those of a servlet engine.

As with servlets, it's perfectly legitimate to implement your business logic entirely within the Web service, particularly if the application is relatively simple. A Web services container offers performance characteristics comparable to those of a servlet engine. If your application is simple and doesn't require complex transactions, you can run your Web services using a lightweight servlet engine.

You can implement your business logic entirely within the Web service

If your application requires complex transactions, you'll probably want to implement your business logic using EJB components. EJBs use a complex, low-level API, so you'll definitely want to build a business interface for these applications. You would deploy the business interface in the Web service container.

You should build a business interface for your EJB applications

A Web service adapter for a legacy application might run entirely within the Web service container, or it might call a **JCA adapter** running in the EJB container. The J2EE Connector Architecture (**JCA**) defines a standard plug-in architecture for application adapters in J2EE application servers.

An adapter can use JCA or call the application directly

J2EE or Servlet Engine?

As mentioned earlier, quite a few Java SOAP implementations don't require a full J2EE application server. Most of these products have built the SOAP server as a servlet, and this means that the SOAP container actually runs in the servlet engine. This architecture ensures that the SOAP server is portable across multiple application servers. The SOAP server can also use the existing HTTP processing services, as well as clustering and load balancing capabilities, offered by the servlet engine.

A Java SOAP server normally runs as a servlet

A number of free or low-cost, lightweight application servers—such as Apache Tomcat, Caucho Resin, and Jetty—support servlets. Most of the independent Java SOAP implementations will run in any of

You can run your Web services in a low-cost servlet engine

Chapter 8   Web Services Infrastructure

these servlet engines, so you can use these application servers to host your Web services.

You may prefer to use a full J2EE environment

Still, there are many reasons you might prefer to deploy your Web services in a full-fledged J2EE application server. You may already have a J2EE application server. You may implement your business logic as EJB components. You may prefer to use commercial products rather than open source technology, or you may need the increased performance, reliability, availability, and scalability provided by an industrial-strength product.

The third-party platforms offer features that aren't available in most built-in containers

If you decide to use a J2EE application server, you can use the built-in Web services container that comes with the server, or you can use one of the portable third-party Web services platforms. The third-party platforms offer a number of competitive features that aren't available with most built-in containers. Also, services written for the built-in container generally can run only within that particular J2EE application server. If you need portability across application servers, you'll want to use a third-party platform. See Chapter 9 for platform evaluation guidelines.

Web Services Management Extensions

A Web services management extension adds advanced capabilities to a basic platform

The next major category of Web services infrastructure products is what I call the Web services management extensions.[5] You may also hear these products referred to as Web services management systems or Web services management platforms. Don't let the name of this category confuse you. Most of these products are not associated with traditional network management frameworks such as BMC Patrol, CA Unicenter, HP OpenView, and IBM Tivoli. Instead

---

[5] Actually, my preferred name for this category is Web services platform extensions because these products invariably extend a Web services platform. I find the term "management" to be confusing. But most of the industry uses that term, so I follow the trend.

a Web services management extension adds advanced capabilities to a basic Web services platform. For the most part, these products can work with any Web services platform. This product category is a popular market segment for startups because very few platform vendors offer all these extended services.

Quite a few products fall into this category, offering a variable set of features such as monitoring, security, reliability, transactions, and performance. Typically these products serve two functions. On one hand they provide middleware extensions, and on the other hand they supply a monitoring framework. Most products in this market segment provide both middleware and monitoring capabilities.

Extensions provide services such as monitoring and security

Middleware Extensions

A middleware extension augments a basic Web services platform with advanced middleware functionality, such as load balancing, content-based routing, version control, reliable message delivery, and security.

They add advanced functionality

Perhaps because there are no standards for middleware extensions, these products often operate using an intermediary architecture, as shown in Figure 8-10. When you send a message, the management framework intercepts the message before it reaches the SOAP runtime. The framework can monitor messages, execute security policies, redirect a message, or transform a message according to the capabilities and policies defined by the framework.

They intercept messages en route

Middleware extension frameworks—such as those from AmberPoint, Blue Titan, Confluent, Digital Evolution, Flamenco Networks, Talking Blocks, and WestGlobal—intercept and process SOAP messages in transit and take appropriate action based on content. Each of these vendors focuses on its own set of capabilities. For example, Talking Blocks focuses on message routing and transformation, and WestGlobal focuses on performance management.

They perform actions based on message content

Chapter 8   Web Services Infrastructure

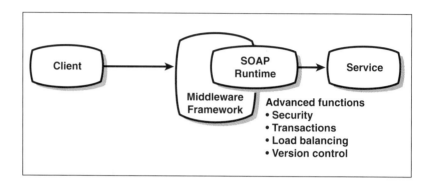

Figure 8-10: A middleware extension intercepts messages and adds extended functionality in transit.

Security extensions support authentication, authorization, and other security functions

Nearly all middleware extensions provide some type of security framework. Some vendors, such as Hitachi Quadrasis, Reactivity, Vordel, and WestBridge, focus exclusively on security. These security frameworks enable a variety of security functions, such as authentication, authorization, encryption, auditing, and key management. You'll also find that many of the traditional security vendors, such as Netegrity and VeriSign, offer products in this space. Netegrity has extended its products to encompass Web services security. VeriSign has developed a series of toolkits specifically to support Web services security.

They augment your core Web services platform

These middleware frameworks are especially helpful if you are using a Web services platform that doesn't provide a lot of advanced middleware capabilities. You can use these systems to augment the capabilities of your core Web services platform to make it more secure and robust.

These products may impose significant overhead

Although these products provide tremendous incremental value to the current crop of Web services platforms, I must caution you about overhead. As mentioned earlier, most of these products run as an intermediary that intercepts and processes the SOAP messages in transit. This intermediary can run as a filter in your Web server or as a separate proxy server. In either configuration I refer to this architecture as "the big fat proxy." SOAP message processing can constitute as much as 90 percent of a Web services message exchange. If you add a SOAP processing intermediary to the message path, it can nearly double the invocation response time.

Rather than run as an intermediary, a middleware extension can instead run as an interceptor in the SOAP runtime server. In this architecture the message is processed only once by the SOAP message processor in the SOAP runtime server, which calls out to the middleware extension at the appropriate moment to perform the requested functions. From a performance perspective, it's much more efficient to perform all middleware functions in the SOAP runtime server rather than in an intermediary.

It's more efficient to perform these functions in the SOAP runtime server

To support the runtime interceptor architecture, a vendor must build a unique interceptor for each Web services platform; as a result, many vendors may elect to support only the most popular platforms. The JAX-RPC API defines a standard interceptor model called JAX-RPC handlers, so a vendor can build a generic interceptor for all Java platforms that support JAX-RPC.

JAX-RPC defines a standard interceptor model

I tend to think of middleware extensions as a stopgap solution, though. Over time many of the Web services platform vendors will provide built-in support for features such as security, load balancing, transactions, and version control. A number of platforms already have quite a few advanced features, and they implement them in the SOAP processing layer.

Middleware extensions are a stopgap solution

Monitoring Frameworks

A monitoring framework is closer in nature to a traditional systems management framework. The reason that the middleware extension products are associated with the term "management" is that most of them also provide monitoring facilities. A monitoring

Most products also do monitoring

Chapter 8   Web Services Infrastructure

framework monitors SOAP message traffic to give you visibility into your runtime environment.

Monitoring frameworks provide critical information to your operations staff

These monitoring frameworks are aimed at two audiences: your operations staff and your business analysts. From an operations perspective, these frameworks provide critical information needed by your operations staff to keep your systems up and running. Products such as Actional SOAP station Adjoin SOMMA and Service Integrity SIFT focus on this operations perspective. These systems capture SOAP message traffic as it streams by and actively analyze the information in an out-of-band process, imposing very little overhead. The analyzers identify trends, define thresholds, and take action when unusual conditions arise. For example, if the average message response time exceeds a threshold, the framework can page an administrator or send an alert to HP OpenView. Monitoring frameworks can also collect information needed for metering and billing purposes and can monitor conformance to service level agreements. I view this type of monitoring framework as a critical piece of your core Web services infrastructure.

You can also analyze the message traffic for business reasons

The monitoring frameworks also give you the opportunity to analyze the SOAP message traffic for business purposes. You can archive the captured message traffic and perform statistical and heuristic analysis of it. For example, you can identify business trends, track regional sales fluctuations, and predict traffic peaks and valleys.

Infrastructure-Level Web Services

This part of the infrastructure is implemented as a grid of Web services

The last major category of the core Web services infrastructure products is what I call infrastructure-level Web services. This part of the infrastructure is implemented as a grid of Web services that support other Web services. This **service grid** provides a diverse set of enabling functionality for your entire Web services environment. For example, infrastructure-level Web services can support these kinds of functions:

Core Products

- Reliable message delivery
- Advertising and discovery
- Security and trust functions
- Metering and billing

Because these infrastructure components are Web services, your applications access these services using SOAP. Some grid services may be included as part of a Web services platform, but in most cases they are sold or licensed separately. You may host some of these services yourself, and you may license others from a third-party provider. For example, you might operate your own UDDI registry, and you might use a reliable network provider to support reliable messaging.

Your applications access these services using SOAP

Note that infrastructure-level services make excellent candidates for the software-as-a-service business model. But as with any ASP-style service, to be successful the service provider must offer a compelling business advantage in licensing a hosted service rather than licensing the software.

Infrastructure services may be licensed software-as-a-service

Reliable Network Providers

A reliable network provider (RNP), such as Flamenco Networks and Grand Central, provides an infrastructure-level Web service that supports reliable message delivery. These companies supply ASP-style services that ensure that your SOAP messages get delivered reliably to their intended target.

RNPs guarantee message delivery

When an application sends a message, as shown in Figure 8-11, the SOAP runtime system routes the message through an RNP proxy, which takes responsibility for delivering the message via the reliable network. The proxy stores the message in a persistent file before sending it on. It then monitors the delivery of the message and automatically resends it if it goes astray. An RNP may also offer additional services, such as authentication and authorization checks, message encryption, message auditing, and service level monitoring.

All messages are logged, monitored, and tracked

Chapter 8 Web Services Infrastructure

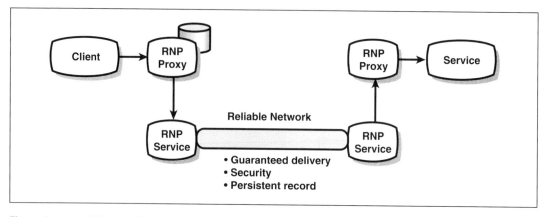

Figure 8-11: An RNP proxy intercepts SOAP messages and routes them through a reliable network.

An RNP isolates users from a proprietary network

RNPs are particularly useful when you need reliable messaging but can't dictate a proprietary networking environment. For example, they are popular for B2B applications and e-marketplaces. Many Web services platforms provide basic support for reliable message delivery by using a reliable transport, such as IBM WebSphereMQ or JMS. But this choice restricts your options. If you use a MOM technology as a transport, everyone that wants to talk to you must also use that MOM technology. The RNP services isolate the users from the proprietary network.

UDDI Registries

You will probably access many UDDI registries

A UDDI registry is an infrastructure-level service. You are likely to use a variety of UDDI registries, including the public UBR, a private e-market registry, your partners' registries, and your own internal private registries.

Look for advanced security and administrative features

Many Web services platforms include a lightweight UDDI service for development and testing purposes, although you may find that these systems aren't sufficient for production use. If you intend to use a private UDDI in production, you might want to look for an

Core Products

implementation that has extended features to support security, administration, and taxonomy management.

Trust Services

You're likely to use a number of trust services in your service grid, including a single sign-on service, an entitlement service, a key management service, and a digital signature processing service. These trust services make it easier to implement global security policies for your environment.[6]

Trust services centralize security management

A single sign-on (SSO) service helps facilitate the authentication process within your Web services infrastructure. A user can sign on to the SSO service and obtain an identity credential. Your SOAP runtime can then pass this credential in a SOAP header on all subsequent requests, alleviating the need to repeatedly perform authentication tests. SAML defines a standard XML format for authentication credentials. Many of the traditional security companies, such as Netegrity and Oblix, are extending their current single sign-on products to support SAML.

An SSO service facilitates authentication

An entitlement service provides a central coordination point to implement access control policies. An entitlement service may support one or more of the developing OASIS security standards, including SAML, XACML, and XrML. Most traditional access control vendors, such as IBM and Netegrity, are enhancing their systems to support access control for Web services.

An entitlement service implements access control policies

If you plan to use digital signatures in your environment, you may want to deploy trust services to help manage signature creation and verification as well as key registration and retrieval. PKI management is notoriously arduous. The OASIS DSS and W3C XKMS

DSS and XKMS services help you manage digital signatures

---

[6] See Chapter 5 for a discussion of trust services and Web services security.

Chapter 8   Web Services Infrastructure

specifications show some promise for making the technology more accessible.

Some services come packaged with hardware

Some infrastructure-level Web services come packaged as a hardware appliance. For example, DataPower and Forum Systems supply appliances that give you application-level XML security in a box. Using hardware acceleration technology, these appliances support high-performance XML encryption and XML signature services.

A billing service meters and charges for service utilization

A metering and billing service keeps track of a user's service utilization and accrues billing information. You'll need this type of service if you intend to charge users to use your services. As of this writing, few vendors or service providers are working in this area. Metra-Tech and Schemantix are early entrants. A number of companies provide ASP-style billing presentment and payment services, and perhaps these services will be adapted to support Web services.

Associated Products

Many types of products use or rely on Web services

The associated products are products that use or rely on Web services. There are lots of different types of associated Web services products. Many of them existed long before Web services came onto the scene, and they have been adapted or extended to work with and exploit the power of Web services. Others are new types of products that are emerging to exploit the opportunities provided by this new technology. Here are some examples of associated products:

- XML tools
- Application adapters for Web services
- Message switching systems
- Multichannel user interface systems and portals
- Integrated development environments (IDEs)
- Web services testing, diagnostic, and optimization tools

Associated Products

- Web services applications
- Web services business process management (BPM)

You may want to get a few XML tools to augment your design and development environment. XML and WSDL editing tools—such as Altova XMLSpy, Kodiak OmniOpera, and Tibco Extensibility—help you create and validate XML documents, schemata, style sheets, and WSDL descriptions. XML design tools, such as Swingtide QoB Assistant, help you design SOAP message formats that ensure the highest degree of interoperability.

XML tools augment your design and development environment

As I've mentioned a few times, many EAI vendors provide adapter frameworks that you can use to create Web APIs for your legacy application systems. A Web service gives you an open, outward-facing interface that can be called by any application written in any programming language and running on any platform. But somehow that interface needs to talk to the inner workings of your corporate application systems. You still need application adapters that speak the internal language of your legacy applications. Most of the traditional EAI and B2Bi vendors, such as Mercator and webMethods, have enhanced their application adapters to support Web services.

Use an application adapter to create a Web API for legacy applications

To some degree a message switching system looks and feels similar to a Web services management extension. Message switching systems act as intermediaries along a message path. They provide extended middleware services, such as reliability, security, content-based routing, and load balancing. What makes these systems different from Web services management extensions is that they aren't focused exclusively on Web services. Message switching systems, such as those from Actional, Kenamea, KnowNow, Sonic Software, and Talking Blocks, act as a centralized hub or message bus, providing a point of integration among multiple messaging systems, including Web services, JMS, RMI, CORBA, DCOM, and proprietary communication protocols.

A message switch integrates Web services and other messaging systems

Chapter 8   Web Services Infrastructure

Many portal systems support Web services

A number of vendors have developed Web services products that specialize in supporting multichannel applications and portal development. For example, the Jarna Enterprise Event Management Platform is a framework for extending your Web services to a broad range of mobile devices. Similarly, WebCollage Syndicator helps you build interactive Web services that can execute in a portal. Many of the leading enterprise information portal (EIP) suppliers are adding support for Web services portlets and WSRP to their products. For example, CA is adding WSRP support to CleverPath Portal.

Tools vendors are building IDEs that exploit Web services

Quite a few companies are producing application development environments that support Web services technologies. For the most part, these tools are full-solution environments that hide the complexities of Web services technology from the developer. Most of these IDEs focus on component-based development, and a Web service is treated like any other type of component. In some cases the IDE works only with Web services. Many of these tools include user interface designers, proprietary scripting languages, embedded application servers, integrated processing engines, and application adapter frameworks. Examples of these tools are BEA WebLogic Workshop, Bowstreet Factory, and Altio AltioLive.

Testing tools help you prepare your services for deployment

In addition to the basic tools that come with your Web service platform, you probably also want testing, diagnostic, and optimization tools. These tools allow you to prepare your Web services for deployment. They provide services to test individual Web services and composite services. They assist you in performance, scalability, and reliability testing. Market leaders such as Mercury Interactive and Parasoft are expanding the scope of their products to support Web services. Also, a number of startups and specialty companies, such as Altova, Empirix, Mindreef, and Optimyz provide Web services specific tools.

A number of ERP, CRM, and HR application vendors, such as Peoplesoft, SAP, and Siebel, are starting to include Web services interfaces in their application systems. Some startup application vendors are taking a slightly different approach; rather than try to provide a comprehensive application solution, they focus on supplying best-of-breed application modules that are designed from the ground up to be integratable. For example, Webify is developing a set of loosely coupled enterprise applications, implemented as Web services, for the financial services and healthcare industries.

Many application vendors are adding Web APIs to their systems

One category of associated products is the focus of a great deal of attention and activity. As described in Chapter 5, there is strong interest in using Web services for business process management. People hope to use BPM to realize the vision of dynamic assembly of Web services.

BPM is tied to the idea of dynamic assembly

A number of vendors are developing Web services orchestration and choreography tools. Microsoft was one of the first players in this space, with BizTalk Server. Many EAI and message broker vendors, such as IBM, Mercator, Tibco, and Versata, now have offerings in this space. A host of startup companies, including AptSoft, Carnot, and Fuego, also offer this type of product.

Many vendors provide orchestration and choreography tools

As with earlier BPM products, these systems give you a rules language to define a choreographed interchange of messages among a set of Web services. Also, they usually supply a runtime processor that executes your rules and ensures that the interchange runs as defined. Unfortunately, each of these products uses a proprietary rules language to define the business process coordination information. Lack of a standard rules language makes it hard to support the dynamic assembly of Web services. When the choreography standards efforts get sorted out, let's hope that these vendors adopt open languages and protocols.

Rules languages are proprietary

Chapter 8   Web Services Infrastructure

Quite a few vendors support BPEL4WS

Of all the potential contenders, the BPEL4WS specification from BEA, IBM, and Microsoft seems to have achieved the widest adoption, at least for now. IBM provides a preliminary implementation of a BPEL4WS process engine called BPWS4J, which is available on alphaWorks. Meanwhile Collaxa, Momentum, Vitria, webMethods, and WebV2 all say that their products support BPEL4WS.

Don't jump into orchestration unless you have a pressing BPM application

I generally view this product segment with caution. If you are experimenting with Web services and just trying to figure out what you can do with them, I don't recommend that you jump into orchestration and choreography. I recommend that you wait it out until the technologies and standards mature.

Recognize that BPM tools are proprietary

On the other hand, if you have a pressing BPM project on your plate, don't hesitate. I definitely recommend that you evaluate some of the Web services-based orchestration tools. But recognize that the rules languages are still proprietary.

9

Evaluation Guidelines

After you've made the decision to develop applications using Web services, how do you go about selecting products? There is no one product that is best for all situations. In fact, you'll almost certainly need multiple products. As a rule, you should always select your products based on the requirements of each application. This chapter provides basic guidelines that you can follow to help you select the right products for your application.

No one product is best for all situations

Appendix A provides a list of many, although not all, of the available Web services platforms and UDDI registries. I have not included all the open source and academic implementations, and I'm sure that I've missed some commercial implementations, too. As you can see from the list, you have quite a few products to choose from.

Appendix A has a list of core platform products

Characterizing Your Project

Before you try to select a product, you first need to understand the requirements of your project. Are you developing a new application, or extending an existing application? Is the application for internal or external use (or both)? Are you building a corporate application, or will you sell the application to others? Will you sell it as packaged software, or as a service? Which programming languages will you use? Which operating systems will the service run on? Will it run on a server, or do you prefer to embed it in an application or device? If it will be server-based, what Web server or application server do you prefer to use? What about the client environment? Keep in mind that you may implement your clients using

Understand your project before trying to select a product

Chapter 9 Evaluation Guidelines

a different Web service platform from the one you use to implement your servers.

Characterize your server platform

In particular, you need to characterize the environment that will host your Web service. Technically, a Web service is simply an interface to an application. The application runs in a specific environment, which I refer to as its **operating platform**. You must find a Web services platform that fits with this operating platform.

Your service needs to work with your existing environment

Your operating platform is an amalgam of infrastructure technologies. Even if you have the luxury of writing a brand new application from scratch, you will probably need to link the application with many parts of your existing operating platform. Key components of your operating platform are as follows:

- Operating system
- Programming language
- Web server
- Application server
- Database server
- Directory server
- Security infrastructure
- Management infrastructure
- Workflow systems
- Business rule engines
- Transaction management infrastructure

Nontechnical factors will affect your decision

You also need to consider a number of nontechnical factors. What is your budget? Do you have existing license agreements with certain vendors? Do you prefer integrated solutions or best of breed? How does your company feel about working with startups? How does your company feel about open source? These factors can definitely affect your product selection.

Making the Initial Cut

Appendix B provides a questionnaire that can help you characterize the key attributes of your project. These attributes will help you understand your requirements, which in turn will help you determine which products best fit your project.

These attributes will help you select the right product

Making the Initial Cut

Start your selection process by identifying your available options. Invariably, you want to make your first cut based on language and operating system. You also should consider licensing and support issues.

Make your first cut based on language and operating system

Language and Operating System

A Web services platform supports a limited set of languages and operating systems. For example, the Microsoft .NET Framework runs on Windows 98, Windows ME, Windows 2000, Windows XP, Windows XP Embedded, Windows CE, and Windows Server 2003. .NET is not available for Linux or UNIX systems, nor does it run on Windows 3.1 or Windows 95. It supports services developed using any of the Visual Studio .NET languages, but it cannot host services developed using Java or previous versions of the Visual Studio languages, such as Visual Basic 6.0. You can deploy .NET services in the IIS Web server and the ASP.NET application server, but you cannot deploy them in a Java application server, such as WebLogic or WebSphere, even if it is running on a Windows operating system.

.NET runs on Windows and supports Visual Studio .NET

The .NET platform is compatible with, but not the same as, Microsoft's previous operating system infrastructure, which was based on the Component Object Model (COM). If you would like to create a Web API for an application running on Windows 95 or an application written using Visual Basic 6.0 or Visual C++ 6.0, then you must use a Web service platform that supports COM. For

You must use a different platform to support Visual Basic 6.0

Chapter 9   Evaluation Guidelines

example, you could use Microsoft SOAP Toolkit or Simon Fell's PocketSOAP.

EntireX supports CICS/COBOL

If you want to create a Web API for an application running on a non-Windows platform, then you need a platform that supports your application programming language on that operating system. For example, if your application is written in COBOL and runs in CICS on OS/390, you must find a Web services platform that supports CICS/COBOL on OS/390. In this situation you might consider using IBM WebSphere Studio Enterprise Edition or Software AG EntireX Communicator, which can generate Web service adapters for CICS COBOL applications.

WASP, LEIF, and gSOAP support C++ on UNIX

If your application is written in C++ and runs on UNIX, you must find a Web services platform that supports C++ on UNIX. For example, Systinet WASP Server for C++, Rogue Wave LEIF, and the open source gSOAP project support C++ on UNIX.

Selecting a Java Platform

There are more than two dozen platforms for Java

If your application is written in Java, you have a much wider array of choices. There are more than two dozen Web services platforms for Java. Although all of them support the Java programming language, each has its platform support limits. You must find a Web services platform that supports Java on your preferred operating platform.

Most J2EE application servers include a Web services platform

Most J2EE application server vendors—including BEA, Borland, IBM, IONA, JBoss, Macromedia, Novell, Oracle, SAP, Sun, and Sybase—provide integrated support for Web services. These Web services platforms are nicely integrated with the application server, but most also have a hard dependency. For example, BEA WebLogic Workshop is designed to work with BEA WebLogic Server. BEA WebLogic Workshop supports only Web services developed with Java, and these Web services can be deployed only within BEA WebLogic Server.

Making the Initial Cut

Although your J2EE platform comes with Web services support, you may prefer to install a third-party Web services platform on your application server. These platforms—from organizations such as Apache, Cape Clear, Indiana University, IONA, Sun, Systinet, The Mind Electric, and Wingfoot—can run in a variety of J2EE application servers. If you have a requirement to support multiple application servers, one of these systems might be best for you. You can also use these platforms with J2EE application servers that don't provide a built-in Web services container, such as Orion Application Server.

You can also use a third-party platform with your J2EE server

You may find that the independent commercial platforms from Cape Clear, IONA, Novell, Systinet, and The Mind Electric offer better tools as well as better performance, scalability, management, and security facilities compared with most of the bundled platforms. Given that these platforms tend to be moderately priced, they are often well worth the added investment.

The independent platforms offer attractive features

If you don't already have a J2EE server, you don't need to get one just to run Web services. The third-party platforms run as a servlet, so you can also deploy them in a lightweight Web server or application server containing only a servlet engine, such as Apache Tomcat, Caucho Resin, Jetty, and Zeus Web Server.

Third-party platforms don't require a full J2EE environment

Some of these platforms permit you to embed a Web services platform in your application so that you don't need any type of Web server or application server. If you are building an application for wide distribution that requires simple administration, you might find this feature very appealing.

Some platforms can be embedded in an application

You'll notice that most Web services platforms for Java require a fairly modern version of Java. Most platforms require at least Java 1.3.1. Some platforms require Java 1.4. If your applications have been developed using an older version of Java, you must use a Web services platform that supports the version you are using.

Make sure that the platform supports the right version of Java

Chapter 9   Evaluation Guidelines

For mobile applications you'll need a J2ME implementation

If you intend to deploy a Web service client or service in a small device, such as a PDA or a mobile handset, then you may need to find a Web services platform that supports the Java 2 Micro Edition (J2ME) platform. In this situation you also want to look for implementations that have a very small footprint.

eSOAP supports RTOS environments

If you'd like to deploy a Web service client or server on an even smaller device, or if you don't have a JVM available for your embedded application, you'll need a SOAP implementation that supports that target platform. For example, EXOR International's eSOAP implementation is designed to run in very constrained environments in real-time operating systems (RTOSs), such as eCos and QNX. eSOAP supports Web services clients and servers written in C++, and clients written in Java.

Web services can run on almost any platform

You can build Web services using almost any programming language on any operating system. See Appendix A for a lengthy list of products organized by supported languages. You can use this list to determine which products match your language and platform requirements. You should consider performing evaluation tests on all products that make this first cut.

Licensing and Support Issues

What are your company policies regarding open source?

As part of your initial selection process, you also should consider licensing and support issues. Licensing issues can be particularly important if you are building a commercial product. Also, your company might have policies regarding open source licensing. The product list in Appendix A includes licensing information.

Web services infrastructure is not very expensive

For the most part, you'll find that Web services infrastructure is not very expensive. Many Web services platforms are available as open source or free software. Some platforms are bundled with other products, such as an operating system, a language platform, an application server, or an application development tool. Other platforms are sold as separate commercial software products. The high-end commercial Web services platforms generally sell for less than $5,000 per CPU on the server. In contrast to other middleware technologies, most vendors don't charge for client runtime systems.

If you intend to create a product based on Web services, you could create your own Web services platform, or you could build a derivative product based on an existing platform. I don't recommend that you build your own platform unless you have extensive expertise in distributed computing technologies. Building a Web services platform requires a significant investment in time and resources. Consider for a moment the amount of effort that has been invested in the Apache Axis project. Apache Axis is an open source project sponsored by the Apache Software Foundation. This project started in February 2001. More than 30 software engineers from companies such as Borland, CA, IBM, Macromedia, Sonic Software, and Systinet have contributed to this project, and many of these people have worked full-time on Axis. Quite a few of them had previous experience building other Web services platforms. Even with this large and experienced team, it took 19 months to complete the v1.0 release.

I don't recommend that you try to build your own platform

In general, I recommend that you build on top of an existing platform. Keep in mind, though, that if you build a derivative product, you must obtain a license to redistribute the platform software.

You need a license to redistribute someone else's software

By definition, you can redistribute any software that is licensed using an open source license. Apache Axis, Apache SOAP, PocketSOAP, White Mesa, gSOAP, XSOAP, kSOAP, and most of the scripting implementations are licensed using an open source license. You should review the terms of each open source license. Some open source licenses, such as the GNU General Public License (GPL), impose strict rules on how you can license your derivative products. Other open source licenses, such as Apache Source License,

The GPL license imposes strict rules on how you can license derivative products

Artistic License, BSD License, CNRI Python License, and MIT License, don't impose the same licensing scheme on derivative products.

Always check the redistribution terms of free software

Many, but not all, free software products permit you to redistribute the software. You should always verify the terms of the free software license. In some cases you may need to get a separate OEM license to redistribute the software.

No one is paid to provide support for open source software

If you use open source or free software, you must be prepared to support the software yourself. Open source projects rarely provide formal support facilities. Users can ask questions on an e-mail discussion list, but no one is paid to answer those questions. Your developers will need to rely on the kindness and dedication of the user community to get answers. If you prefer to have a more structured and dependable support facility, you should consider licensing a Web service platform from a commercial vendor.

Evaluating Your Requirements

Make sure you understand your requirements

After you have made your initial cut, you now want to start evaluating products based on your project requirements. I like to start with performance and scalability. Make sure that you understand what your requirements are for these characteristics. How many concurrent clients will you need to support? What is the maximum acceptable response time? Make sure that you account for both average and peak requirements.

Performance and Scalability

Performance and scalability may vary

You'll find that there can be an enormous difference in performance among the various platforms. For example, among the current crop of products, the independent commercial Java platforms from Cape Clear, IONA, Novell, Systinet, and The Mind Electric perform about an order of magnitude faster than those from

Evaluating Your Requirements

Apache Axis and Sun JWSDP. The discrepancy becomes more pronounced as you scale up the number of concurrent users. You'll get your best possible performance from the portable C++ implementations.

The deployment configuration of an individual product can also affect performance and scalability. For example, Systinet WASP Server for Java achieves its best raw performance (measured as messages per second with one user) when configured as a stand-alone server, but it delivers its best scalability (messages per second with many users) when installed in a cluster-enabled application server.

Scalability may vary based on configuration

I strongly recommend that you perform internal benchmarks. Don't just accept the vendors' published benchmarks. Run your own benchmarks, simulating the requirements of your production applications. SOAP processing performance varies dramatically based on the length and complexity of the messages you exchange. Your benchmarks should test the various products with a variety of messages, in a variety of configurations, with a variety of user load levels. Also, ask your vendors for customer testimonials. Find out from them how well the performance claims match up to real experience.

Run benchmarks that simulate the requirements of your production applications

Standards Support and Interoperability

Web services support cross-platform integration. Chances are extremely high that you will not have a homogenous Web services environment. You want to make sure that your Web services platforms interoperate easily with other platforms. Therefore you want to look for platforms that fully support the Web services standards. The most critical standards to look for are SOAP 1.1, WSDL 1.1, and XML Schema 1.0.[1] A Web services platform should support all

A Web service platform should support SOAP 1.1, WSDL 1.1, XML Schema 1.0, and UDDI 2.0

---

[1] By XML Schema 1.0 I'm referring to the W3C XML Schema Recommendation dated May 2001.

Chapter 9   Evaluation Guidelines

features of these specifications. The XML Schema standard can be especially tricky. Early SOAP implementations predated the formal W3C XML Schema Recommendation that was published in May 2001, and these implementations may use older, prestandard versions of XML Schema rather than the final recommendation. For example, Apache SOAP uses the 1999 XML Schema draft specification. Apache SOAP also does not support WSDL 1.1. If you intend to use UDDI, you should make sure that your platform supports UDDI V2 (or later).

Make sure that the platform supports the WS-I Basic Profile

Even if a Web services platform fully supports the specifications, you still might have trouble with interoperability. The SOAP 1.1 and WSDL 1.1 specifications contain a number of ambiguities that cause integration headaches. WS-I[2] has defined a Basic Profile that provides guidance to ensure interoperable Web services based on SOAP 1.1, WSDL 1.1, and UDDI 2.0. The WS-I Basic Profile prohibits the use of the SOAP Encoding style. You must use Document/Literal or RPC/Literal rather than RPC/Encoded SOAP messaging. As of this writing, a number of platforms still use RPC/Encoded by default, and some of them provide limited or no support for Document/Literal and RPC/Literal. Make sure that the platform supports the WS-I profile.

Look for platforms that use compatible complex type containers

You're very likely to encounter integration headaches when using complex data structures. Mapping complex types is by far the most challenging part of cross-language interoperability. There are no formal standards that specify how to map a complex programming language structure, such as a **linked list** or a **hash table**, to the XML Schema type system, so each vendor must design its own mapping system. Unfortunately WS-I has not yet attempted to tackle this interoperability issue. The complex programming language structures are referred to as **collections**. A corresponding XML Schema

---

[2] See Chapter 4 for information about WS-I.

Evaluating Your Requirements

type structure is referred to as a **container**. The interoperability issue comes into play when one Web services platform cannot properly interpret the containers generated by another Web services platform. In particular, Apache Axis uses containers that are incompatible with those of Microsoft .NET. Developers are forced to write custom serialization routines, and that greatly reduces their productivity. Look for platforms that provide container types that enable compatibility with both Apache Axis and Microsoft .NET.

Extensibility Features

Most Web services platforms provide a basic communications environment that supports simple Web services. Going forward you'll almost certainly want to start using a few advanced features, such as security, transactions, asynchronous invocations, alternative transport facilities, message correlation, reliable delivery, message transformation, and version control. As mentioned in Chapter 3, SOAP provides a built-in extension mechanism that allows you to add extended middleware functionality to the message processing system. But the SOAP specification doesn't define how a Web services platform should implement these extensions. When you're evaluating a platform, determine which facilities it offers to let you extend the environment. Platforms generally support extensibility using proxies and message processing interceptors.

Assess how easy it is to add advanced middleware capabilities

Proxy Interceptors

As mentioned in Chapter 8, you can use a Web services management extension to add extended middleware functionality to a Web services platform. These systems work with most core platforms, and they tend to be easy to configure. They allow you to add security, reliability, load balancing, transactions, and version control functionality.

Proxies can add advanced functionality to any platform

In their simplest configuration, these extensions operate as a proxy that intercepts messages in transit between the client and

Third-party management extensions can add significant overhead

the service. As mentioned in Chapter 8, this configuration imposes significant overhead. These systems operate outside the core platform's SOAP message processing system, and this means that your SOAP messages must be processed twice: once by the management extension and again by the core platform. SOAP message processing is the most time-consuming part of Web services communications, so double processing will impact your performance and scalability.

You should do middleware processing inline with your SOAP message processing

Many of these systems also allow you to configure the framework to work within the application server that hosts the SOAP server. For example, you can configure the interceptor to work as a servlet filter. This configuration is more optimized than the proxy interceptor because it removes an additional network hop, but it still imposes double message processing. A more efficient way to add extended middleware functionality is to use a extension that can plug right in to the core system's message processing system. To use this type of configuration, the core SOAP system must support message processing interceptors.

Message Processing Interceptors

An interceptor interrupts message processing to add custom functionality

A message processing interceptor interrupts the SOAP runtime's standard message processing system and allows you to add custom functionality to the process. Many platforms give you a mechanism to intercept a message at three or more stages as it passes through the SOAP message processor. At each interception point, you can take the message and perform a variety of functions in a predetermined chained sequence; then you hand it back to the SOAP processor to continue processing. Among other things, an interceptor can authenticate messages, validate and transform them, compress and decompress them, reject messages that exceed a certain size, and gather statistics about messages. An interceptor can also perform functions such as message header processing and custom serialization of message contents. This interception methodology is defined as part of the JAX-RPC API specification, so many Java platforms use it.

Some platforms extend the basic interceptor model with a slightly friendlier interception API that supports specific types of interceptors. A typed API passes the message to a specific message handler at a specific point in the message processing sequence. A typed API makes it much easier for the developer or administrator to define and manage the chained sequence of interception handlers. A typed API also makes it easier for the developer to obtain the specific bits and pieces of the message that the handler needs to process. For example, if you are developing a header processor, a typed header processor API allows the developer to quickly and easily pull the required header element from the SOAP message. Without a typed API, the developer would have to write code to parse the entire message to find the specific header to process.

A typed interceptor API passes the message to a specific handler during the process

Multiple Transport Support

The SOAP specification requires only one transport protocol, and that is HTTP. For that reason some Web services platforms support only HTTP. Yet the SOAP specification allows you to use any transport protocol to exchange messages. Quite a few SOAP platforms now support SMTP, JMS, and other transports. Although JMS limits your interoperability, it gives you increased reliability. Keep this point in mind as you evaluate products, especially if you anticipate that you may need to use other transports. Evaluate how much effort is involved in switching from one transport to another.

Many products support multiple transports

Security

As mentioned in Chapter 5, the industry is making great progress in defining security standards for Web services. Although Web services security hasn't yet been fully standardized, that doesn't mean you can't build secure, interoperable Web services. Most Web services platforms provide basic security features. If you need a secure

Most platforms provide basic security features

Chapter 9   Evaluation Guidelines

environment, you can use almost any platform to do it. The question is whether you have enough control to suit your requirements.

You can implement security at various levels in the infrastructure

There are five basic security functions: confidentiality, integrity, nonrepudiation, authentication, and authorization. You can implement these functions at three levels within the infrastructure: transport level, application level, and XML level. As you move up the stack, you get much finer control over security.

Most platforms support transport-level security

Almost every Web services platform provides support for security at the transport level. First, you can encrypt your messages using HTTPS and SSL. Encryption ensures message confidentiality and integrity.

HTTP supports two authentication mechanisms

You can also use the transport to perform authentication. HTTP provides two popular authentication mechanisms: HTTP Basic and HTTP Digest. HTTP Basic offers minimal security because it passes user and password information in clear text. You should always use SSL when using HTTP Basic. HTTP Digest doesn't require SSL because it encrypts the authentication information. If you are using SSL, you can also use public key authentication, which is the strongest transport-level authentication mechanism.

Look for platforms that support multiple authentication mechanisms

For the most part, transport-level security works. It is very easy to use. It operates completely transparently to the client, the service, the developer, and the administrator. The only problem you might encounter is in terms of the authentication mechanisms supported. Microsoft uses HTTP Digest by default. A number of Java platforms support only HTTP Basic. For easiest interoperability, choose a platform that supports multiple authentication mechanisms.

Application-level security gives you more control

Although transport-level security is easy, it doesn't give you very much control. In particular, transport-level security really doesn't support authorization. To implement different access control policies for different groups of users accessing different services, you must also perform security at the application level.

Application-level security augments transport-level security. In addition to the transport-based authentication mechanisms, application-level security supports a number of very strong authentication mechanisms, including Kerberos, X.509 certificates, biometric authorization, and XML tokens.

It supports strong authentication

Regardless of the mechanism used for authentication, the application-level security system associates each authenticated user with a **principal** security identifier. This principal enables authorization. A principal represents a user, and it provides a reference key that can be used to verify the rights and privileges that have been granted to the user. Each time a user makes a request, the application-level security system can check to see whether the user is authorized to perform the action. You can delegate actions using principals—in effect passing the principal information as you route a request through a series of steps and services. Delegation becomes critical when you're using proxies and intermediaries or linking multiple services into a workflow. Application-level security also permits you to define trust domains, which simplify security administration.

It supports authorization

Many of the commercial Web services platforms now provide application-level security features. Compare and contrast the capabilities of each of your prospective platforms. How well does the Web services security management system fit in with your security infrastructure? Make sure that the Web services platform can work with your corporate security information store, such as LDAP, Active Directory, or Netegrity SiteMinder.

Make sure the product works with your system

XML-level security allows you to implement security at the message level. For example, you can use XML-level security to encrypt

Chapter 9 Evaluation Guidelines

XML-level security allows you to encrypt and sign your messages

and digitally sign the entire message or a portion of the message and to pass security authentication and authorization assertions. The evolving Web services security standards, including WS-Security and SAML, operate at this level. These standards are critical for comprehensive security in heterogeneous communications. Look for vendors that support WS-Security and SAML.

Add advanced security capabilities using third-party products

If your preferred platform doesn't provide the built-in security facilities you need, you can use a third-party Web services management extension, an XML firewall, or a hardware XML security appliance to add these capabilities. These solutions tend to be a bit more expensive than most Web services infrastructure products.

Tools

Tools are tied to a specific platform

Each Web services platform offers its own assortment of development, deployment, administration, and management tools. As I've said before, the tools are tied to a specific platform, so your platform selection determines which tools you can use.

Development Tools

Most platforms include class libraries and command line tools

Most platforms include a basic set of class libraries and command line tools. The class libraries contain the APIs and the code that a developer uses to build Web services. The command line tools consist of code generators, WSDL compilers, build utilities, deployment tools, and message monitoring tools. The Java platforms usually provide a set of Apache Ant tasks. Ant is the most popular Java build utility.

Evaluate how well the tools map complex types

The capabilities and the amount of automation supplied by these tools vary from product to product. Pay particular attention to how well the tools handle complex type mapping. Some tools can automatically generate all your serialization routines, regardless of the complexity of the data structures. Others can generate serialization routines only for simple structures or for structures that conform to certain conventions (such as JavaBeans). Also evaluate how well the tools support Document/Literal bindings versus RPC/Encoded bindings. Some tools generate serialization routines only for RPC/Encoded bindings.

Although an advanced developer often prefers to work with command line tools, some of your less experienced developers might find them a bit cryptic. These developers would probably prefer to use a visual programming tool. Some Web services platforms include visual development tools. Other vendors sell separate visual development tools. Still other vendors provide free plug-in tools that work with one or more popular integrated development environments. The IDE plug-ins add integrated support for Web services to the developer's native development environment. I prefer this last option, but that's my opinion. What counts is how your developers feel about it.

Choose tools based on your developers' experience and preferences

If you intend to use UDDI, you should look for platforms that include UDDI browsers, wizards, and utilities. These tools make it easy for developers to query a UDDI registry looking for service information or to publish service information to a registry. In particular, you should look for tools that include a UDDI browser that can view both public and private UDDI registries. You should also look for a UDDI registration utility that can generate UDDI registrations from a service's WSDL description. The OASIS UDDI-spec Technical Committee has published a set of WSDL-to-UDDI best practice documents that define a standard methodology to map WSDL descriptions to UDDI. Look for tools that automatically register services according to this methodology.

If you intend to use UDDI, look for UDDI wizards

Deployment and Administration

All Web services platforms provide some basic deployment and administration tools that you use to deploy and configure your Web services. Be aware that some platforms package the administration

Look for separation of development and administrative tools

Chapter 9   Evaluation Guidelines

tools with the development tools, and they don't really distinguish between the developer role and the administrator role.

Look for comprehensive administrative tools

As your efforts with Web services scale up, you'll need a reasonable way to manage and coordinate your Web services. Take a look at the administrative capabilities of each platform. It's nice if you can administer all your Web services across multiple platform servers from a single console. You should be able to start and stop platform servers. You should be able to deploy, undeploy, and redeploy services without restarting the server. You should be able to manage and administer service deployment options, such as interceptors, header processors, serialization routines, transformation routines, session management, and security access options. You should be able to see the status of all running services, and you should be able to turn on tracing and logging facilities for individual services. You'll find that commercial products tend to have much better administration facilities than the open source and free software products.

UDDI Registries

You should evaluate a UDDI server in the same way you assess your platform

If you intend to deploy a private UDDI registry, you should go through the same evaluation process as you do for your Web services platform. You should always select a product based on your requirements. In this situation, though, there are fewer options to evaluate. As of this writing, there are only 10 product-quality UDDI registries on the market.[3]

Some products are bundled with a Web services platform

Acumen, IBM, Select, and Systinet sell their UDDI registries as separate commercial products. Microsoft includes its registry with Windows Server 2003. Cape Clear, IONA, Oracle, and The Mind

---

[3] By "product-quality," I mean that a version 1.0 or later is available. I expect SAP to release a product-quality registry in 2003.

Electric bundle their registries with their Web services platforms, and they are not available as separate products. BEA and Pramati include Acumen AUDDI with their respective platforms. Sun provides a UDDI registry as part of JWSDP, although Sun's license prohibits you from using it for commercial purposes. Two open source registries are available, including Novell Nsure UDDI server (product quality) and jUDDI (not product quality).

Platform Considerations

As with a Web services platform, I suggest you start your selection process based on platform considerations. A UDDI registry server is an infrastructure-level Web service. It is an application that runs within a specific Web services platform on a specific operating system. It manages and provides access to UDDI registry information, which it stores in some type of data storage facility. The registry's underlying platform influences its performance and scalability. For optimum performance, you want to select a registry based on a fast Web services platform and an industrial-grade database.

A UDDI server runs in a Web service platform and uses a data store

Operating System

Most UDDI registries are implemented in Java, and they can run on Windows, Linux, and UNIX. Novell Nsure also runs on NetWare. Two products are limited to Windows: Microsoft's Enterprise UDDI Services is implemented using .NET and runs only on Windows Server 2003, and Select UDDIServer is implemented using Visual Basic and C++ and runs on all Windows platforms.

Most UDDI servers can run on Windows, Linux, and UNIX

Web Services Platform

Acumen, Novell, Select, and Systinet built their products as standalone applications. For the most part, you don't really see the Web services platform if you don't want to. Systinet gives you the option of deploying WASP UDDI in a wide choice of application servers if you prefer. IBM sells its registry separately from the WebSphere platform, but you must deploy it in WebSphere. Obviously, the

Acumen, Novell, Select, and Systinet are standalone products

Chapter 9 Evaluation Guidelines

embedded registries from Cape Clear, IONA, Oracle, and The Mind Electric are designed to run in their associated Web services platforms.

Data Store

Most registries use a relational database to store data

A UDDI registry uses some type of data store to manage and maintain the registry data. Because of the relational nature of the UDDI registry information, most implementations use a relational database management system (RDBMS). IBM requires that you use DB2. Oracle requires that you use Oracle 9i. Microsoft lets you use the Microsoft Data Engine or SQL Server. Cape Clear, jUDDI, and Systinet let you use any JDBC-compatible RDBMS. Select uses an object repository. Sun JWSDP and The Mind Electric GLUE use an XML database. Novell Nsure uses an LDAP directory. IONA can use either Cloudscape or LDAP.

UDDI and LDAP are very different applications

Some folks argue that it makes sense to consolidate UDDI with LDAP because both are directories of resources. But this idea makes about as much sense as storing your HR data in LDAP because they are both directories of employees.

A UDDI registry contains relational information

A UDDI registry is much more than a directory. It is a complex, multidimensional index of information about businesses, services, and service types. It contains a tremendous amount of relational information.

LDAP isn't suited to manage relational information

LDAP is a hierarchical directory and thus is not especially suited to this relational information. LDAP doesn't provide some of the basic capabilities that you need to manage relational data, such as multistep transactions, referential integrity, and query joins. You can make LDAP host this information, but I don't see the point. It's not as if you are really integrating the information. You still need to use two different programming APIs and two different browsing

UDDI Registries

utilities to see UDDI data versus LDAP data. I see no advantage to consolidating the information.

Some argue that LDAP provides better retrieval performance than a relational database, but this argument doesn't hold water in this situation. Many UDDI queries involve complex joins, and LDAP doesn't support joins. The registry application must implement this functionality, and its performance can't compare to that of a relational database.

An RDBMS provides better performance for complex joins

I also caution you against overburdening your production LDAP directory with this much relational work. I do think that it's a good idea to use LDAP (or Active Directory) to manage the security aspects of your UDDI registry and your Web services. For more on this idea, see the section on security later in this chapter.

Use LDAP to manage the security aspects of UDDI

Standards Support

All the UDDI registries that I've mentioned support UDDI V2 or later. I suggest that you not even consider a UDDI V1 registry. The UDDI V2 specifications define two programming APIs (inquiry and publication), an operators specification, and a replication specification. All UDDI registry servers should fully support the UDDI V2 inquiry and publication APIs.

A registry should support the UDDI V2 inquiry and publication APIs

The operators specification defines the behavior and operational parameters required of node operators in the public UDDI Business Registry (UBR). It doesn't apply to private registries. The replication specification describes the data replication process and programmatic interface used to replicate data across nodes in the UBR. You could use the replication specification to implement a replicated multinode private registry, but there are much more efficient ways to manage a replicated registry. (My first choice would be to use the database replication services supplied by a commercial database

The operators and replication specifications don't apply to private registries

system.) You cannot use the replication specification to replicate data from the UBR to a private registry. UDDI V2 does not support this capability. To my knowledge, no private UDDI implementations support replication.

UDDI V3 adds a subscription API

UDDI V3 adds a number of valuable features. In particular, it adds a subscription API, which allows a user (or registry) to subscribe to changes made in a UDDI registry. You can use the subscription API to keep two nodes synchronized. You can also use it to notify service users of any change to a service.

UDDI V3 adds cross-registry references

UDDI V3 also allows you to publish information across multiple registries. For example, a binding template in one registry can reference a tModel in another registry. You also can move a registry entry from one registry to another. For example, you can promote a business service from a test registry to a production registry.

UDDI V3 adds security policies

Perhaps most important of all, UDDI V3 adds support for security policies. The security architecture permits you to define and enforce policies for authentication, access control, data integrity, publication limits, and more.

UDDI V3 products should appear in 2003

As of this writing, only Systinet WASP UDDI supports the UDDI V3 subscription API. Select UDDIServer supports the UDDI V3 inquiry and publish APIs. None of the implementations supports the UDDI V3 cross-registry publishing and security APIs. UDDI V3-compliant products should appear in 2003.

User Interfaces

You can use any client API to talk to any UDDI registry

Applications communicate with a UDDI registry using the UDDI inquiry and publication SOAP APIs. You can construct those SOAP messages using any SOAP implementation, but the UDDI SOAP APIs are fairly complex. Therefore most UDDI registries include a UDDI client programming interface that automatically generates the appropriate UDDI SOAP APIs on behalf of the client. Microsoft and Select provide APIs for COM and .NET clients. The other vendors provide APIs for Java. You'll also find that many Web services platforms include a UDDI client API. Some vendors provide JAXR-compliant APIs. Most UDDI client APIs are free or open source. Because you can use any UDDI V1 or V2 client API to talk to any UDDI V2 registry, the client API isn't a particularly important selection factor. Have your developers experiment with the various APIs to see which one they like best.

API Extensions

The only reason you might want to consider the client API is if the vendor provides proprietary extensions to the basic API to improve usability and performance. In all cases, these extensions are optional, so you are never forced to use them. Keep in mind, though, that the extensions work only with the associated UDDI registry. You must make a judgment call as to whether you're willing to use proprietary extensions in order to take advantage of these features.

API extensions improve usability and performance but don't work with other systems

Visual Interfaces

Most UDDI registries provide a Web interface to support interactive access to the registry. You can use this interface to query or publish information to the registry. The UDDI browser should let you browse taxonomies. As mentioned earlier, many visual Web services development tools provide UDDI wizards to help developers browse the registry and publish services. These wizards don't usually come with the UDDI registry, though.

Most registries include a UDDI browser interface

Administration and Management

All registries should provide a set of administrative utilities. The UDDI specification does not define standards for UDDI administration, so each implementation will be unique. These administration

Each UDDI registry has its own administration tools

Chapter 9　Evaluation Guidelines

utilities should let you manage the UDDI application, its database, and the Web services hosting environment.

Taxonomy Management

Custom taxonomies are critical to a private UDDI

Custom taxonomies are a critical part of a private UDDI. You'll want to develop a number of taxonomies to help you properly categorize your services and service types. Without taxonomies, your UDDI registry is really nothing more than a directory.

You need administration tools to help you manage taxonomies

A private UDDI registry should give you administration tools to help you manage and maintain your taxonomies. A UDDI registry should let you define custom taxonomies and specify valid values for them. You should be able to maintain the taxonomies either within the registry or in an external taxonomy service. You also need a validation service that can perform validation checks at runtime.

Security

The Publication API uses HTTPS

The last area to evaluate in a UDDI registry is its support for security. All UDDI V2.0 registries must support transport-level security. According to the specification, the UDDI inquiry API communicates over HTTP, and the UDDI publication API communicates over HTTPS. If you are operating a private registry, though, you should be able to establish your own transport security policies. For example, you could require HTTPS for the inquiry API.[4]

Each registry uses its own mechanism for authentication

Every UDDI registry must also support authentication. The UDDI publication API requires that a user obtain an authentication token before storing any information to the database. The UDDI specification doesn't mandate any particular mechanism to

---

[4] UDDI V3.0 gives you much more control over registry security options.

manage and maintain user information, though, so each implementation uses a different method. For example, Microsoft uses Active Directory, and Novell uses LDAP. Some systems maintain a simple user/password database. There are obvious advantages to a system that supports your existing user account management system.

Authentication gives you only the simplest form of access control. Either users are authorized to access the registry, or they aren't. It gives you no control over what the user can do. Many registries permit you to assign users to user groups and then to assign privileges to those groups. You can use the groups to establish and enforce coarse-grained control policies. For example, you can say that members of a particular group can register no more than 10 services. Most UDDI registries give you this level of access control for administrative functions and the publication API. Acumen, Oracle, and Select give you more fine-grained control for update functions. These implementations permit you to define update rights by user for every element in the registry.

Most UDDI registries give you coarse access control for updates

As of this writing, only two registry implementations provide granular access control facilities that apply to both update and query operations: Novell Nsure and Systinet WASP. These two products give you the ability to define specific access rights, by user or group, for every element in the registry. For example, suppose you want to set up a UDDI registry for your distributor network. You can offer different services to your different distributors based on geographic location, sales volume, or some other criteria. With inquiry-based access control facilities, you can segregate your services automatically. A user from one distributor would be able to find only the services that pertain to that distributor. When selecting a product, consider your access control requirements.

Novell and Systinet give you fine-grained access control for inquiry and update operations

Chapter 9   Evaluation Guidelines

Executive Summary

You don't need much to start

To build Web services, you need to select some products. I wouldn't be surprised if you found the blizzard of Web services products intimidating. Fortunately, you don't need a lot of products for your pilot project. At a minimum you need Web services platforms for the client and server environments. Depending on your integration needs, you may need an adapter framework to help you build application adapters. You might also find it helpful to use some XML tools and testing and diagnostic tools.[5]

Requirements increase as your portfolio grows

When you begin to deploy multiple systems, you'll start to need a few more pieces. I strongly recommend that you get an operations-oriented Web services management extension. Your operations staff will certainly appreciate it. I also recommend that you set up a private UDDI registry to help manage your service assets, although not necessarily immediately. UDDI becomes more important as your portfolio of services increases and when you want to start offering these services to a wider constituency.

Base Your Selection on Project Requirements

Always select products based on project requirements

I can't stress enough how important it is that you select your products based on your project requirements. Before you start your product evaluation process, make sure that you understand your requirements, including factors such as operating platform, performance, scalability, reliability, availability, security, asynchrony, and transactions. Don't forget to characterize your nontechnical requirements, too. These requirements will influence your core platform selection. They will also help you determine whether you need any additional middleware-oriented management extensions or infrastructure-level services.

---

[5] See Chapter 8 for a definition of these product categories.

Executive Summary

Some of the most basic characteristics that I look for in a Web services platform are as follows:

- Standards support. Standards compliance ensures easier interoperability. At a minimum a platform should support SOAP 1.1, WSDL 1.1, UDDI 2.0, and XML Schema 1.0. Also look for WS-I Basic Profile compliance. If you're investigating solutions for Java, look for JAX-RPC compliance.
- Performance and scalability. You need to make sure that the platform will support your requirements. Run benchmarks that represent realistic applications and loads.
- Security. Figure out what your immediate security requirements are. Also consider what your future requirements might be. Investigate which security features are built into the platform, and which options are available to extend those features. For maximum flexibility, you'll want support for multiple authentication mechanisms and application-level authorization services. Determine what it would take to integrate the supplied security features with your security infrastructure. Look for support for WS-Security and SAML.
- Extensibility. Extensibility allows you to add functionality to the platform. I always assume that at some point I'm going to want to make the system do more than originally expected. Figure out which mechanisms the platform has that will help you extend or enhance the platform. How easy is it to write and configure interceptors and header processors? What's involved in adding support for emerging standards, such as SOAP 1.2, WSDL 1.2, WS-Security, WS-RM, WSDM, and others? What transports does the platform support beyond HTTP?
- Development. Make sure that your developers feel comfortable with the environment. What kinds of tools does the platform supply? How well do they fit with your developers' usual toolbox? How much of the development effort is

These are the most crucial evaluation factors

Chapter 9   Evaluation Guidelines

automated? How often does a developer have to tweak the generated code to make the applications work in real world scenarios?

❑ Management and administration. Make sure that your operations staff feels comfortable with the administrative tools supplied. What facilities are available to manage the Web services runtime using your traditional system management framework?

See for yourself and network with others to learn what you can

Don't just blithely believe the vendor claims. Run your own tests and benchmarks. Experiment with multiple products. Most vendors will give you a free evaluation period. Get feedback from both your development staff and your operations staff. Make your vendors give you references. It's especially nice if these organizations are doing projects somewhat similar in scope to yours. Take advantage of these contacts to learn whatever you can. Join user groups. Participate in discussions. Make the effort to get educated.

Charting Your Course

Start with a noncritical yet visible project

I hope this book has been helpful to you and that you are now prepared to start your voyage. My advice is that you take it easy and start slowly. Identify a noncritical but reasonably visible project. For your first pilot, I suggest that you choose a simple point-to-point integration project. It will give you a chance to learn the basics about the technology. Make sure that you constrain the scope of the project. Break it into attainable tasks, and chart your course.

Web services should support your business model

Don't build Web services just because they're cool. Make sure that you have a viable business model to go with the service. As a rule, your Web services should support or augment your existing business model. Web services should do things such as enhance sales, improve customer relationships, simplify customer or partner interaction, and streamline business processes.

Executive Summary

Don't get distracted by the software-as-a-service business model. If you don't have a viable ASP-style business model today, Web services won't help you create one. If you do have a viable ASP-style business model, you should definitely use Web services technology to provide programmable Web APIs to the business service. Just keep in mind that you are selling a business service, not the Web service. The Web service is simply one of many mechanisms you provide to your customers to use the business service. The technology and the business model are separate things.

Web services can support the ASP-style business model, too

For the time being, I recommend that you focus on integration. First and foremost, Web services help you integrate applications. And they do so at a fraction of the cost of traditional middleware technology.

Focus on integration

After you get comfortable with the concepts, you can start tackling some really high-payoff initiatives.[6] Here are examples:

After you get comfortable, tackle some high-payoff initiatives

- ❏ Use Web services to support collaboration, allowing your people to more effectively share information so that they can be better and more efficient at their jobs.
- ❏ Use Web services to give your staff a 360-degree view of your customers, resulting in higher productivity, stronger customer relationships, and lowered attrition rates.
- ❏ Use Web services to integrate your business process across departmental and organizational boundaries, eliminating friction, reducing costs, and improving quality.
- ❏ Use Web services to provide programmable access to your business process for your customers and business partners, making it easier for them to do business with you and producing higher sales.

---

[6] See Chapter 7 for case studies of high-payoff initiatives.

Chapter 9   Evaluation Guidelines

- Use Web services to consolidate redundant application systems, resulting in substantial savings from streamlining systems operations and increasing process efficiencies.
- Use Web services to make it easier to manage your legacy application assets, significantly lowering the total cost of ownership of these systems.
- Use Web services to coordinate your portal initiatives, making it easier for your staff, your partners, and your customers to interact with you. Web services also make it easier for your portal to support multiple user access channels such as IVR and the wireless Web.

Web services are lubrication for your business

I'm sure you can think of other ways to exploit Web services. They have enormous potential. Web services simplify integration. Integration helps your business operate better. Think of Web services as lubrication for your business.

Appendix A

Web Services Product List

Quite a few products are available that you can use to implement Web services. This appendix provides a list of many of these products. For brevity's sake, I am constraining this list to only the basic SOAP platforms and UDDI registry servers. I am aware of more than 90 SOAP implementations, although many of them are research projects, and some are no longer available. For the most part I have listed only platforms that are "product quality"—meaning that a version 1.0 or later is available. The products are organized by supported language or platform and are listed in alphabetical order.

More than 90 SOAP implementations are available

.NET Platform

Microsoft is the only provider of a .NET platform. The .NET platform is available for Windows CE, Windows XP Embedded, Windows 98, Windows ME, Windows NT 4.0, Windows 2000, Windows XP, and Windows Server 2003. Ximian and GNU are developing open source implementations of the .NET platform for Linux and UNIX operating systems, although these implementations are not yet product quality.

Microsoft is the only supplier of a .NET platform

Vendor	Microsoft Corporation
Product	.NET Framework
OS Support	Windows 98, ME, NT, 2000, XP, Server 2003
	Requires IIS and ASP.NET for deployment
Languages	Visual Basic .NET, Visual C++ .NET, Visual C# .NET, Visual J# .NET, Visual FoxPro, other .NET languages
Licensing	Free and redistributable (not open source)

Microsoft .NET Framework

Appendix A   Web Services Product List

Microsoft .NET Compact Framework

Vendor	Microsoft Corporation
Platform	.NET Compact Framework
OS Support	Windows CE / CE .NET
Languages	Visual Basic .NET, Visual C# .NET
Licensing	Commercial

COM Platform

Visual Studio 6.0 uses COM

A COM platform is a Windows platform that predates or does not use the .NET platform. Applications developed using Visual Studio 6.0 execute in a COM platform.

Microsoft SOAP Toolkit

Vendor	Microsoft Corporation
Product	SOAP Toolkit
OS Support	Windows 98, ME, NT, 2000, XP, Server 2003
Languages	Visual Basic, Visual C++, Visual J#, other COM languages
Licensing	Free and redistributable (not open source)

PocketSOAP

Provider	Simon Fell
Products	PocketSOAP (client)
OS Support	PocketPC, Windows 95, 98, ME. NT4, 2000, XP
Languages	VBScript, Visual Basic, Visual C++, Visual C#, eMbedded Visual Basic, eMbedded Visual C++, other COM languages
Licensing	Open Source (Mozilla Public License)

4s4c

Provider	Simon Fell
Product	4s4c (server)
OS Support	Windows NT4, 2000
Languages	Any COM component (uses OLE Automation)
Licensing	Open Source (Mozilla Public License)

SQLData SOAP Client

Vendor	SQLData Systems
Product	C++ Library for SOAP Client

OS Support	Windows 95, 98, NT4, 2000
Languages	Visual C++ 6.0
Licensing	Commercial and OEM

Vendor	SQLData Systems	*SQLData*
Product	SOAP Server	*SOAP Server*
OS Support	Windows 95, 98, NT4, 2000	
Languages	Visual C++ 6.0, COM	
Licensing	Commercial and OEM	

Vendor	White Mesa Software	*White Mesa*
Product	White Mesa SOAP Services	
OS Support	Windows NT4	
Languages	Visual C++ 6.0	
Licensing	Open Source (modified MIT license)	

Portable C and C++ Platforms

A few Web services platforms are designed to support C and C++ applications on Windows, Linux, UNIX, and other operating systems. These platforms deliver the best performance of all SOAP implementations.

Cross-platform products for C and C++

Vendor	EXOR International Consortium	*eSOAP*
Product	eSOAP (designed for embedded systems)	
OS Support	RTEMS, eCos, QNX, Linux, Solaris, Windows	
Languages	C++	
Licensing	Commercial	

Provider	Florida State University	*gSOAP*
Product	gSOAP	
OS Support	Windows, Linux, Mac OS X, UNIX	
Languages	C and C++	
Licensing	Open Source (gSOAP Public License, based on MPL)	

Appendix A Web Services Product List

Rogue Wave LEIF

Vendor	Rogue Wave
Product	Lightweight Enterprise Integration Framework (LEIF)
OS Support	Windows, Linux, UNIX
Languages	C++
Web Server	LEIF application server (included)
Licensing	Commercial

Systinet WASP Server for C++

Vendor	Systinet
Product	WASP Server for C++
OS Support	Windows (Win 32 and CE), Linux, UNIX
Web Servers	Apache Server, Microsoft IIS, Sun ONE Web Server
	Supports stand-alone and embedded configurations
Languages	C, C++
Licensing	Commercial, OEM, and Source

Java Platforms

Java products for J2EE, J2SE, or J2ME

There are more than two dozen SOAP implementations for the Java platform. Some implementations are packaged with a J2EE application server; other implementations can be deployed in a J2SE environment or in a third-party J2EE application server; still other implementations can be deployed in a J2ME environment.

J2EE Platforms

Most J2EE application servers support Web services

Most J2EE application servers now include integrated support for Web services. Management and security for these systems are integrated with the application server environment. BEA, IONA, Novell, Oracle, and Sybase have developed their own SOAP implementations. Borland, IBM, JBoss, Macromedia, and Pramati use the Apache Axis platform. Sun uses the Java APIs for XML (JAX) reference implementations, collectively known as the Java Web Services Development Pack (JWSDP). You can also get the Axis, IONA, Novell, and Sun JWSDP platforms separately. Although

Java Platforms

these application servers include a SOAP implementation, you can also install a third-party platform in these systems.

Vendor	BEA Systems	*BEA WebLogic*
Product	WebLogic Server, WebLogic Workshop	
OS Support	Windows, Linux, UNIX, Mid-range, and Mainframe	
Languages	Java 1.3.1 or later	
UDDI	Includes Acumen AUDDI	
Licensing	Commercial	

Vendor	Borland Software Corporation	*Borland Enterprise Server*
Product	Enterprise Server (Apache Axis)	
OS Support	Windows, Linux, UNIX	
Languages	Java 1.3.1 or later	
Licensing	Commercial	

Vendor	IBM Corporation	*IBM WebSphere*
Product	WebSphere Application Server (Apache Axis)	
OS Support	Windows, Linux, UNIX, iSeries, zSeries (Linux)	
Languages	Java 1.3.1 or later	
UDDI	Network edition includes WebSphere UDDI	
Licensing	Commercial	

Vendor	IONA	*IONA Orbix E2A ASP*
Product	Orbix E2A Application Server Platform (IONA XMLBus)	
OS Support	Windows, Linux, UNIX, OpenVMS, OS/390, z/OS	
Languages	Java 1.3.1, CORBA (C++ and Java)	
UDDI	Included	
Licensing	Commercial	

Provider	JBoss Group	*JBoss.net*
Product	JBoss.net (Apache Axis)	
OS Support	Windows, Linux, UNIX	

Appendix A   Web Services Product List

	Languages	Java 1.3.1 or later
	Licensing	Open source (GNU Lesser General Public License)
Macromedia JRun	Vendor	Macromedia
	Product	JRun (Apache Axis)
	OS Support	Windows, Linux, UNIX
	Languages	Java 1.3.1 or later
	Licensing	Commercial
Novell exteNd	Vendor	Novell
	Product	exteNd Application Server (jBroker Web)
	OS Support	Windows, Linux, UNIX
	Languages	Java 1.3.1
	Licensing	Commercial
Oracle 9i	Vendor	Oracle
	Product	Oracle 9i Application Server
	OS Support	Windows, Linux, UNIX
	Languages	Java 1.3.1 or later, PL/SQL
	UDDI	Included
	Licensing	Commercial
Pramati Server	Vendor	Pramati
	Product	Pramati Server (Apache Axis)
	OS Support	Windows, Linux, UNIX
	Languages	Java 1.3.1 or later
	UDDI	Includes Acumen AUDDI
	Licensing	Commercial
SAP Web Application Server	Vendor	SAP
	Product	Web Application Server
	OS Support	Windows, Linux, UNIX, Mid-range, and Mainframe
	Languages	Java, ABAP
	Licensing	Commercial

Vendor	Sun Microsystems	*Sun ONE*
Product	Sun ONE Application Server (Sun JWSDP)	*Application Server*
OS Support	Windows, Linux, UNIX	
Languages	Java 1.4.0_02 or later	
UDDI	Includes JWSDP UDDI (noncommercial)	
Licensing	Platform Edition is free (not open source)	
	Commercial licensing for Standard/Enterprise Editions	
	OEM licensing required for redistribution	

Vendor	Sybase	*Sybase EAServer*
Product	EAServer	
OS Support	Windows, Solaris	
Languages	Java 1.3.1	
	Connectors for Stored Procedures, CICS, ERP adapters	
	PowerBuilder (client only)	
Licensing	Commercial	

J2SE Platforms

A number of Web services platforms for Java do not require a complete J2EE application server environment. These platforms can be deployed in a stand-alone fashion on J2SE or as a plug-in to a Web server or an application server. The commercial products offer excellent performance.

Many Java platforms don't require J2EE

Provider	Apache Software Foundation	*Apache Axis*
Product	Axis	
OS Support	Any J2SE platform	
App Servers	Any Servlet 2.2 or later servlet engine	
Languages	Java 1.3 or later	
Licensing	Open Source (Apache Software License)	

Provider	Apache Software Foundation	*Apache SOAP*
Product	SOAP (superceded by Axis)	
OS Support	Any J2SE 1.2 or later platform	

Appendix A   Web Services Product List

	App Servers	Any Servlet 2.2 engine
	Languages	Java 1.2 or later
	Licensing	Open Source (Apache Software License)
Cape Clear	Vendor	Cape Clear
	Product	Cape Clear Server
	OS Support	Windows, Linux, Solaris
	App Servers	WebLogic, WebSphere, JBoss, others on request
		Supports stand-alone configuration
	Languages	Java 1.3.1 or later
	UDDI	Included with Enterprise edition
	Licensing	Commercial
IONA XMLBus	Vendor	IONA
	Product	XMLBus
	OS Support	Windows, Linux, UNIX
	App Servers	WebLogic, WebSphere, Orbix
		Supports stand-alone configuration
	Languages	Java 1.3.1, J2ME (client only)
	UDDI	Included
	Licensing	Commercial
Killdara Vitiris	Vendor	Killdara
	Product	Vitiris
	OS Support	Windows, Linux, and Solaris
	App Servers	Embedded configurations only
	Languages	Java 1.4
	Licensing	OEM
Novell jBroker Web	Vendor	Novell
	Product	exteNd jBroker Web
	OS Support	Windows, Linux, Solaris
	App Servers	Any Servlet 2.1 or later servlet engine
		Supports stand-alone configuration

Java Platforms

Languages	Java 1.2 or later	
Licensing	Commercial	

Vendor	Sun Microsystems	*Sun JWSDP*
Product	Java Web Services Developer Pack (JWSDP)	
OS Support	Windows, Linux, Solaris	
App Servers	Any Servlet 2.1 or later servlet engine	
Languages	Java 1.3.1 or later	
UDDI	Included (noncommercial)	
Licensing	Free (not open source) and redistributable	
	Restricted license for JWSDP Registry	

Vendor	Systinet	*Systinet WASP*
Product	WASP Server for Java	*Server for Java*
OS Support	Most operating systems with Java 1.3.1 or higher	
App Servers	Any Servlet 2.1 or later servlet engine	
	Supports stand-alone and embedded configurations	
Languages	Java 1.3.1 or later	
Licensing	Commercial and OEM; free single CPU license	

Vendor	The Mind Electric	*The Mind*
Product	GLUE	*Electric GLUE*
OS Support	Windows, Linux, UNIX	
App Servers	Any Servlet 2.1 or later servlet engine	
	Supports stand-alone and embedded configurations	
Languages	Java 1.1.8 or later	
UDDI	Included with Professional edition	
Licensing	Standard edition: Free (not open source)	
	Professional edition: Commercial and OEM	

Vendor	Wingfoot	*Wingfoot Parvus*
Product	Parvus	
OS Support	Windows, Linux, UNIX	
App Servers	Any Servlet 2.2 or later servlet engine	

Appendix A   Web Services Product List

	Languages	Java 1.2 or later
	Licensing	Free and redistributable (not open source)
XSOAP	Provider	Indiana University Extreme! Computing Lab
	Product	XSOAP
	OS Support	Any system running J2SE 1.3 or later
	App Servers	Any Servlet 2.2 or later servlet engine
	Languages	Java 1.3 or later
	Licensing	Open Source (IU Extreme! Lab Software License)

J2ME and KVM Platforms

Web services can run on consumer devices such as mobile phones and PDAs

Some Web services platforms are designed for consumer devices, embedded systems, and smart cards. These tiny-footprint systems can run on the J2ME and KVM platforms. The KVM is an extremely small Java Virtual Machine that requires as little as 128K of memory.

eSOAP	Vendor	EXOR International/Embedding.net
	Product	eSOAP
	OS Support	RTEMS, eCos, QNX, Linux, Windows
	Languages	J2ME, C++
	Licensing	Commercial
kSOAP	Provider	Enhydra
	Product	kSOAP (subset of SOAP1.1 features)
	OS Support	Any platform with J2ME CLDC
	Languages	Java 1.4
	Licensing	Open Source (Enhydra Public License)
Wingfoot SOAP Client	Vendor	Wingfoot
	Product	SOAP Client
	Platforms	J2ME, J2SE, J2EE
	Languages	Java 1.2 or later
	Licensing	Free and redistributable (not open source)

Other Languages and Platforms

Web services platforms are available for many other languages, including scripting languages (such as AppleScript, Perl, and Python) and programming languages (such as COBOL, Delphi, and Smalltalk). Many of these platforms are not product quality, although quite a few people manage to use them in production mode, so I have included a few pre-version 1.0 products in this section.

Web service platforms are available for many other languages

Scripting Languages

Vendor	Apple Computer	*AppleScript*
Product	AppleScript Studio (client)	
OS Support	Mac OS X	
Languages	AppleScript	
Licensing	Free with Mac OS X	

Vendor	Macromedia	*ColdFusion*
Product	ColdFusion SOAP (part of ColdFusion MX)	
OS Support	Windows, Linux, Solaris	
Languages	ColdFusion ActiveScript	
Licensing	Commercial	

Vendor	Userland	*Frontier*
Product	Frontier	
OS Support	Windows, Mac OS 7.5.5 or later, Mac OS X	
Languages	Frontier	
Licensing	Commercial	

Vendor	Active State	*Perl*
Product	ActivePerl	
OS Support	Windows, Linux, Solaris	
Languages	Perl 5.8.0.804	
Licensing	Free and redistributable (partially open source)	

Appendix A   Web Services Product List

Perl
- Provider: Paul Kulchenko
- Product: SOAP::Lite for Perl
- OS Support: Windows, Linux, UNIX
- Languages: Perl 5.004 or later
- Licensing: Open Source (Artistic License)

PHP
- Provider: Dietrich Ayala
- Product: NuSOAP
- OS Support: Windows, Linux
- Languages: PHP
- Licensing: Open Source (GNU Lesser General Public License)

PHP
- Vendor: eZ Systems
- Product: eZ SOAP (part of eZ publish SDK)
- OS Support: Windows, Linux, UNIX
- Languages: PHP
- Licensing: Open Source (GNU General Public License)
- OEM source license for closed source applications

Python
- Providers: Cayce Ullman and Brian Matthews
- Product: SOAP.py
- OS Support: Windows, Linux, UNIX
- Languages: Python
- Licensing: Open Source (CNRI Python License)

Python
- Provider: Rich Salz
- Product: ZSI–Zolara SOAP Infrastructure
- OS Support: Windows, Linux, UNIX
- Languages: Python 2.0 or later
- Licensing: Open Source (CNRI Python License)

Ruby
- Provider: Hiroshi Nakamura
- Product: SOAP4R

Other Languages and Platforms

OS Support	DOS, Windows, Mac OS X, BeOS, Amiga, Acorn, OS/2, Linux, UNIX	
Languages	Ruby 1.6 or later	
Licensing	Open Source (GNU General Public License)	

Provider	Pat Thoyts	*Tcl*
Product	TclSOAP	
OS Support	Windows, Linux, UNIX	
Languages	Tcl	
Licensing	Open Source (MIT License)	

Programming Languages

Vendor	IBM Corporation	*COBOL*
Product	Enterprise COBOL for z/OS and OS/390 v3.2	
OS Support	z/OS and OS/390	
Languages	COBOL	
Licensing	Commercial	

Vendor	Microfocus	*COBOL*
Product	EnterpriseLink	
OS Support	Access from Windows, Solaris, AIX	
	Access to OS/390, z/OS	
Languages	COBOL	
Licensing	Commercial	

Vendor	Software AG	*COBOL and*
Product	EntireX Communicator	*other languages*
OS Support	Windows, UNIX, Linux, OS/400, OpenVMS, OS/390, VSE, BS2000	
Languages	COBOL, Natural, RPG, C, C++, Java, COM, etc.	
Licensing	Commercial	

Appendix A   Web Services Product List

Delphi

Vendor	Borland
Products	DataSnap, BizSnap, WebSnap (part of Delphi/Kylix)
OS Support	Windows, Linux
Languages	Delphi
Licensing	Commercial

Cincom Smalltalk

Vendor	Cincom
Product	VisualWorks Opentalk SOAP (part of VisualWorks)
OS Support	Windows, Mac OS 9, Mac OS X, Linux, UNIX
Languages	Smalltalk
Licensing	Commercial

IBM Smalltalk

Vendor	IBM
Product	VisualAge Smalltalk Web Services (part of VisualAge)
OS Support	Windows, Linux, UNIX
Languages	Smalltalk
Licensing	Commercial

UDDI Registry Servers

A UDDI server can be embedded in a Web services platform or sold separately

Some Web services platforms include a UDDI registry server, although most do not. I've broken this list into two groups: those that are embedded in a Web services platform, and those that are available as separate commercial products. A UDDI registry is a Web service, so it must run in a specific Web services platform. The commercial products include a stand-alone Web services environment. A UDDI registry also requires some type of data store to house the registry information. Most implementations use a relational database, although some use an XML database, an object repository, or an LDAP directory.

UDDI Registry Servers

Embedded UDDI Registries

Cape Clear, IONA, Oracle, Sun, and The Mind Electric provide an embedded UDDI registry server with their Web services platform. (BEA and Pramati include the Acumen AUDDI registry, which is listed with the commercial implementations.) You can get these embedded UDDI registries only with their associated Web services platform. For the most part, these registries are basic UDDI implementations without a lot of extra features. Sun's implementation is not intended for commercial use. IONA's implementation offers some extended security features. Oracle's implementation provides extended security, synchronization, and taxonomy management features.

Embedded UDDI registries are supplied with a Web services platform

Vendor	Cape Clear	*Cape Clear*
WS Platform	Cape Clear Enterprise	
Data Store	Lutris InstantDB (included), Oracle 8i, any JDBC DB	
Licensing	Commercial	

Vendor	IONA	*IONA*
WS Platform	XMLBus and Orbix E2A ASP	
Data Store	Cloudscape (included) or LDAP	
Licensing	Commercial	

Vendor	Oracle	*Oracle*
WS Platform	Oracle 9iAS	
Data Store	Oracle 9i	
Licensing	Commercial	

Vendor	Sun Microsystems	*Sun*
WS Platform	Sun Java WSDP	
Data Store	Xindice (included)	
Licensing	Free; restricted use: noncommercial	

Vendor	The Mind Electric	*The Mind Electric*
WS Platform	The Mind Electric GLUE Professional	

Appendix A Web Services Product List

	Data Store	GLUE XML storage engine (included)
	Licensing	Commercial

Standalone UDDI Registries

These UDDI registries can be used with any Web services platform

Acumen, IBM, Microsoft, Novell, Select, and Systinet provide stand-alone UDDI registry implementations. Although the registry service is built using a specific Web service platform, the administration of the platform is mostly hidden. These registries can be used with any Web services platform. For the most part, these registries are commercial-grade systems with advanced features. Microsoft's UDDI registry is included as part of Windows Server 2003. It is not available for other operating systems. Select's UDDI registry runs on all Windows platforms. The other implementations are cross-platform solutions.

Acumen AUDDI

	Vendor	Acumen Technologies
	Product	AUDDI-SE
	OS Support	Most operating systems with Java 1.3.1 or higher
	WS Platform	AUDDI Engine (included)
		Runs stand-alone or in your choice of app server
	Data Store	iPlanet Directory Server, other JNDI-compliant LDAP servers
	Features	User management, access control (publish), usability
	Licensing	Commercial

IBM WebSphere UDDI Registry

	Vendor	IBM Corporation
	Product	WebSphere UDDI Registry
	OS Support	Windows, Linux, Solaris
	WS Platform	IBM WebSphere Application Server
	Data Store	IBM DB2 v7.2 or later
	Features	Usability
	Licensing	Commercial

Microsoft Enterprise UDDI Services

	Vendor	Microsoft
	Product	Enterprise UDDI Services (part of Windows Server 2003)

UDDI Registry Servers

OS Support	Windows Server 2003
WS Platform	.NET
Data Store	Microsoft Data Engine (default) or SQL Server 2000
Features	Integration with MCC and Active Directory
Licensing	Commercial

Vendor	Novell	*Novell Nsure*
Product	Nsure UDDI Server	*UDDI Server*
OS Support	Windows, NetWare, Linux, UNIX	
WS Platform	Apache Tomcat application (included)	
Data Store	Novell eDirectory (LDAP)	
Features	Access control (inquiry and publish)	
Licensing	Open Source (BSD License)	

Vendor	Select Business Solutions	*Select UDDIServer*
Product	Select UDDIServer	
OS Support	Windows	
WS Platform	ISAPI module (included)	
Data Store	Fujitsu Enabled (included)	
Features	Access control (publish), usability	
Licensing	Commercial	

Vendor	Systinet	*Systinet WASP*
Product	WASP UDDI	*UDDI*
OS Support	Most operating systems with Java 1.3.1 or higher	
WS Platform	Systinet WASP Server for Java (included)	
	Runs stand-alone or in your choice of app server	
Data Store	Oracle 8i, Microsoft SQL Server 2000, IBM DB2, IBM Cloudscape, Sybase ASE, Pointbase, PostgreSQL, or Hypersonic SQL (included)	
Features	User management, access control (inquiry and publish), usability, taxonomy management, V3 subscription API	
Licensing	Commercial and OEM	

Appendix B

Requirements Questionnaire

This questionnaire should help you identify your requirements as you evaluate products.

Operating Platform Attributes

1. Which operating system(s) will you use to host the service?
2. Which programming language(s) will you use to write the service?
3. Will you need an adapter to connect to a legacy application?
4. Which Web server(s) will you use?
5. Which application server(s) will you use?
6. Which database system(s) will you use?
7. Which user management system(s) do you use?
8. Which access control system(s) do you use?
9. Which management infrastructure(s) do you use?

Client Platform Attributes

1. Will you support internal or external clients (or both)?
2. Is there a chance that you will add new clients over time?
3. Will you have control over the client environment?
4. Which software distribution tool(s) do you have?
5. Which operating system(s) will host the clients?
6. Which programming language(s) will be used to write the clients?

Licensing Requirements

1. Are you developing an application for commercial use?
2. How many servers will you use to deploy the application?

Appendix B   Requirements Questionnaire

3. Are you developing a commercial product for resale?
4. Will you need to redistribute Web services platform software?
5. Does your company have any policies regarding open source software?
6. What are your support requirements?

Performance and Scalability Requirements

1. What do you view as the minimum acceptable latency for an online query?
2. What do you view as the minimum acceptable number of transactions per second that your service must perform?
3. What is your estimate for the average and peak number of concurrent users that will access the service?
4. When will you need to support these performance requirements?

Extensibility Features

1. Do you need to support transactions?
2. Do you need guaranteed message delivery?
3. Do you need to support asynchronous communications?
4. Do you need to support security? (See the next section for details.)
5. Do you need to support logging or auditing?
6. Do you need to support alternative transports?
7. Do you need to support automatic message transformation or version management?

Security Requirements

1. What type of authentication mechanism(s) do you need to support?
2. Is transport-level security sufficient to address your needs?

3. Do you need to restrict access to certain services?
4. Do you have an existing access authorization system?
5. Do you need to digitally sign your messages?
6. Do you need to support single sign-on?
7. Do you have an existing single sign-on solution?

Developer Preferences

1. How experienced is your developer staff?
2. How comfortable are they with command line tools?
3. Do they prefer to use visual tools?
4. What integrated development environments do they use?
5. Will you be using UDDI?

UDDI Requirements

1. Which operating system(s) will you use to host your registry?
2. Which database or data storage facility would you prefer to use?
3. What are your performance requirements?
4. Will you need to replicate the registry across multiple systems?
5. Will you need to federate the registry across multiple systems?
6. Will your users want to subscribe to registry updates?
7. Will you define custom taxonomies?
8. Will you need to customize the UDDI browser interface?
9. Will you need inquiry-based access control?

Glossary

abstract interface
A description of the functionality supported by a service, but not the protocols used to access the service. An abstract interface corresponds to a service type. In a Web service, the abstract interface defines the operations the service supports and the formats of the messages that must be exchanged. A WSDL portType defines the abstract interface.

API
See **application programming interface**.

application adapter
A program that provides an interface to a legacy application. It maps an open API to a proprietary API.

application programming interface
A programming mechanism that allows an application or system function to expose its capabilities to other applications. An API supports application-to-application communication.

application server
A server that provides a runtime framework for application services. An application server manages an application's life cycle and coordinates the utilization of resources. An application server enables optimized performance, scalability, reliability, and availability.

asymmetric encryption
A process in which a message is encrypted and decrypted using two keys (one public, one private). If the message is encrypted with the

Glossary

public key, it can be decrypted only with the private key. Similarly, if the message is encrypted with the private key, it can be decrypted only with the public key. Also known as public key encryption.

asynchronous

Not at the same time. In asynchronous application communication, the two applications don't need to communicate simultaneously. One application sends a message. The other receives the message when it's ready. Used with MOM systems.

atomic transaction

A transaction in which all tasks must complete successfully or else the entire transaction must be reset.

authentication

The process used to verify a user's or application's identity.

authorization

The process used to determine whether an authenticated entity has permission to perform a particular action or function.

binary data format

A format in which information is encoded as a series of 0's and 1's. Binary formats can be processed only by applications that understand the format. Binary formats are more compact than text formats.

bind

The operation that a service consumer performs to connect a client to a service. One of three basic operations in the SOA.

binding

The WSDL *how* part. A WSDL element that maps a portType to a concrete set of protocols. The binding specifies the technical details of how to communicate with a service.

BPEL4WS
Business Process Execution Language for Web Services. A Web services orchestration language developed by BEA, IBM, and Microsoft.

BPMI
Business Process Management Initiative. A consortium dedicated to the development of business process management standards.

BPML
Business Process Modeling Language. A BPMI standard. An XML vocabulary for modeling business processes. BPML relies on WSDL and WSCI to describe Web services interactions. It defines an execution language that specifies the runtime semantics of interactions, and it defines an abstract execution model to manage the orchestration of those interactions.

BPSS
Business Process Specification Schema. Part of the ebXML framework. Managed by UN/CEFACT. An XML language used to describe the choreographed interchange of messages that must be exchanged to complete the specified business transaction.

BTP
Business Transaction Protocol. An OASIS Committee Specification. An XML-based transaction coordination system that supports asynchronous, loosely coupled, long-term transactions. BTP supports atomic and cohesive transactions.

business model
The way in which a company operates and makes money.

bytecode
The Java intermediate code. Bytecode executes in a JVM.

Glossary

canonical

The simplest way to represent something. You must transform an XML document into its canonical form before you can create a digital signature.

choreography

The planning and arrangement of movements into a meaningful whole. In Web services, choreography refers to the planning and arrangement of interactions among multiple Web services, especially the structured composition of services to effect a business process. See also **orchestration**.

CIL

Common Intermediate Language. The C# intermediate code. All .NET languages compile into CIL. CIL executes in a VES.

CIM

Common Information Model. A DMTF standard that defines a common management data model that is independent of any particular management framework. This data model defines the structure and format of management information.

circle of trust

An agreement among business affiliates to support a federated identity scheme according to defined trust relationships. The term is associated with the Liberty Alliance federal identity scheme.

CLI

Common Language Infrastructure. An ISO international standard for the C# language runtime platform.

client

An application that calls a service. The requester in a client/server relationship.

Glossary

client/server
A style of communication between two computer programs in which one program (the client) sends a request to another program (the server), which responds to the request.

CLR
Common Language Runtime. Microsoft's runtime environment for C# and .NET on Windows. The CLR implements the CLI international standard.

cohesive transaction
A transaction in which a certain set of tasks must complete successfully or else the entire transaction must be reset.

collection
A programming language structure containing a group of objects.

command line tools
Nonvisual development tools executed from a command line prompt or invoked through a script. Command line tools are typically very powerful but cryptic.

communication middleware
A form of middleware used for application-to-application communication.

confidentiality
The ability to prevent unauthorized access to data or the contents of a message.

container
An XML Schema type structure containing a group of simple or complex types. Also a runtime framework for application servers. See **EJB container**, **runtime container**.

Glossary

context
Information about the current state of an activity.

CORBA
Common Object Request Broker Architecture. An RPC-style distributed object middleware system developed and standardized by OMG. Available for most platforms, supporting many languages.

CPPA
Collaboration Protocol Profile and Agreement. An OASIS standard. Part of the ebXML framework. An XML language for specifying the details of how a company supports B2B integration.

datatype
The definition of the kind of data within an object or element, such as text, integer, decimal number, or date.

DCE RPC
Distributed Computing Environment Remote Procedure Call. An RPC-style middleware system developed and standardized by OSF (now The Open Group). Available for most platforms, supporting C, C++, and Java.

DCOM
Distributed Component Object Model. Microsoft's native distributed object technology for Windows that predates .NET. DCOM communicates using Microsoft RPC. Available for all Windows platforms, supporting any programming language. Available but rarely seen on other platforms.

deployment descriptor
A file that describes the deployment configuration of a service.

Glossary

digital signature
A digital value that represents someone's handwritten signature used for nonrepudiation. A digital signature is the value produced when you apply a signing algorithm to some data using the signatory's private key. The receiver can verify the signature by applying a verification algorithm to the same data, this time using the signatory's public key. The generated value should match the digital signature.

DMTF
Distributed Management Task Force. An industry organization focused on developing standards for the management of desktop, enterprise, and Internet environments.

DNS
Domain Name System. An essential piece of the Internet infrastructure. DNS maps an abstract network address to a physical TCP/IP network location

document-style
An unconstrained way to structure SOAP messages. Document-style messages do not indicate what operation to invoke.

DotGNU
An open source project sponsored by the Free Software Foundation and the GNU Project to port C# and .NET to Linux and UNIX.

DSS
Digital Signature Service. A trust service that can create and verify XML signatures. An OASIS work-in-progress.

dynamic binding
The act of mapping an abstract interface to specific protocols and a specific service implementation at runtime.

Glossary

dynamic proxy

A client proxy generated at runtime.

EAI

Enterprise application integration. A comprehensive framework for integrating multiple application systems. EAI solves a much larger problem than just basic application integration. EAI uses extraction, aggregation, routing, and dissemination of information based on business rules. EAI tends to operate outside the production process and communicates using MOM and message brokers.

ebMS

ebXML Message Service protocol. An OASIS standard. Part of the ebXML framework. An XML protocol that extends SOAP to add support for attachments, security, and reliable message delivery.

ebXML

Electronic Business using Extensible Markup Language. A standard XML-based Web services framework designed to support B2B integration. It greatly expands the power of electronic data interchange (EDI). It was a joint effort of OASIS and UN/CEFACT. See **ebMS**, **CPPA**, **BPSS**, **ebXML Registry and Repository**.

ebXML Registry and Repository

A registry and repository for Web services. An OASIS standard. Part of the ebXML framework. It manages information about service types and service providers. It also provides a repository for service descriptions, schemata, CPPA descriptions, BPSS specifications, and other metadata. An ebXML registry is an ebXML Web service.

ECMA

ECMA International. An industry association dedicated to the standardization of information and communications systems. Responsible for standardizing C#.

Glossary

encoded
Data that have been processed according to a set of encoding rules. See **encoding**.

encoding
A set of unambiguous rules used to represent data.

encryption
The process of changing data to make it indecipherable to all except the intended recipient. Encryption ensures message integrity and confidentiality.

endpoint
The networking access point of an application.

EJB
Enterprise JavaBeans. A J2EE component model for industrial-strength, secure, transactional business applications.

EJB container
A J2EE application server container that hosts EJB components.

federated identity
A single identity credential that can map to different identity information on different systems within a circle of trust. Enables single sign-on across security domains. The term is associated with the Liberty Alliance.

find
The operation that a service consumer performs to find or discover a service through a service broker. One of three basic operations in the SOA.

firewall

A mechanism used to protect a corporate network from unauthorized or unwelcome access. A firewall screens incoming messages and determines whether to let them pass.

framework

An environment that provides a partial solution, usually automating a particularly tedious or difficult part of an application project. There are development frameworks and runtime frameworks. A development framework provides prebuilt code and application skeletons that developers can use to implement solutions quickly and consistently. A runtime framework often implements middleware functionality.

FTP

File Transfer Protocol. An IETF standard application protocol used to transfer files.

GXA

Global XML Web Services Architecture. A set of Microsoft technologies and SOAP extensions for advanced Web services functionality associated with attachments, discovery, routing, security, and transaction coordination.

hash table

A complex datatype structured as a table of keys associated with values.

HTML

Hypertext Markup Language. A W3C standard markup language used to create and format Web pages. The HTML vocabulary defines formatting information.

HTTP
Hypertext Transfer Protocol. An IETF standard application protocol for distributed, collaborative, hypermedia information systems. HTTP is the protocol that Web browsers use to communicate with Web servers. Most Web services communicate using HTTP.

HTTPS
Hypertext Transfer Protocol Secure. HTTP running over SSL/TLS. A secure, encrypted, authenticated version of HTTP.

IDL
See **Interface Definition Language**

IETF
Internet Engineering Task Force. The standards organization that develops and maintains Internet protocols and technologies, such as TCP/IP, DNS, SSL/TLS, HTTP, SMTP, and FTP. The IETF also works with NIST on encryption and digital signature technologies.

implementation
An occurrence of a thing, as opposed to the definition of the thing. See **type.**

infrastructure-level Web service
A Web services infrastructure product that is implemented as a Web service. Examples include a UDDI registry service and a single sign-on service. The collection of Web services that supports your infrastructure forms a shared service grid.

integrity
The ability to prevent unauthorized modification of data or a message.

Glossary

Interface definition language

IDL. A machine-readable language used to describe the interfaces to a service. Many RPC-style middleware systems use IDL to describe a service contract. The IDL defines a service's signature. IDL can be compiled to generate a client proxy. Sample IDL languages include OMG IDL (for CORBA), Microsoft IDL, and DCE IDL.

ISO

International Standards Organization. A *de jure* international standards organization. ISO has published the CLI international standard.

Java Community Process

JCP. The formal process used to develop and revise Java technology. The JCP is organized by Sun. Anyone can participate.

JAX-RPC

Java APIs for XML based RPC. A WSDL-aware RPC-style Java API for SOAP. JAX-RPC makes SOAP look and feel like RMI.

JAXM

Java API for XML Messaging. An XML-centric, message-oriented Java API for SOAP. JAXM does not support WSDL.

JAXR

Java API for XML Registries. A Java API that can be used to access either UDDI or ebXML registries.

JCA

J2EE Connector Architecture. A standard plug-in architecture for application adapters in J2EE application servers.

JCA adapter

An application adapter that conforms to JCA and can plug in to a J2EE application server.

JCP
See **Java Community Process**.

JMS
Java Messaging Service. A standard Java API for MOM middleware.

JRE
Java Runtime Environment. The runtime environment for Java. A JRE consists of a JVM, a class loader, and the Java runtime security framework. JREs are available for most operating systems and hardware platforms.

JSP
JavaServer Pages. A Java component model that permits you to embed Java code within an HTML page. JSPs execute within a servlet engine.

JVM
Java Virtual Machine. The virtual machine in the Java runtime environment that interprets Java bytecode.

JWSDL
Java API for WSDL. A Java API used to create, inspect, and manipulate WSDL documents.

Kerberos
An authentication protocol first developed at MIT and standardized by OSF (now The Open Group). It is the primary authentication mechanism used in Windows and DCE. A Kerberos authentication token is called a ticket. (In Greek mythology, Kerberos is the three-headed dog that guards the gates to the underworld.)

key management
The process used to manage encryption keys, including secret keys and public and private keys.

Liberty

An infrastructure that supports federated identity. Liberty permits you to create a circle of trust with select business partners to simplify cross-domain security management.

lifecycle

The management of an application program, including loading it into memory, allocating the system resources it needs, and removing it when it's complete.

linked list

A complex datatype in which multiple data objects are arranged in a list, and each object maintains a reference to the next object in the list.

literal encoding

An encoding system for SOAP messages in which the messages are encoded using a specified XML Schema description.

loosely coupled

Refers to the relaxed dependency between two communicating applications. If you modify either application, it usually doesn't cause the connection to break.

markup language

A language syntax that uses tags to structure a document or to indicate layout and styling. Examples include XML, HTML, WML, and VoiceXML.

meta-markup language

A markup language used to define other markup languages. XML is a meta-markup language.

Glossary

Microsoft RPC
The native RPC-style communications system for Windows platforms. DCOM communicates using Microsoft RPC.

middleware
A software package that sits between your application code and its underlying platform, providing easy access to core system facilities such as the network, storage, and processors.

message-oriented middleware
MOM. A middleware system that uses an asynchronous, peer-based style of communication. Applications send and receive messages. Examples include IBM WebSphereMQ, Microsoft MQ, and Tibco Rendezvous.

MOM
See **message-oriented middleware**.

Mono
An open source project sponsored by Ximian to port C# and .NET to Linux and UNIX.

NASSL
Network Accessible Service Specification Language. A Web service description language for SOAP, developed by IBM, predating WSDL.

.NET
Microsoft's application platform based on the C# programming language. .NET provides integrated support for SOAP-based Web services.

NIST

National Institute of Standards and Technologies. A nonregulatory U.S. federal agency that, among other things, develops encryption and digital signature standards.

nonrepudiation

The ability to prove that a particular action occurred—for example, that a particular user or application sent a message. Digital signatures support nonrepudiation.

OASIS

Organization for the Advancement of Structured Information Standards. A consortium that develops standards for Web services and e-business, including UDDI, DSS, WS-Security, WS-RM, WSRP, and ebXML.

OASIS Committee Specification

An OASIS specification that has been approved by its technical committee but not yet approved as an OASIS standard.

OASIS Standard

An approved OASIS standard.

OMI

Open Management Interface. A management framework specification from HP and webMethods. OMI manages distributed applications systems using Web services. Submitted to OASIS. The OASIS WSDM Technical Committee may use OMI as input.

ONC RPC

Open Network Computing Remote Procedure Call. An RPC-style middleware system developed by Sun and standardized by IETF. Available for most platforms, supporting C, C++, and Java.

Glossary

operating platform
An amalgam of the many different infrastructure technologies that host your application systems, such as operating system, programming language, application server, and security infrastructure.

orchestration
The arrangement of events to achieve a certain goal or effect. In Web services, orchestration refers to the arrangement of interactions among multiple Web services, especially the structured composition of services to effect a business process. See also **choreography**.

peer
An equal participant in peer-to-peer communications. A peer can act as either a sender (client) or a receiver (server).

PKI
Public key infrastructure. A security infrastructure for the Internet designed by IETF and based on digital certificates and public key cryptography. PKI relies on a system of registration authorities that verify the validity of the parties involved in a secure Internet transaction.

port
The WSDL *where* part. A WSDL element that defines the endpoint of a Web service implementation. The Web service implements a specific binding of a portType.

portlet
An application running with a portal.

portType
The WSDL *what* part. A WSDL element that defines a Web service. A portType describes the abstract interface of the Web service. A portType represents a Web service type.

Glossary

principal

A security identifier. A principal represents a user, and it provides a reference key that can be used to verify the rights and privileges that have been granted to the user.

protocol

A set of rules for information exchange. You use a number of different protocols at different levels of communication (message, application, network, etc.).

proxy

An intermediary application or routine that acts as a liaison between a client and a server. In Web services, a client proxy is a communications routine, generated from a WSDL file, that a client application uses to invoke a service. You can also use proxies to intercept messages to perform various security or other middleware functions.

reference architecture

A description of the design of a system. An architecture identifies the functional components of a system. It also defines the relationships among those components and establishes a set of constraints upon each.

register

The operation a service provider uses to register or advertise a service with a service broker. One of three basic operations in the SOA.

registry

A database that provides information about registered resources. A registry supports the advertising and discovery function in an SOA. A service provider advertises its services in the registry.

Service consumers can search the registry to discover services that match their needs.

reliable message delivery
The ability to guarantee the proper delivery of messages, in the right sequence, within an acceptable time frame. See **WS-RM**.

remote procedure call
RPC. A middleware system that uses a synchronous, client/server-based style of communication. A client uses RPC to invoke a procedure on a remote system. RPC makes the remote procedure appear as if it were a local procedure.

RMI
Remote Method Invocation. The native RPC-style communication system used by Java.

RNP
Reliable network provider. A service provider that provides a reliable messaging service.

RPC
See **remote procedure call**.

RPC-style
A constrained way to structure SOAP messages to simulate an RPC invocation. The request message contains a method name and a set of parameters. The response message contains a return value.

runtime container
A runtime framework in an application server that hosts applications and manages application lifecycle. Some examples are EJB container, servlet engine, and SOAP runtime container. A SOAP

runtime container hosts the applications that implement Web services.

SAAJ
SOAP with Attachments API for Java. A low-level Java API for SOAP.

SAML
Security Assertions Markup Language. An OASIS standard. An XML syntax for representing security assertions for authentication, authorization, and attributes. Also defines a set of trust services for single sign-on and entitlement.

SCL
SOAP Contract Language. A Web services description language for SOAP, developed by Microsoft, predating WSDL.

screen scraping
A technique used to create an application adapter by encapsulating a human-oriented user interface. The adapter simulates human interaction.

security token
A token that represents a decision made by a security authority.

service
An application that exposes its functionality through an application programming interface (API). A service is designed to be consumed by software rather than by humans.

service broker
An entity that facilities the advertising and discovery of services. A role within the SOA.

Glossary

service consumer

An entity that consumes a service. One of three roles within the SOA.

service contract

A machine-readable description of the API used to access a service. A service contract can be compiled into client proxy code.

service grid

A set of Web services that implements part of your Web services infrastructure.

Service-Oriented Architecture

SOA. A set of common practices for service-based applications. The SOA defines mechanisms for describing services, advertising and discovering services, and communicating with services. Most RPC-based middleware systems use the SOA.

service provider

An entity that provides a service. One of three roles within the SOA.

servlet

A lightweight Java component model for Web applications. A servlet executes in a servlet engine.

servlet engine

An application server or container that hosts JSPs and servlets.

signature

The concrete definition of a service interface, including the procedure name, an ordered list of parameter names and types, the return type, and permitted exceptions. See also **digital signature**.

Glossary

single sign-on
A single sign-on service allows a user to log in once with a recognized security authority and use the returned login credentials to access multiple resources for some predefined period of time.

SMTP
Simple Mail Transfer Protocol. An IETF standard application protocol used to send electronic mail.

SNMP
Simple Network Management Protocol. An IETF standard application protocol used to monitor and manage devices connected to a TCP/IP network.

SOA
See service-oriented architecture.

SOAP
Simple Object Access Protocol. The most popular XML protocol used to support communication in Web services. SOAP provides a simple, consistent, and extensible mechanism that allows one application to send an XML message to another application. Being standardized by W3C.

SOAP body
A mandatory part of a SOAP message that contains the message payload.

SOAPbuilders
An informal organization of SOAP vendors working to solve SOAP interoperability issues.

SOAP encoding
An encoding system for SOAP messages in which the messages are encoded using the SOAP encoding data model.

SOAP engine
A Web services platform. A product that implements the SOAP specification. Also known as a SOAP stack, SOAP server, or SOAP implementation.

SOAP envelope
The root element in a SOAP message. The SOAP message container.

SOAP header
An optional part of a SOAP message that usually contains system-level information, such as security credentials, transaction context, message correlation information, session identifiers, or management information. If no system-level information is required, the SOAP header can be omitted from the message.

SOAP header processor
A routine that processes SOAP headers, usually performing middleware functionality.

SOAP implementation
A Web services platform. A product that implements the SOAP specification. Also known as a SOAP stack, SOAP server, or SOAP engine.

SOAP intermediary
An application or service that is both a SOAP receiver and a SOAP sender. An intermediary sits between the sender and the receiver. It usually processes SOAP headers and performs middleware functions.

Glossary

SOAP message processor
A part of a SOAP runtime system that is responsible for processing SOAP messages. It listens for requests and processes them according to the settings defined in the associated deployment descriptor.

SOAP receiver
An application that receives a SOAP message.

SOAP RPC convention
Also called SOAP RPC representation. An optional SOAP convention used to simulate RPC requests and responses. The convention uses the RPC-style message structure.

SOAP sender
An application that sends a SOAP message.

SOAP server
A Web services platform. A product that implements the SOAP specification. Also known as a SOAP stack, SOAP engine, or SOAP implementation.

SOAP stack
A Web services platform. A product that implements the SOAP specification. Also known as a SOAP engine, SOAP server, or SOAP implementation.

software-as-a-service
A business model in which a software provider licenses software as a hosted service.

SSL/TLS
Secure Sockets Layer/Transport Layer Security. A secure network protocol that supports encrypted, authenticated communications across the Internet. SSL was developed by Netscape. TLS is the IETF

standard. It provides message integrity and confidentiality at the network layer. It also optionally supports strong authentication.

style sheet
A document that provides instructions on how to display, modify, or restructure a document.

symmetric encryption
An encryption process in which a message is encrypted and decrypted using the same key. The key must be exchanged in a separate transmission. Also known as single key or secret key encryption.

synchronous
At the same time. In synchronous application communication, the two applications must communicate simultaneously. A client issues a request and waits for a response. The server must handle the request immediately. If the server is not available, the request fails.

tag
A markup language construct that provides a label and container for an element. An element has a start tag and an end tag.

taxonomy
A classification scheme. In the UDDI and ebXML registries, you can categorize businesses, services, and service types using any number of taxonomies.

TCP/IP
Transmission Control Protocol/Internet Protocol. The pervasive network protocol that supports the Internet.

Glossary

tightly coupled
Refers to the tight dependency between two communicating applications. If you modify either application, it often causes the connection to break.

tModel
Technical model. A UDDI entity that represents an abstract or reusable resource. You use tModels to represent service types. The tModel points to the specification (WSDL) that defines the service type. You also use tModels to represent identifier and categorization taxonomies.

token
A digital value that represents something, such as a login credential. See **security token**.

traditional middleware
Middleware systems such as RPC, DCOM, CORBA, RMI, and MOM.

trust service
A Web service that provides security functions for your applications. Examples include a single sign-on service, a key management service, and a digital signature service.

type
The definition of a thing as opposed to an actual occurrence of a thing. Also see **implementation**.

UBR
See **UDDI Business Registry**.

UBR node
A node within the UBR. All nodes contain identical information.

UDDI
See **Universal Description, Discovery & Integration**.

UDDI4J
An open source UDDI client API for Java.

UDDI.org
An informal consortium of vendors that developed the UDDI specifications. The group submitted the specifications to OASIS and has since disbanded.

UDDI Business Registry
UBR. A public UDDI Web services registry. The UBR is replicated across multiple nodes operated by IBM, Microsoft, NTT, and SAP.

UDDI Operators Council
A formal business partnership among the companies that operate nodes in the UBR.

UML
Unified Modeling Language. An OMG standard for modeling software artifacts.

Uniform Resource Identifier
URI. A compact, formatted name that identifies a Web resource. You use this name to reference, access, and share a resource.

Uniform Resource Locator
URL. A URI that can be resolved to a physical network address.

Uniform Resource Name
URN. A URI that is simply a name. It cannot be resolved to a physical network address.

Glossary

Universal Description, Discovery & Integration
UDDI. An OASIS standard. A registry for Web services. A UDDI registry manages information about service types and service providers. A UDDI service is a Web service.

URI
See **Uniform Resource Identifier**.

URI scheme
The first part of a URI. Indicates the application protocol used to access the resource.

URL
See **Uniform Resource Locator**.

URN
See **Uniform Resource Name**.

VES
Virtual Execution System. The virtual machine in the .NET runtime system (CLR) that interprets CIL.

vocabulary
The set of words within a language. In markup languages, a vocabulary defines the set of tags that can be used within the language. A meta-markup language permits you to define your own tags.

VoiceXML
A W3C standard markup language for use with interactive voice response (IVR) applications and other telephony systems.

Glossary

W3C
The World Wide Web Consortium. A consortium that develops standards for the World Wide Web, including HTML, XML, SOAP, and related technologies.

W3C Candidate Recommendation
A W3C draft specification that is two steps from being a standard. From the W3C site: "A Candidate Recommendation is work that has received significant review from its immediate technical community. It is an explicit call to those outside of the related Working Groups or the W3C itself for implementation and technical feedback."

W3C Note
A specification that has been submitted to and published by the W3C. Publication of a Note does not imply endorsement from W3C. From the W3C site: "A Note is a dated, public record of an idea, comment, or document. A Note does not represent commitment by W3C to pursue work related to the Note."

W3C Proposed Recommendation
A W3C draft specification that is one step from being a standard. From the W3C site: "A Proposed Recommendation is work that (1) represents consensus within the group that produced it and (2) has been proposed by the Director to the Advisory Committee for review."

W3C Recommendation
A W3C standard. From the W3C site: "A Recommendation is work that represents consensus within W3C and has the Director's stamp of approval. W3C considers that the ideas or technology specified by a Recommendation are appropriate for widespread deployment and promote W3C's mission."

Glossary

W3C Working Draft

A W3C draft specification representing work in progress. From the W3C site: "A Working Draft represents work in progress and a commitment by W3C to pursue work in this area. A Working Draft does not imply consensus by a group or W3C."

WBEM

Web-Based Enterprise Management. A DTMF standard that extends CIM to bring it more in line with the Web. The xmlCIM specification defines CIM in terms of XML. The CIM Operations over HTTP specification defines a transport mechanism that allows you to send CIM commands to management agents over HTTP.

Web

See **World Wide Web**.

Web API

An API for a Web service. A Web API lets applications communicate using XML and the Web.

Web resource

Any type of named information object, such as a word processing document, a digital picture, a Web page, an e-mail account, or an application. Every Web resource is identified by a URI.

Web server

A server that hosts and provides access to Web resources. A Web server contains an HTTP server.

Web service

An application that provides a Web API. A Web service is a Web resource that is designed to be accessed by applications. It supports application-to-application communications using XML and the Web.

Web service implementation
A specific Web service. A Web service implementation implements a Web service type.

Web service type
A definition of a Web service. The type corresponds to its abstract interface, as defined by a WSDL portType. Multiple service providers can implement the same Web service type.

Web services application templates
The types of applications and initiatives that you can build using Web services.

Web Services Description Language
WSDL. An XML language that describes a Web service. A WSDL document describes *what* functionality a Web service offers, *how* it communicates, and *where* to find it. A WSDL file is the service contract for a Web service. WSDL is being standardized by W3C.

Web services infrastructure
Products that implement XML and Web services technologies. You use these products to build, deploy, manage, and use Web services.

Web services management extension
A Web services infrastructure product that adds advanced features to a Web services platform, such as security, version control, and monitoring.

Web services platform
A Web services infrastructure product that consists of a SOAP runtime environment and the tools you need to develop, deploy, and manage Web services.

Glossary

Web services technologies
The technologies that provide the foundation for Web services. These technologies include SOAP, WSDL, UDDI, and related technologies.

Web site
A group of Web resources that are designed to be accessed by humans.

white space
Any characters in an XML document that have no semantic meaning, such as blanks and line feeds.

WML
Wireless Markup Language. A standard markup language for specifying content and formatting information for display in browsers on a wireless device. WML is managed by the Open Mobile Alliance.

World Wide Web
The Web. An Internet application that supports an immensely scalable information space filled with interconnected Web resources.

WS-Choreography
A W3C effort to define a standard Web services choreography language. The WS-Choreography Working Group may base its work on WSCI.

WSCI
Web Services Choreography Interface. A choreography language developed by BEA, Intalio, SAP, and Sun. A W3C Note. The W3C WS-Choreography Working Group may base its work on WSCI.

WS-Coordination
A SOAP extension from BEA, IBM, and Microsoft. It defines a coordination framework that allows multiple participants to reach agreement on the outcome of a distributed activity.

Glossary

WSDL
See **Web Services Description Language**.

WSDL compiler
A tool that compiles a WSDL definition and generates application code.

WSDM
Web Services Distributed Management. A management framework that uses Web services to manage Web services. An OASIS work-in-progress.

WSFL
Web Services Flow Language. A Web services orchestration language from IBM used as input to BPEL4WS. See **BPEL4WS**.

WSIA
Web Services Interactive Applications. Part of the OASIS WSRP specification that defines Web services standard behaviors for interactive interfaces to Web services. An OASIS technical committee. See **WSRP**.

WS-I
Web Services-Interoperability Organization. A vendor-sponsored consortium focused on promoting Web services interoperability across platforms, operating systems, and programming languages.

WS-I Basic Profile
A WS-I profile, based on SOAP 1.1, WSDL 1.1, and UDDI 2.0, that defines a set of constraints that reduce interoperability problems.

WS-RM
Web Services Reliable Messaging. A SOAP extension for reliable message delivery. An OASIS work-in-progress.

Glossary

WSRP

Web Services for Remote Portals. A Web services framework that enables "pluggable portlets." It defines a generic adapter that enables any WSRP-compliant portal to consume and display any WSRP-compliant Web service, without the need to develop a specific portlet for each service. An OASIS work-in-progress.

WSS

Web Services Security. A SOAP extension that defines a standard way to represent security information in a SOAP message. An OASIS work-in-progress based on WS-Security.

WS-Security

A SOAP extension that defines a standard way to represent security information in a SOAP message. Based on a specification developed by IBM, Microsoft, and VeriSign. An OASIS work-in-progress. See **WSS**.

WS-Transaction

A SOAP extension defined by BEA, IBM, and Microsoft that works in conjunction with WS-Coordination to define the protocols used to implement atomic transactions and loosely coupled business activities.

XACML

XML Access Control Markup Language. An OASIS standard. A policy-oriented XML language for defining access policies and rules.

XCBF

XML Common Biometric Format. An OASIS Committee Specification. An XML vocabulary for representing and exchanging biometric information in XML.

XKMS
XML Key Management Service. A set of trust services that can manage the registration and distribution of public keys. A W3C work-in-progress.

XLANG
A Web services orchestration language from Microsoft. Used as input to BPEL4WS. See **BPEL4WS**.

XML
Extensible Markup Language. A W3C standard data format for electronic documents and messages. It is a self-describing meta-markup language. XML provides a universal data format that can be interpreted, processed, and transformed by any application running on any platform.

XML document
A structured electronic document written in XML.

XML Encryption
A W3C standard that defines a process for encrypting and decrypting all or part of an XML document. It also defines an XML syntax for representing encrypted content in an XML document and an XML syntax for representing the information that you need to decrypt the content.

XML element
A distinct piece of information within an XML document. An element is bounded by a set of tags.

XML protocol
A protocol for XML messages. A set of rules that govern the format and processing of XML messages. Examples include SOAP, ebMS, and XML-RPC.

Glossary

XML Schema
A W3C standard that defines an XML grammar for defining the contents and structure of an XML document. Web services use XML schema to define the format of XML messages.

XML Signature
A W3C standard that defines an XML syntax to represent signed data in XML and a set of processing instructions to canonicalize XML, sign data, and interpret signatures.

XrML
Extensible Rights Markup Language. A content-centric XML language for specifying access rights and permissions. An OASIS work-in-progress.

XSLT
Extensible Stylesheet Language Transformations. An XML-based programming language for transforming XML documents into other XML documents or other data formats.

Index

A

Abstract interface, Web services, 60
Accenture
   history, UDDI, 92
   WS-Interoperability, 86
ACORD, 67
   XML standards for insurance industry, 144
Adapters, 9–11, 214–215
   frameworks, 11
   JCA adapters, 205
Adjoin SOMMA, 210
Administration tools, project evaluation guidelines, 235–236
alphaWorks, BPWS4J, 129
Amazon, Web APIs, 40–41
Apache Software Foundation, SOAP history, 85
   Axis, 88,
   Licensing and support issues, 225
   Evaluating your requirements, 227-229
APIs (application programming interfaces), 8–9
Application adapters, 9–11, 214–215
   frameworks, 11
   JCA adapters, 205
Application integration
   APIs, 8–9
   application-level, 7–9
   B2B, 5
   business intelligence systems, 4
   CRM, 4
   data-level, 7–8
   DCM, 4
   ERP, 2, 4
   external integration, 7
   FFA, 4
   heterogeneous integration, 158–159
   implementation difficulties, 6–7
   KM systems, 4
   PLM, 4
   point-to-point integration, 162–163
   portals, 4
   SCM, 4
   SFA, 4
   tactical and strategic advantages, 3
   Web services as solution, 6
Application-level application integration, 7–9
Application programming interfaces (APIs), 8–9
Application servers, 31
Ariba, history of UDDI, 92
ASP-style business model, 173–174
Asymmetric encryption, 106
Asynchronous communication, 14
Atomic transactions, 123
AT&T, 165
Attunity, application adapter frameworks, 11
Authentication and authorization, 110–112, 114–115
   SOAP messaging, 74–76
Aventail, BPM standards, 128

B

B2B (business-to-business)
   application integration, 5, 20–21
   ebXML, 78
   electronic procurement, 170–171
   Web service technologies, 77
BEA Systems
   BPEL4WS, 91–92, 129, 218
   BPM standards, 128
   orchestration and choreography, 126
   reliable message delivery, 130
   SOAP extension specifications, 134
   WebLogic Server, 88, 201, 222

Index

BEA Systems (*cont.*)
  WS-Coordination and -Transaction specifications, 124–126
  WS-Interoperability, 86
  WS-ReliableMessaging, 131
  WSCI, 91, 127
Binary data formats, 13
Bind Systems, ebXML, 80
Binding, SOA operation, 58, 6067
Black Pearl, BPM standards, 128
Blaze Software, BPM standards, 128
BMC Patrol, 118, 206
  BPM standards, 128
Borland
  SOAP integration into programming languages, 98
  .NET language support, 185
  Web services development tools, 193
Bowstreet, BPM standards, 128
BPEL4WS (Business Process Execution Language for Web Services), 91–92, 129, 218
BPM (business process management) standards, 128, 215, 217–218
BPMI (Business Process Management Initiative), orchestration and choreography, 126, 128
BPML (Business Process Modeling Language), 128
BPSS (Business Process Specification Schema), 126–127, 130
Browser interfaces, 10
BTP (Business Transaction Protocol), 123–126
Business models
  Amazon, 40–41
  Google, 38–39
  Kinko's, 39–40
Business Process Execution Language for Web Services. *See* BPEL4WS
Business process management (BPM) standards, 128
Business Process Management Initiative (BPMI), 126, 128
Business Process Modeling Language (BPML), 128
Business Process Specification Schema (BPSS), 126–127, 130
Business-to-business. *See* B2B
Business Transaction Protocol (BTP), 123–126
Bytecode (Java), 184

C

CA Unicenter, 118, 206
Canonical form, XML documents, 109
Cap Gemini Ernst & Young, BPM standards, 128
Cape Clear, 162–163
Cell Directory Service, DCE, 64
Certificate authorities, 75
Choreography
  BPEL4WS, 92
  standardization efforts, 126–130
  vendors, 217
  WSCI, 91
CICS (Customer Information Control System) applications, 44
CIL (Common Intermediate Language), 183–185
CIM (Common Information Model), 119–120
Circle of trust, 113–114
CLI (Common Language Infrastructure) specification, 186
Client/server-based communication, 14–16, 31
  client development tools, 198–199
  client SOA roles, 58
ClinicStation, 169–170
CLR (Common Language Runtime), 183–184
Cobalt Group, ebXML, 80
Cohesive transactions, 123
Collaboration Protocol Profile and Agreement (CPPA) specification, 79

Index

Collaborative Planning, Forecasting and Replenishment (CPFR) standards, 147
Collaxa, BPEL4WS, 129, 218
Collections, programming language structures, 228
Coloplast, 164
ComCARE (Communications for Coordinated Assistance and Response to Emergencies), 145–146
Command line tools, 191, 193
CommerceOne
  BPM standards, 128
  ebXML, 80
  history, UDDI, 92
Common Information Model (CIM), 119–120
Common Intermediate Language (CIL), 183–185
Common Language Infrastructure (CLI) specification, 186
Common Language Runtime (CLR), 183–184
Common Object Request Broker Architecture. *See* CORBA
Communication middleware
  basics, 12–13
  challenges, 16–20
  message-oriented, 14
  RPC-style, 14–16
Compaq, history of UDDI, 92
Component Object Model (COM), 221
Computer Sciences Corporation, BPM standards, 128
Con-Way Transportation Services, 159–160
Containers
  EJB containers, 203–205
  runtime, 200–202
Context, Web services, 124
CORBA (Common Object Request Broker Architecture), 15–17
  CORBA Naming Service, 64
  versus SOAP, 76
  tightly coupled connections, 19, 29
  versus UDDI, 69
  versus WSDL, 63
  versus XML, 55, 57
Costs, ownership of middleware, 18–20
Country Codes standard, 66
CPFR (Collaborative Planning, Forecasting and Replenishment) standards, 147
CPPA (Collaboration Protocol Profile and Agreement) specification, 79
CRM (customer relationship management), 4
Customer Information Control System (CICS), 44
Cyclone Commerce, BPM standards, 128

D

D-U-N-S numbers, UDDI, 66
Data confidentiality, 107
Data integrity, 107
Data-level application integration, 7–8
Database servers, 31
Databases, UDDI registries, 238–239
DataChannel, BPM standards, 128
Datatypes, XML, 53
DCE (Distributed Computing Environment) RPC, 15–16
  Cell Directory Service, 64
  versus SOAP, 76
  versus WSDL, 63
DCM (demand chain management) application integration, 4
DCOM (Distributed Component Object Model) RPC, 15, 17
  NT Registry, 64
  tightly coupled connections, 19, 29
  versus WSDL, 63
  versus XML, 55, 57
DealerSphere, ebXML, 80

Index

DECnet, 50
   versus SOAP, 76
Demand chain management (DCM), 4
Deployment tools, 191, 193–194
   descriptors, 197–198
   project evaluation guidelines, 235–236
Descriptors, deployment, 197–198
Deutsche Telekom, T-Mobile International, 41
Development tools, 191, 193–194
   clients, 198–199
   project evaluation guidelines, 234–235
   services, 194–198
DevelopMentor, SOAP project, 78, 84
Diagnostic tools, 214, 216
Digital certificates, 75
Digital Signature Services (DSS), 110, 117
Digital signatures, 106, 108–109
   managing, 110, 213
   SOAP messaging, 74
Distributed Component Object Model. *See* DCOM
Distributed Computing Environment. *See* DCE
DMTF (Distributed Management Task Force), 119
DNS (Domain Name System), 48
Document-style SOAP messaging, 72
Documentum, ebXML, 80
Domain Name System. *See* DNS
DotGNU project, 186
DSS (Digital Signature Services), 110, 117
Dynamic binding, 62, 147–150
Dynamic discovery, 140–143
Dynamic proxies, 62

E

E-Gov Task Force, 165–169
E-Travel, 166–167
EAI (enterprise application integration), 11, 20
   potential replacement by Web services, 176
ebMS (ebXML Message Service), 79
   JAXM, 100
ebXML (Electronic Business using Extensible Markup Language), 78–80
   CPPA specification, 79
   JAXR, 102
   orchestration and choreography, 126–127, 130
   Registry and Repository, 79
ECMA
   CLI, 186
   technology ownership, 187–189
EDI (Electronic Data Interchange), 170–171
EDS
   BPM standards, 128
   ebXML, 80
Einstein, 160–161
EJBs (Enterprise JavaBeans), 202–205
Electronic Business using Extensible Markup Language. *See* EbXML
Electronic Data Interchange (EDI), 170–171
Encoding, 61
Encryption, 106–108
Endpoints, 61
Enterprise application integration. *See* EAI
Enterprise JavaBeans (EJBs), 202–205
Enterprise resource planning. *See* ERP
Entricom, BPM standards, 128
Equifax, history of UDDI, 92
ERP (enterprise resource planning)
   application integration, 4
   Hershey Foods Corporation, 2

Index

eSOAP platform, 199
EXOR platform, 199
Extensible Business Reporting Language (XBRL) International, 146
Extensible Markup Language. *See* XML
Extensible Rights Markup Language. *See* XrML
Extensible Stylesheet Language Transformations. *See* XSLT

F

Federated identity, 113
FedEx, software-as-service business model, 138
Fell, Simon, 85
FFA (field force automation), 4
Field force automation. *See* FFA
File servers, 31
File Transfer Protocol (FTP), 49
Find SOA operation, 58
Firewalls
   definition, 21, 22
   Web services, 50
FirstGov portal, 169
Forrester Research, 153
Frameworks, 11
Free Software Foundation, 186
FTP (File Transfer Protocol), 49
Fujitsu
   history, UDDI, 92
   reliable message delivery, 130
   WS-Interoperability, 86

G

Gartner, 152
GE Global eXchange Services, 11
Global Web Services Architecture (GXA), 134
GNU Project, 186
Google Web APIs, 38–39
Graphical user interfaces, 10
GUIs (graphical user interfaces), 10
GXA (Global Web Services Architecture), 134

H

Hash tables, 228
Hershey Foods Corporation, application integration, 2–3
Heterogeneous integration, 158–159
Hewlett-Packard
   history, UDDI, 92
   HP OpenView, 118, 206
   OMI, 121
Hitachi, reliable message delivery, 130
HR-XML Consortium, 146
HTML (Hypertext Markup Language), 34
   vocabulary, 52
HTTP (Hypertext Transfer Protocol), 49, 50
   authentication, 110–111
HTTPS (Hypertext Transfer Protocol Secure), 73–74
Hypertext Markup Language. *See* HTML
Hypertext Transfer Protocol. *See* HTTP
Hypertext Transfer Protocol Secure. *See* HTTPS

I

i2 Technologies, history of UDDI, 92
IBM
   BPEL4WS, 91–92, 129, 218
   BPM standards, 128
   ebXML, 80
   history, SOAP, 84
   history, UDDI, 92
   history, WSDL, 88–89
   orchestration and choreography, 126
   reliable message delivery, 130
   Tivoli, 118, 206
   UDDI4J, 102
   Web Services Developer Kit (WSDK) 191-192
   WebSphere, 159-161
   WebSphereMQ, 14, 71, 212

Index

IBM *(cont.)*
  WS-Coordination and -Transaction specifications, 124–126
  WS-Interoperability, 86
  WS-ReliableMessaging, 131
  WS-Security specification, 115
  WSFL, 129
IDEs (integrated development environments), 214, 216
IDLs (interface definition languages), 63
IdooXoap (Systinet), 85
IETF (Internet Engineering Task Force)
  encryption standards, 106
  Web services technologies, 90
IIS (Internet Information Services), 183
Implementation of types, Web services, 60–61
Information technology (IT), 2, 4
Infrastructure-level Web services, 210–211
  reliable network providers, 211–212
  trust services, 213–214
  UDDI registries, 212–213
Intalio
  BPM standards, 128
  BPML-based products, 128
  WSCI, 91, 127
Integrated development environments (IDEs), 214, 216
Integrated Shipbuilding Environment Consortium (ISEC), 171–172, 173
Integration hooks, 9–11
Intel
  history, UDDI, 92
  WS-Interoperability, 86
Interactive applications, portlets, 132–133
Interface definition language. *See* IDLs
International Standards Organization (ISO)

ISO 3166 Country Codes standard, 66
technology ownership, 188
Internet, 49
  application integration, 20–22
  versus traditional middleware, 21
Internet Engineering Task Force. *See* IETF
Internet Information Services (IIS), 183
Internetwork Packet Exchange (IPX) *versus* SOAP, 76
Interoperability, projects evaluation guidelines, 227–229
IONA
  application adapter frameworks, 11
  XMLBus, 165
IPX (Internetwork Packet Exchange) *versus* SOAP, 76
ISDA (International Swaps and Derivatives Association), 145
ISEC (Integrated Shipbuilding Environment Consortium), 171–172, 173
ISO (International Standards Organization)
  ISO 3166 Country Codes standard, 66
  technology ownership, 188
IT (information technology), 2, 4
iWay Software, application adapter frameworks, 11

J

Jacada Integrator, 164
Java
  API for WSDL (JWSDL), 101
  APIs for XML-based RPC (JAX-RPC), 99
  API for XML Messaging (JAXM), 99–100
  API for XML Registries (JAXR), 102
  EJBs, 202–205
  JAX-RPC, 99, 209

Index

JCA, 205
JCP, 98–99
JCP, technology ownership, 188–189
J2EE application server, 202–205
J2EE application server, *versus* servlet engines, 205–206
JMS, interfaces to MOM products, 14
JNDI, 64
JRE, 184
JSPs, 203
JVM, 184
JWSDL, 101
versus .NET framework, 182, 184–190
platform selection for projects, 222–224
Remote Method Invocation (*See* RMI)
Java Community Process. *See* Java, JCP
Java Message Service. *See* Java, JMS
Java Naming and Directory Interface. *See* Java, JNDI
Java Runtime Environment. *See* Java, JRE
Java Virtual Machine. *See* Java, JVM
JavaServer Pages. *See* Java, JSPs
J2EE Connector Architecture. *See* Java, JCA
JPMorgan, 158–159
Jupiter Research, 152

K

Kerberos tickets, 75, 111
  WS-Security bindings, 116
Key management, 106, 109–110
Killdara, ebXML, 80
Kinko's "File, Print . . . Kinko's" Web service, 39–40
kSOAP platform, 199
Kulchenko, Paul, 85

L

Liberty Alliance Project, 113–114
Lifecycle of applications, 201
Linked lists, 228
Linux platform
  deploying .NET applications, 186
  RPC-style middleware, 15, 17
Literal encoding, 72
Loosely coupled connections, 19–20, 29
  document-style SOAP messaging, 72
  versus XML, 57
Lotus, SOAP history, 84

M

Macromedia, XML protocols, 77
Merrill Lynch, CICS environment, 44
Message-oriented middleware. *See* MOM
Message switching systems, 214–215
META Group, 153
Meta-markup languages, XML, 53
Microsoft
  BPEL4WS, 91–92, 129, 218
  DCOM RPC, 15, 17
  history, SOAP, 78, 84
  history, UDDI, 92
  history, WSDL, 88–89
  Intermediate Language (*See* CIL)
  Microsoft MQ, 14, 17
  .NET framework, 85, 88, 98, 182–183
  .NET framework, *versus* Java, 182, 184–190
  orchestration and choreography, 126
  reliable message delivery, 130
  SOAP Toolkit, 85, 98
  WS-Coordination and -Transaction specifications, 124–126
  WS-Interoperability, 86
  WS-ReliableMessaging, 131
  WS-Security specification, 115

Index

Microsoft (cont.)
  XKMS, 110
  XLANG, 129
Middleware. *See also* traditional middleware
  challenges, 16–20
  communication middleware, 12–13
  communication middleware, styles, 13—16
  network APIs, 11–13
  SOA, 30
  versus SOAP, 175–176
  Web service management extensions, 207–209
MOM (message-oriented middleware), 14, 57
  challenges, 16
  difficulty to use, 17
  loosely coupled connections, 19–20
  RNPs, 212
Momentum, BPEL4WS, 129, 218
Monitoring frameworks, 209–210
Mono project, 186
Multichannel user interfaces, 214, 216

N

NAICS (North American Industry Classification System), 66
NASSL (Network Accessible Service Specification Language), 89
National Industrial Infrastructure Protocols Consortium (NIIIP), 171–172, 173
National Institute of Standards and Technologies. *See* NIST
NDR (Native Data Representation), CORBA, 55
NEC, reliable message delivery, 130
.NET framework (Microsoft), 85, 88, 98, 182–183
  versus Java, 182, 184–190
Network Accessible Service Specification Language (NASSL), 89

Network APIs
  middleware, basics, 11–13
  middleware, challenges, 16–20
  middleware, styles of communication, 13–16
  protocols, 13
NIIIP (National Industrial Infrastructure Protocols Consortium), 171–172, 173
NIST (National Institute of Standards and Technologies), 106, 107
North American Industry Classification System (NAICS), 66
NT Registry, DCOM, 64

O

OASIS (Organization for Advancement of Structured Information Standards)
  BTP, 123–126
  DSS, 110
  ebXML, 78, 79
  history, SOAP, 88
  history, WSDL, 90
  SAML, 75, 111–112
  SNMP, 119
  SOAP history, 88
  SSTC, 111–112
  UDDI, 91
  UDDI, OASIS Standard, 93
  Web services security standards, 106
  WS-RM, 131
  WSDM, 122
  WSIA, 132
  WSRP, 132–133
  WSS, 115
  XCBF, 111
  XML security exchange, 75
OMA, 67
OMG (Object Management Group)
  CORBA, 15
  UML, 120
OMI (Open Management Interface), 121–122

Index

ONC (Open Network Computing) RPCs, 15, 17
 versus WSDL, 63
 versus XML, 55
Ontology.Org, BPM standards, 128
Open Application Group, ebXML, 80
Open Management Interface (OMI), 121–122
Open Network Computing. *See* ONC
OpenTravel Alliance (OTA), 67, 145
 ebXML, 80
Optimization tools, 214, 216
Oracle
 history, UDDI, 92
 reliable message delivery, 130
 WS-Interoperability, 86
Orchestration
 standardization efforts, 126–130
 vendors, 217
Organization for Advancement of Structured Information Standards. *See* OASIS

P – Q

Patricia Seybold Group, 153
Peer-based style communication, 14
PeopleSoft, ebXML, 80
PKI (public key infrastructure), 109–110
 managing, 213
PLM (product lifecycle management), 4
PocketSoap (Simon Fell), 85
Point-to-point integration, 162–163
Portals, 214, 216
 managing portal initiatives, 167–169
 portal presentation logic (*See* portlets)
Portlets (portal presentation logic), 55
 interactive applications, 132–133
Ports, 61
portTypes (WSDL), 60
 versus service types, 65

Premier Farnell, 170–171
Principal security identifiers, 233
Print servers, 31
Product lifecycle management. *See* PLM
Projects, evaluation guidelines
 administration tools, 235–236
 characterizing projects, 219–221
 deployment tools, 235–236
 development tools, 234–235
 requirements, extensibility features, 229–231
 requirements, interoperability, 227–229
 requirements, performance, 226–227
 requirements, scalability, 226–227
 requirements, security, 231–234
 requirements, standards support, 227–229
 selecting Java platform, 222–224
 selecting languages and operating systems, 221–222
 UDDI registries, 236–243
Proxies, 61
 interceptors, 229–230
Public key (asymmetric) encryption, 106
Public key infrastructure (PKI), 109–110

R

RDBMS (relational database management systems), 238
Reference architecture, 90–91
Register SOA operation, 58
Registries. *See* UDDI
Registry and Repository, ebXML, 79
Relational database management systems (RDBMS), 238
Reliable message delivery, 130–131
Reliable network providers (RNPs), 181, 211–212

Index

Remote Method Invocation. *See* RMI
Rendezvous (TIBCO), 14
Return on investment (ROI), 5–6
RMI (Remote Method Invocation), 15, 17
  registry, 64
  tightly coupled connections, 19, 29
  versus WSDL, 63
  versus XML, 55, 57
RNPs (reliable network providers), 181, 211–212
ROI (return on investment), 5–6
RosettaNet
  ebXML, 80
  Web service technologies, 77
  XML-based standards, 67
RPC-style (remote procedure call) middleware, 14–16
  challenges, 16–20
  SOA, 30
  SOAP, 72
  versus Web services, 29, 57
Runtime architecture, 191, 199–202

S

S1 Corporation, BPM standards, 128
SAAJ (SOAP with Attachments API for Java), 100
Sales force automation. *See* SFA
Salesforce.com, 162–163
SAML (Security Assertions Markup Language), 75, 111–112, 117
  single sign-on services, 112–114
  WSS bindings, 116
SAP
  BPM standards, 128
  history, UDDI, 92
  WS-Interoperability, 86
  WSCI, 91, 127
Scalability, project evaluation guidelines, 226–227
SCL (SOAP Contract Language), 89
SCM (supply chain management), 4
Screen scraping, 10
Secure Sockets Layer/Transport Layer Security. *See* SSL/TLS
Security
  authentication and authorization, 110–112, 114–115
  data confidentiality and integrity, 107
  digital signatures, 106, 108–109
  digital signatures, managing, 110
  encryption, 106–108
  expressing and exchanging information in XML, 111–112
  key management, 106, 109–110
  middleware, 208
  project evaluation guidelines, 231–234
  security tokens, 111
  single sign-on services, 75, 112–114, 117
  SOAP, 73–76
  standardization efforts, 105–106
  XML security, 115–117
Security Assertions Markup Language. *See* SAML
Security Services Technical Committee (SSTC), 111–112
SeeBeyond, BPML-based products, 128
Semantic Web project, 143
Service brokers, 58
Service consumers, 58
  standard international taxonomies, 66
Service contracts
  IDL, 63
  SOA roles, 58
Service grids, 210–211
Service Integrity SIFT, 210
Service-Oriented Architecture. *See* SOA
Service providers
  SOA roles, 58
  UDDI, 65, 67

Index

Service types
  UBR, 94
  UDDI, 65
  UDDI, tModel, 66–68
Services, definition, 30
Servlets/servlet engines *versus* J2EE application server, 205–206
SFA (sales force automation), 4
Short Message Service. *See* SMS
Siebel Call Center, 164
SIIA (Software Information Industry Association), 151
Simple Mail Transfer Protocol. *See* SMTP
Simple Network Management Protocol (SNMP), 119
Simple Object Access Protocol. *See* SOAP
Single key (symmetric) encryption, 106
Single sign-on services, 75, 112–114, 117
SMS (Short Message Service), 42
SMTP (Simple Mail Transfer Protocol), 49, 50
SNA (System Network Architecture), 50
  versus SOAP, 76
SNMP (Simple Network Management Protocol), 119
SOA (Service-Oriented Architecture), 30
  core technology of Web services, 47–48, 57–59
  technologies implementing SOA patterns, 59
  versus UDDI, 69–70
SOAP Contract Language (SCL), 89
  extensions, specifications, 134
SOAP messages
  body, 71, 117
  document-style, 72
  encoding, 73
  envelopes, 70
  header processors, 76, 117
  headers, 71, 117
  processors, 200–201
  receivers, 72
  RPC-style, 72
  runtime containers, 200–202
  senders, 72
SOAP (Simple Object Access Protocol), 27, 59
  development challenges, 85–86
  engines, 181
  extensions, 73
  history, 84–85
  implementations, 83, 181
  versus middleware technologies, 175–176
  versus other communication systems, 76–77
  programming standards, 97–98, 103
  programming standards, Java, 99–100
  security, 73–76
  servers, 181
  versus SOA systems, 77
  stacks, 181
  standards, 190–191
  W3C and OASIS, 88
  WS-Interoperability, 86–88
SOAP Toolkit (Microsoft), 85, 98
SOAP with Attachments API for Java (SAAJ), 100
SOAPbuilders, 86
SOAP::Lite (Paul Kulchenko), 85
Software AG, application adapter frameworks, 11
Software-as-service business model, 27, 172–174, 211, 247
  versus Web services, 37–38
  Web services potential, 137–140
Software Information Industry Association (SIIA), 151
Sonic Software
  reliable message delivery, 130
  SonicMQ, 14
SSL/TLS (Secure Sockets Layer/Transport Layer Security), 73

Index

SSTC (Security Services Technical Committee), 111–112
Standards for Technology in Automotive Retail (STAR), 145
Sterling Commerce, ebXML, 80
Style sheets, XSLT, 54–55
Sun Microsystems
   BPM standards, 128
   ebXML, 80
   history, UDDI, 92
   orchestration and choreography, 126
   reliable message delivery, 130
   technology ownership, 188–189
   WSCI, 91, 127
Supply chain management. *See* SCM
Sybase, SOAP integration into programming languages, 98
Symmetric encryption, 106
Synchronous communication, 14–16
System Network Architecture. *See* SNA
Systinet
   adoption of Web services, 151
   IdooXoap, 85
   WASP, 88, 158–159

T

T-Mobile International, T-Mobile Online, 41–43
Taxonomies, UDDI, 65, 242
TCP/IP (Transmission Control Protocol/Internet Protocol), 48, 50
TechRepublic surveys, 152
Testing tools, 214, 216
Thomas Register supplier identifier, 66
TIBCO Software
   application adapter frameworks, 11
   reliable message delivery, 130
   Rendevous, 14
   Web Services SDK, 88
   WS-ReliableMessaging, 131

Tightly coupled connections, 19, 29
   SOAP RPC convention, 72
   versus XML, 57
TIRKS (Trunks Inventory Record Keeping System), 165
Tivoli (IBM), 118, 206
tModels, UDDI, 66–68
Tokens, security, 75
Trading partner networks, 171–172, 173
Traditional middleware. *See also* middleware
   challenges, 16–20
   inability to work across Internet, 21
   versus Internet, 21
   styles, 13–16
   versus WSDL, 64
   versus XML, 57
Transactions, 122–126
Transmission Control Protocol/Internet Protocol. *See* TCP/IP
Trunks Inventory Record Keeping System (TIRKS), 165
Trust services, 109–110, 213–214
Types, Web services, 60

U

UBR (UDDI Business Registry), 93–95, 239–240
   dynamic discovery of business partners, 140, 142
   nodes, 93–94
UCC (Uniform Code Council)
   business XML standards, 146–147
   Core Order business message, 147–148
   RosettaNet, 77
UDDI Business Registry. *See* UBR
UDDI (Universal Description, Discovery & Integration), 59, 65–69
   dynamic binding, 149–150
   history, 92–93

versus other description languages, 69–70
programming standards, 97, 103
programming standards, Java, 101–102
project evaluation guidelines, 236–243
registries, 35, 212–213
registries, for ISEC, 172, 173
registries, private, 95–97
registries, wizards, 192, 198
UDDI Business Registry, 93–95
UDDI Operators Council, 93–95
UDDI4J (UDDI Java client APIs), 101–102
UML (Unified Modeling Language), 120
UN/CEFACT (United Nations Centre for Trade Facilitation and Electronic Business), 78, 79
Unified Modeling Language (UML), 120
Uniform Code Council. *See* UCC
Uniform Resource Identifiers. *See* URIs
Uniform Resource Locators. *See* URLs
Uniform Resource Names. *See* URNs
United Nations Centre for Trade Facilitation and Electronic Business (UN/CEFACT), 78, 79
United Nations Standard Products and Services Codes (UNSPSC), 66
United Parcel Service, UPS OnLine Tools, 41
Universal Description, Discovery & Integration. *See* UDDI
Universal Product Code (UPC), 146–147
University of Texas M.D. Anderson Cancer Center, 169–170
UNIX platform
  deploying .NET applications, 186
  RPC-style middleware, 15, 17

UNSPSC (United Nations Standard Products and Services Codes), 66
UPC (Universal Product Code), 146–147
URIs (Uniform Resource Identifiers), 48–49
URLs (Uniform Resource Locators), 48–49
URNs (Uniform Resource Names), 48
U.S. Navy, private UDDI registries, 95–96
Userland, SOAP project, 78, 84

V

VeriSign
  history, UDDI, 92
  WS-Security specification, 115
  XKMS, 110
Versata, BPM standards and products, 128
VerticalNet, BPM standards, 128
Verve, BPM standards, 128
VES (VIrtual Execution System), 184
VICS (Voluntary Interindustry Commerce Standards) Association, 147
Virtual Execution System (VES), 184
Vitria, BPEL4WS, 218
VoiceXML, 54–55

W

Wachovia, 160–161
Wal-mart, effective use of information technology, 138
WAP (Wireless Application Protocol), 54–55
WASP (Web Applications and Services Platform), 88, 158–159
WBEM (Web-Based Enterprise Management), 120

Index

W3C (World Wide Web Consortium)
  Semantic Web project, 143
  SOAP history, W3C Note, 84
  SOAP history, W3C Recommendation, 88
  Web architecture development and standards, 30
  Web services security standards, 106
  WSDL history, W3C Note, 89
  WSDL history, W3C Working Draft, 90
  XKMS, 110
  XML Encryption, 108
  XML Schema, 53–54
Web. *See* World Wide Web
Web Applications and Services Platform (WASP), 88, 158–159
Web-Based Enterprise Management (WBEM), 120
Web servers, 31, 33
Web services
  adoption, 151–153
  application integration, 6, 22–23
  application integration, advantages, 23–25
  application templates, 36–37
  basics, 27–32
  benefits, 153–155
  building, 32–33
  business models, 33–44
  characteristics, 35
  combining advantages of MOM and RPC-style middleware, 20
  core technologies, 47
  domain-specific industry standards, 143–147
  dynamic binding, 147–150
  dynamic discovery of business partners, 140–143
  employees sharing information, 169–170
  firewalls, 50
  inappropriate uses, 174–176
  infrastructure, 36–37
  internal integration, 163–165
  managing portal initiatives, 167–169
  multichannel client formats, 160–161
  pervasiveness, 17–18
  potential uses, hype, 135–136
  programming standards, basics, 97–99
  programming standards, Java, 99–102
  reasons for using, 28–29
  reducing duplicative applications, 165–167
  scope, 35–37
  service grids, 210–211
  software-as-service, 137–140, 172–174
  versus software-as-service business model, 37–44
  standardization efforts, 133–134
  standardization efforts, management, 117–122
  superpowered PDAs, 136–137
  technologies, 36
  trading partner networks, 171–172, 173
  versus traditional middleware, 28
  unknown client environments, 159–160
  XML, 21–22
Web services, evaluation guidelines
  administration tools, 235–236
  characterizing projects, 219–221
  deployment tools, 235–236
  development tools, 234–235
  project requirements, extensibility features, 229–231
  project requirements, interoperability, 227–229
  project requirements, performance, 226–227
  project requirements, scalability, 226–227
  project requirements, security, 231–234

Index

project requirements, standards support, 227–229
selecting Java platform, 222–224
selecting languages and operating systems, 221–222
UDDI registries, 236–243
Web services, infrastructure-level, 210–211
   reliable network providers, 211–212
   trust services, 213–214
   UDDI registries, 212–213
Web services, management extensions
   basics, 206–207
   middleware, 207–209
   monitoring frameworks, 209–210
Web services, platforms
   basics, 181–182
   deployment tools, 191, 193–194
   deployment tools, descriptors, 197–198
   development, clients, 198–199
   development, services, 194–198
   development, tools, 191, 193–194
   features, 190–192
   J2EE application server, 202–205
   J2EE application server, *versus* servlet engines, 205–206
   .NET framework, 182–183
   .NET *versus* Java, 182, 184–190
   runtime architecture, 191, 199–202
Web Services Architecture Working Group, 90, 133
Web Services Choreography Interface. *See* WSCI
Web Services Coordination Group, 90
Web Services Description Language. *See* WSDL
Web Services Description Working Group, 90
Web Services Distributed Management (WSDM), 122
Web Services Flow Language (WSFL), 129
Web Services for Remote Portals (WSRP), 132–133
Web Services Interactive Applications (WSIA), 132
Web Services Interoperability Organization. *See* WS-I
Web Services Reliable Messaging (WS-RM), 131
Web Services SDK (TIBCO Software), 88
Web Services Security Technical Committee, 91
Web Services Security (WSS), 115–116
Web sites
   evolution, 33
   versus Web services, 34
WebForms, 183
WebLogic Server (BEA), 88
webMethods
   application adapter frameworks, 11
   BPEL4WS, 218
   OMI, 121
   XKMS, 110
   XML protocols, 77
WebSphereMQ (IBM), 14
WebV2, BPEL4WS, 218
White space, XML documents, 108–109
WhiteMesa Server, 88
Winer, Dave, 84
WinForms, 183
Wingfoot, 199
Wireless Application Protocol. *See* WAP
Wireless Markup Language. *See* WML
WML (Wireless Markup Language), 54–55
World Wide Web
   DNS, 48

321

Index

World Wide Web (*cont.*)
  evolution, 33–35
  FTP, 49
  HTTP, 49
  versus other networks, 50
  SMTP, 49
  TCP/IP, 48
  URI schemes, 49
  URIs, 48
  URLs, 48–49
  Web application protocols, 49
  Web services, 17
  Web services, core technology, 47
World Wide Web Consortium. *See* W3C
Wrapping services, 195–196, 201
WS-Addressing, 131
WS-Coordination specification, 124–126
WS-I (Web Services Interoperability Organization), 86–88
WS-ReliableMessaging, 131
WS-Reliability, 131
WS-RM (Web Services Reliable Messaging), 131
WS-Security specification, 115
WS-Transaction specification, 124–126
WSCI (Web Services Choreography Interface), 91, 127
WSDL (Web Services Description Language), 59–63
  building new services, 194–195
  challenges, version 1.1, 89–92
  versus EAI, 176
  history, 88–89
  JWSDL, 101
  versus other description languages, 63–65
  programming standards, 97, 103
  programming standards, Java, 101
  SOAP messages, 71, 75
  standards, 190–192
WSDM (Web Services Distributed Management), 122
WSFL (Web Services Flow Language), 129
WSIA (Web Services Interactive Applications), 132
WSRP (Web Services for Remote Portals), 132–133
  dynamic discovery of business partners, 143
WSS (Web Services Security), 115–116

X – Z

X.509 certificates, 111
  WS-Security bindings, 116
XACML (XML Access Control Markup Language), 115
XBRL (Extensible Business Reporting Language) International, 146
XCBF (XML Common Biometric Format), 111
  WS-Security bindings, 116
Ximian, Mono project, 186
XKMS (XML Key Management Specification), 110, 116–117
XLANG (Microsoft), 129
XML Access Control Markup Language (XACML), 115
XML Common Biometric Format (XCBF), 111
XML documents, 51–52
  canonical form, 109
  transforming with XSLT, 54–55
  white space, 108–109
XML elements, 51
  datatypes, 53
XML Encryption, 108
XML (Extensible Markup Language), 51
  definition, 21–22
  HTML vocabulary, 52
  meta-markup languages, 53
  OASIS, 75
  versus other data representations, 55–57
  SAML, 75

SOAP, 70–73
tags, 51
tokens, 111
tools, 214–215
Web service core technology, 47, 50–53
XML Fund, BPM standards, 128
XML Global, ebXML, 80
XML Key Management Specification (XKMS), 110
XML Protocol Working Group, proposals to W3C, 88, 90
XML-RPC protocol, 78, 84
XML Schema, 53–54, 56
element's datatypes, 53
RPC messages, 73
XML Signature Recommendations, 109
XrML (Extensible Rights Markup Language), 115
WS-Security bindings, 116
XSLT (Extensible Stylesheet Language Transformations), 54–55
versus XML, 56
Yahoo, 174

Register Your Book

at www.awprofessional.com/register

You may be eligible to receive:

- Advance notice of forthcoming editions of the book
- Related book recommendations
- Chapter excerpts and supplements of forthcoming titles
- Information about special contests and promotions throughout the year
- Notices and reminders about author appearances, tradeshows, and online chats with special guests

Contact us

If you are interested in writing a book or reviewing manuscripts prior to publication, please write to us at:

Editorial Department
Addison-Wesley Professional
75 Arlington Street, Suite 300
Boston, MA 02116 USA
Email: AWPro@aw.com

Visit us on the Web: http://www.awprofessional.com